MISSING IN ACTION

THE 465TH BOMB GROUP IN COMBAT WORLD WAR TWO

BY

GENE F. MOXLEY

ISBN: 0-7596-9272-6

This book is printed on acid free paper.

1stBooks - rev. 06/21/02

FORWARD

By

John Charlton, Major 782nd Squadron

This is a compilation of the stories of missing in action crews, told in their own words. Their stories were brought to light by the dedicated research of Gene Moxley. These are the crews of the 465th Bomb Group, B-24s from the 15th AAF based at Pantanella, Italy. Nine hundred and fifty four men were shot down in combat in this Group in action during the last year of World War Two. These stories will, no doubt, be similar to those of other missing in action American Airmen (sum 79,265 total), and many of the 79,281 missing in action British Airmen from the European theater.

There is no more poignant reading than the last statements passed between many of these crewmembers in the act of escaping from a shot down bomber, jumping through a fiery bomb bay to probable capture by mad citizens below, and a career in a German prison camp.

These stories were compiled from debriefing records, which were gathered after return to group, or return to the U.S. following the war, and from memories of some surviving veterans. Stories include ground experience after being shot down, but are much abridged in this area in order to avoid redundancy. This book will acquaint the reader with the tremendous sacrifices made by the crews, and the level of honor attained by some men in the choices they made in their final hour.

To: Frank V. Williams Jr.
best wishes
Gene F. Moxley
19 August 2003

I hereby wish to acknowledge the following sources, without which, this history could not have been written:

General Dynamics Corporation, San Diego California
Headquarters, Air Force Historical Research Agency, Maxwell Air Force Base, Alabama
The National Archives at College Park, 8601 Adelphi Road, College Park, Maryland.
Suitland Reference Branch (NNRR) National Archives, Washington, D. C.
U. S. Army Total Personnel Command, Alexandria, VA.
465th Bombardment Group (H) History
780th Squadron History Book
781st Squadron History Book
782nd Squadron Microfilmed History
783rd Squadron History Book
Mr. John R. Beitling, B-24 Historian and Archivist
1st Lt. Carl V. Dahl, Pilot, Crew # 280, 781st Squadron
Lt. Delbert E. Forsberg, Pilot, 783rd Squadron
Major John F. Charlton, Pilot & Operations Officer, 782nd Squadron
Major General Richard Bodycombe, Pilot, USAF (Ret), 782nd Squadron
1st Lt. Norman R. Stickney, Co-Pilot, 782nd Squadron, Lt. Gemmato Crew
1st Lt. Sam Marie, Bombardier, USAF (Ret), 783rd Squadron, Lt. Greenwood and Lt. Petranek Crew
1st Lt. Joseph Spontak, Navigator, 780th Squadron, Lt. Crane Crew
Lt. Frank C. Diederichs, Bombardier, 780th Squadron, Lt. Shreve Crew
S/Sgt. Robert Babcock, 780th Squadron, 465th Group Public Relations Photographer, Cover Photo
T/Sgt. Vincent A. Beeson, Flight Engineer-Gunner, 781st Squadron, Lt. Martz Crew
Sgt. Richard A. Keenan, Ball Turret Gunner, 782nd Squadron, Lt. Ayres Crew
T/Sgt. Alvin M. Murphy, Flight Engineer-Gunner, 783rd Squadron, Lt. Elliott Crew
S/Sgt. Andy Snyder, Nose Turret Gunner, 783rd Squadron, Lt. Johnson Crew
S/Sgt. Cecil L. Sammons, Top Turret Gunner, 782nd Squadron, Lt. Pemberton Crew
S/Sgt. Weyland B. Feely, Tail Turret Gunner, 783rd Squadron, Col. Clark Crew
S/Sgt. Robert N. Windom, Assist. Engineer-Top Turret Gunner, 782nd Squadron, Lt. Johns Crew
Sgt. Theodore A. Butler, Tail Turret Gunner, 782nd Squadron, Lt. Johns Crew

This book is dedicated to my wife Mary, for all of her help, and encouragement, in its completion and to her uncle, S/Sgt. Frank Hutchcraft and all of his comrades in the 780th, 781st, 782nd and 783rd Squadrons of the 465th Bombardment Group (H.)

THE B-24 LIBERATOR

"ANATOMY OF A HEAVYWEIGHT"

The fuselage was divided into five major compartments: nose, nose wheel, flight deck, bomb bay, and rear fuselage. Most crewmembers climbed into the cabin through the bomb bay, which they opened by pulling the emergency handle on the right side of the nose. Other entrances were through the nose wheel compartment and entry hatch in the underside of the rear fuselage. The four engines served a number of functions other than spinning the propellers. Number three drove the main hydraulic system, while numbers one and two drove instrument and de-icer system vacuum pumps. Four hydraulic systems powered the many B-24 subsystems. The main system operated the landing gear, wing flaps, bomb bay doors, power brakes, and gun-charging mechanism on the belly turret. The three other systems cushioned landing impact, dampened nose wheel shimmy, and controlled tail turret gun elevation, gun-charging, and rotation.

Mechanical linkages ran throughout the aircraft. In all, nearly a mile of cable was involved in the various control systems. A small gasoline-powered auxiliary power unit (APU) in the nose wheel compartment backed up the 24 vdc electrical system, making the B-24 fully self-contained. The sputtering APU, nicknamed "putt putt," was notorious for flooding the flight deck with exhaust fumes. The two-kilowatt auxiliary generator provided electrical power to start the engines and for emergency power if the main generator failed in flight. Oxygen, always a critical factor at high altitudes, was supplied by 10 to 18 yellow bottles. Flow was regulated by dials at each station's outlet, marked in thousands of feet of altitude. Loss of this system during a high-altitude mission could mean aborting the mission and returning to base.

Early B-24Ds used an eight-step procedure for emergency nose gear lowering. Later aircraft replaced this formal document with words that said, essentially, "just kick it out." Twin life rafts were stowed outside, just aft of the top turret under spring-loaded covers. The rafts were deployed by pulling a T-handle inside the crew compartment or the two handles outside on top of the fuselage. After ejection, the rafts inflated automatically.

Much of the credit for the Liberator's ability to maintain speed and range while hauling ever-increasing loads of armament and equipment goes to the Pratt and Whitney R-1830 Twin-Wasp engines. The powerful radial engines lived up to expectations. B-24s operated in every rigorous climate a global war could offer, from the 110-degree heat and sand storms of North Africa to the ice and snow of the Aleutians.

The Twin-Wasp was a 14-cylinder, two-row, air-cooled radial engine of 1,830 cubic inch displacement. Originally designed in 1930, "Old Faithful" represented one of the oldest and most reliable items of major equipment on the B-24. Aside from its mechanical soundness, designer Mac Laddon liked the engine for its small frontal cross-section, an attribute that reduced aerodynamic drag significantly. Beginning with the B-24C, a turbo-supercharger was added to enhance operation at high altitudes.

All but a few of the B-24 series used Hamilton Standard Hydromatic three-bladed, full-feathering propellers, painted black with a distinctive four-inch yellow stripe on the tips that helped the pilots synchronize the engines. These "paddle props" combined to form a propeller assembly over 11 feet in diameter.

The workhorse of America's bomber command, the Liberator made its contributions quietly, with little fanfare, but it carried more ordnance faster and farther than any of its counterparts. 19,256 Liberators were built during WWII.

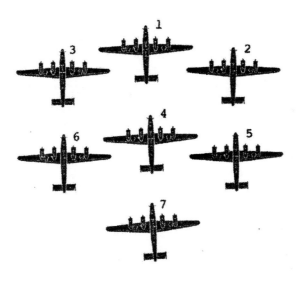

Typical 15th Air Force Squadron Formation.
Top—Front View, **Middle**—Top View, **Bottom**—Left side view
Number Shows Formation Position

Gene F. Moxley

Although each mission was different, they all contained elements that were similar or repetitive. This is an attempt to describe a typical mission, flown early in 1945, along with general comments concerning various phases of the trip, as told by S/Sgt. Andy Snyder, Nose Turret Gunner on Lt. Max Johnson's Crew, 783rd Squadron.

Bomber Command continually reviewed bomb strike photos, recon photos, crew interrogation reports, weather maps and everything at their disposal to determine which targets needed a raid from our heavy bombers. A primary and several alternate targets were chosen for the next days raid by the entire 15th Air Force, a Wing or a Group, and wheels put in motion in the early evening hours for bomb loads, number of planes, take off times, lead groups, rendezvous areas, bombing altitude, etc. Returning weather planes during the night would give reports on weather to and from targets and help layout our routes.

Planning was done assuming that the exact timing of all events could be carried out. Murphy's Law and the old saying that "The best laid plans of mice and men often go astray" were both very much operational. Weather was always the culprit. Due to fog, clouds or rain, take off times of the various Groups could not be carried out as planned. This in turn delayed rendezvous and locations and ultimately lead positions, number of planes going to various targets and even flight routes. In short, weather made a mess out of detailed planning - pure bedlam and confusion reigned rather than the orderly mission as planned. Once airborne, command passed to Group or Squadron leaders and they were forced to make critical decisions that might not correspond with what was planned at headquarters. Many times, primary targets could not be bombed, leaving some portion of the 15th Air Force's 21 Groups prowling the skies over southern Europe looking for alternate targets or even targets of opportunity. If several Groups were in such circumstances, it was not uncommon for two or three of them to be making a run on the same target at the same time and from different directions - causing much confusion in the skies. Weather may have been as great an enemy to the big bombers as the Germans were.

There were enough crews in the squadron to give each a day of much needed rest after flying two to four days in a row, so each evening, Squadron Headquarters posted a list of the next days crews on the bulletin board. Late in the evening we would check the board to see if tomorrow was our day or not. If so, we would normally try to go to bed at a reasonable hour in order to be prepared for a long day. Sometimes sleep came easily but at other times, a deep, restful sleep was nowhere to be found. Rain splattering against the tent and dripping to the soggy ground, the muffled roar of engines from planes along the strip where ground crews worked on them all night - things that normally induced sleep seemed to be of no help. As the night wore on, the anticipation of the arrival of Sgt. Walker, who always woke us at 2:30 to 3:30 AM, began to replace any thoughts of sleep. Finally his footsteps could be heard in the mud as

4

he approached our tent, opened the entrance and announced that briefing would be at 0500. He then quietly moved to the next tent so as not to disturb the non-flying crews who were in a deep sleep. This scene would be repeated in some 1200 to 2500 tents across southern Italy each morning.

In keeping with the reverence of the hour for those still sleeping, we silently stumbled to breakfast, then across the hill to Group Headquarters for briefing. There, in the same room that was used for the theater in the evenings, we took a seat on the cold metal stools that had once been covers for the tail fins on 500 and 1000 pound bombs. A curtain was withdrawn from a large wall map of Europe that had a long, red string drawn tautly from our base to some target many hundreds of miles away. We were told what the target was, how many Groups were going there, our bombing altitude, what the weather was expected to be and what defense from flak and fighters might be encountered. After the Chaplain led us in prayer, we loaded into GI trucks that took us to the equipment shack where parachutes, flak suits and other heavy equipment were picked up, then out to our plane for the day. Since there were more crews than planes, none of us had a regular plane but were assigned a different one from the pool each day.

At the hardstand, we load our gear in the appropriate spots, walk around the plane with Max, C.J. and John looking her over, and then climb aboard. All planes have a unique and distinct odor of oil, high-octane gas, rubber and hydraulic fluid. At times, in the early morning hours and rain, it is almost nauseating. The engines are run up for the last time, gasoline trucks have been by to top off the tanks and it becomes very quiet across the valley. All eyes are turned toward the tower to see if they will fire a red flare signaling that the mission is being called off, or a green flare, telling us to start engines. Shortly after daybreak, a green flare finally arches out across the misty sky, so the mission is on. The quietness in the valley is suddenly shattered by the whine, cough and roar of some 220 big engines coming to life and warming up as the 464th and 465th Bomb Groups prepare to leave Pantanella one more time.

In a few minutes, the signal to taxi and start taking off is given and the sound of squealing brakes and engines under full power join the tumult. One of the big planes with its heavy load slowly starts down the runway every 20 to 30 seconds, gradually gains speed and finally lifts into the very turbulent air created by other planes that have preceded them. This can tax the ability of the pilots when wind and other weather conditions are not right.

With 600 to 1200 planes taking off and assembling over a reasonably small area, each group must have an assigned space and pattern of flight. Our position is to always take off to the west, fly up the valley until enough altitude is gained to circle left over the same range of foothills that we live on. At times, there are only a few feet to spare as we turn into the hills. One morning we were <u>very</u> low over a small field where a farmer was plowing with a donkey. The donkey became frightened and ran away, pulling the farmer and plow the wrong direction across the field. The man thought we were playing games with him and shook his fist at us.

Our Squadron leader starts a slow, gradual left turn and the five or six planes following that will make up our box, each fly a tighter circle behind him until we have formed two V shaped formations, one slightly ahead of and above the other. The lead ship is in the center of the top V with plane number two being slightly behind and on his right wing, number three on his left wing, number four slightly below and behind him, number five on the right wing of number four, number six on the left wing of number four and finally seven - tail last Charlie - being slightly behind and below number four. This allows each plane a small space in which to fly without colliding with another plane or flying in the rough turbulence created by their big props, and at the same time, keeps them in a tight formation for concentration of their defensive firepower against enemy fighters.

In a circular manner, our Squadron rendezvous with the other three Squadrons of the 465th, then with the 55th Wing and we all finally head north. Weather permitting, this process takes roughly an hour and a half and uses many gallons of fuel. If the weather is bad at rendezvous altitude of 5,000 to 9,000 feet, it can take much longer and present a completely different set of problems. At times, the clouds become so thick that other planes cannot be seen. If this condition persists for any length of time, planes become badly scattered and the possibility of mid air collision increases greatly.

As we climb north over the Adriatic, it is time to finish dressing, complete routine duties, use the urinary relief tube for the last time, get in our turrets, test fire all the guns and be on oxygen at 10,000 feet. The human bladder was not designed for long hours in the thin, cold air under conditions of anxiety and stress so becomes very uncomfortable during a mission. A completely dressed and equipped airman starts out with a regular GI woolen uniform and leather combat boots. (Low cut shoes would snap off when a parachute opens, leaving a bare foot on a rough and cold ground.) The next items put on are a 45 caliber automatic pistol in a shoulder holster, a thin satin suit with electric heating cords, a heavy, lined flying suit and boots, fur lined gloves over thin, electrically heated ones, an inflatable life jacket called a "Mae West," a helmet and goggles and finally a parachute harness. All this is quite cumbersome, making it difficult to move freely but is essential for safety and comfort in the hostile environments being worked in. The pilot and copilot are the only crewmembers who wear their parachutes. The others have the harness on at all times but, to provide ease of movement about the plane and room to get in their turrets, have a small chest pack somewhat like a loaf of bread that is hung at a specific, handy location for each person. The pack can be quickly snapped on the harness front. Those who have used them report that they give quite a slap in the face as the chute billows out.

On a clear day, the Yugoslavian coast soon comes into view off to our right. It is a mountainous area with many signs of the last ice age some 10,000 years ago still plainly visible, especially along the near shore islands. They look as though a giant hand has scooped out long, smooth valleys, leaving the ridges intact. Before long, we can see the snow capped Alps towering above any clouds in the area. They are a beautiful sight but are our enemy. They breed much bad weather and are a formidable obstacle to a crippled bomber losing altitude and trying to find its way home.

Our fighter escort joins us after we have made landfall at the end of the Adriatic. They fly above us and are a comfortable sight. As we continue climbing to our bombing altitude of 23,000 to 25,000 feet, Europe lays out before us like a map. Compared to North America, it is a small continent. Several of the larger cities such as Munich, Vienna and Prague are visible in the distance - all under smoke screen. Our adversary knows we are coming but is not sure of our target so tries to hide them all.

Over the snow-covered Alps, the sky is indescribably blue, clear, and cold. Temperature at our altitude is some 30 to 50 degrees below zero. Some of the nose turrets are quite drafty and cold. I discover that the heaters installed on my guns, to keep them from freezing, are a perfect place to warm my hands.

In all directions the air is filled with hundreds of planes, some nearby and others stretched out across the vast expanse of space with the sun glinting off their silver wings, some streaming contrails and others leaving no tracks, but all creating much turbulence in the endless sea of air. The only apparent motion, outside our Group, is the fighters crisscrossing back and forth several thousand feet above us. The distant bombers, drifting through space at the same speed, seem to be in a state of suspended animation - hanging there but not moving. Such awe-inspiring sights make us realize that we are playing a finite roll in the very large production of human history. Those sights and emotions will be forever inscribed in our memories.

In the distance, each Squadron and Group seems to be one vast, smooth flow of planes. The constant bouncing and jockeying for position in our own Group makes us realize that this distant view of grace and poise is only a mirage. The sky is no longer calm and smooth but is churned into a mass of invisible white water rapids, turbulence, vortexes and prop wash created by natural conditions and the passage of hundreds of other planes. In order to stay in formation, the pilots must constantly struggle with those forces to keep their 30 tons of machine and men in the assigned, limited, thin air space. The Group and Squadron leaders can make or break a formation simply by how consistent they fly. Each change they make is magnified as it progresses back through the formation, not unlike the game of "crack the whip" we played in grade school. The further back in the formation you are, the more difficult it becomes not to intrude into another bombers air space, creating a terrible mid air collision. We each feel the plane shudder as it hits those invisible pockets of disturbed air in the sky and as it skids to right or left. We can hear the giant engines roar as Max and C.J. change their power settings in order to close a gap or slack off to keep from chewing up the wing that is just ahead of us. It is this constant change that rattles windows on the ground, wears engines out before their time and, after many hours, extracts every ounce of energy from the pilots.

As our target is approached, we can see the black blotch in the sky and on the ground where other Groups are dropping their bombs and being shot at by flak guns. At times, a burning bomber can be seen in the distance as it spins and falls to earth. Anxiety and fear had stowed away on our ship this morning before we climbed into the murky skies over Pantanella. Anxiety had visited with us all the way up but fear had kept hidden in some remote part of our mind until now, when it suddenly makes its personal appearance. The desire to live becomes so very strong, yet there seems to be nothing we can do to control what might happen. I learn that I am not as brave a young man, as I had always perceived. The thought of turning back seems to never enter our minds, or if it did, is quickly discarded. The only thing left to do is pray. Such conditions probably taught more of us to pray than the Chaplain ever could.

Al tells us when we are approaching the IP (Initial Point) and that it is time to put flak suits on. The flak suit, weighing about 50 pounds, is a semi flexible array of steel slats that overlie each other, covering the upper portion of the body where all the vital organs are located. It and the steel, earflap equipped helmet, offer some protection from small chunks of shrapnel but would not deflect a direct hit. Someone has jokingly said that if you could see inside a B-24 over the target, the only thing visible would be several pairs of GI boots hanging out from under a flak helmet. I'm sure we did draw up into as small a size as possible. Donning the flak suit is normally completed prior to the first shells bursting around us, although at times, the large, long range guns are there ahead of us.

Flak is a German acronym for Antiaircraft Artillery, and is the term commonly used by fliers of most nations. Germany has very good guns and highly trained crews that proved to be a scourge to Allied warplanes. During 1944, flak alone accounted for about 2500 plane losses per month. At our altitude, there are four types of guns that can reach us. These are as outlined below.

Size	Millimeters	Inches	Projectile Weight	Effective Altitude
	88	3.5	20.7 Pounds	35,000 feet
	105	4.1	33.3 "	50,000 "
	128	5.04	68.3 "	60,000 "
	150	5.9	95.0 "	60,000 "

All these guns have muzzle velocities of approximately 3,000 feet per second so can reach our altitude in 10 to 15 seconds if fired nearly straight up. At times, the flash from the muzzle of the larger guns can be seen from our position. They are normally fired in batteries of four or six guns, with their firing and shell explosions being well synchronized. The rate of fire for each gun ranged from 15 to 20 rounds per minute for the 88's to 2 rounds per minute for the 150's. The direction from which the projectile came and its relative size could be seen from the slant of the explosion and how large a blotch it made in the sky. The larger shells blew a perfect smoke ring out the base as they exploded.

Flak has different stages. At a safe distance, the explosions are actually very beautiful, looking like flowers suddenly blooming out in the sky. Although the smoke was normally dark gray or black, sometimes colors such as pink, red or orange were used. A color change was reportedly used to let their fighter pilots know that ground fire would cease and they were safe to attack the bombers. As the exploding shells get nearer, you can hear the "whump," feel the ship lurch and hear the shrapnel tearing through the metal skin, making a sound somewhat like that of a hand full of gravel being thrown on the sheet iron roof of a barn. If it doesn't get any closer than that, you are lucky. Some of the flak gunners track us as we go through their air space and aim directly at a Squadron. Others simply pick out a space in the sky ahead of us and lay down a continuous, heavy barrage that we must fly through. The dense wall that we must fly through is probably the most frightening.

Once the IP has been reached, the group turns in on the bomb run, opens bomb bay doors and leaves the flying to the bombardiers. Opening the bomb bay doors causes an extra amount of drag on the plane and it slows down several miles an hour. During the bomb run, the bombardier needs several minutes of straight and level flying in order to properly aim the bombs. This means no evasive action, giving the flak gunners a golden opportunity to increase their score on the "sitting ducks." The bomb run then becomes a very long period for the crews, seeming to last much longer than it actually takes. It is an exasperating period of time - nothing to do but just sit there and take it. One day when the flak was all around us, the unmistakable vibration from machine gun fire was felt by all of us. Max came in on the intercom with "Pilot to crew, where are the bandits." No answer. Again, "Pilot to crew, call out the bandits." A short silence, Then, "Tail to crew, its just me, strafing those darn flak batteries." The frustration had overcome Johnnie and he was doing what he could from 25,000 feet. We all felt the same.

Even on a clear day, the bombardier's job is difficult. He needs a steady, smooth platform from which to aim and drop his bombs and normally none of these conditions prevailed. The ship was flying in turbulent air created by earlier Groups, flak explosions and natural conditions, and the bombardiers mind was being harassed by all these. A few planes were equipped with radar that would allow large targets to be located below cloud and or smoke screen cover, but many targets were off limits unless the drop could be made visually. This was an attempt to prevent unnecessary civilian casualties. In spite of our best efforts to bomb only military targets, photo recon showed that only 60% of our bombs fell within 1,000 feet of their intended target. Many missed by half a mile or more, helping us to understand why the civilian population hated us so much and why they killed so many of our men who had safely bailed out of downed planes.

We were normally on the bomb run and dropping bombs from near noon to 2:00 PM, local time. This was six hours ahead of Eastern Time and nine hours ahead of Pacific Time at home so our families were in various stages of starting their day or were still in dreamland. We often thought of them and wondered what they might be doing at any one time. As soon as bombs were away, the bomb bay doors were closed and we rallied (turned) sharply right or left, to confuse the flak gunners, then headed for home. The navigators always tried to lead us around known flak areas but there were times when we would fly over uncharted gun positions - probably guns mounted on railroad flat cars and moved every few days. Some of them were very accurate.

Once the Alps were crossed, the territory became more friendly and we would gradually start descending toward the Adriatic. The fighter groups would leave us at this point and either return to base or go down to strafe and bomb tactical targets. Out over the water we could relax our alert for enemy fighters, lean back and enjoy listening to music or news on the BBC and try to eat our frozen K Rations. It was always good to get down where it was warmer and where oxygen masks could be removed. There were emergency landing strips in the mountains of Yugoslavia where partisans (people in sympathy with the Allies) might return us to Italy. Another emergency strip on the Isle of Vis in the Adriatic was there but was difficult to land a crippled bomber on.

As the sun was getting low, we would fly over our base in formation. The planes with wounded on board would fire a red flare and be given first priority at landing and be met by an ambulance with medics and supplies. The rest of us would peel off one at a time, circle, land and taxi the plane back to its hardstand where the ground crew would start the process of getting it ready for tomorrows mission. A truck would pick us up, take us to the equipment shack where we would stow our heavy equipment, then take us back to Headquarters for interrogation. Each crew would meet an interrogation officer in a small room and go over the days mission with him. He would ask what we saw in the way of planes going down, how may parachutes were observed, the location and intensity of flak and fighters, weather, and any potential targets such as full railroad marshalling yards, etc.

Red Cross Ladies would always meet us with hot coffee and donuts prior to our going into the interrogation room and it was probably the best coffee ever brewed. Someone also gave each of us two ounces of whiskey if we wanted it, then we headed back to the tent area, a hot meal, mail call and a relaxing evening reading and answering letters from home. Max and C.J. would be wholly expended. Although the rest of us had not worked so hard physically, we were all exhausted and were glad to be back. Tomorrow would be another day. We might fly again or we might sleep in while others manned the Libs. Someplace along the way, without our awareness, anxiety and fear had slipped away. We would meet again but that was of no concern tonight.

11 March 1944: Two crews collided in mid-air while on a practice mission, near Oudna in North Africa where the 465th Bomb Group was stationed while awaiting the completion of their base at Pantanella, Italy. 1st Lt. Robert E. Murphy, flying number 3 position in the lead box, lost control of his plane in the prop wash and collided with 1st Lt. Charles A. Melody. While circling the field at about 500 feet, picking up the formation, Lt. Murphy's plane slid over and his right wing damaged Major Smith's left rudder. Apparently, Lt. Murphy immediately cut the throttles, which resulted in Lt. Melody's plane ramming Lt. Murphy's plane in the rear. Both planes caught fire and seemed to explode in midair killing all crewmembers on both planes, with the exception of two crewmembers from each crew who were not flying that day. The largest piece of wreckage found was a section of the nose and part of the nose turret of Lt. Melody's plane. A search party was organized in the afternoon and fifteen bodies were found. Most of them were hardly recognizable. The following crewmembers were killed:

Lt. Murphy Crew

1st Lt. Robert E. Murphy; Lt. Marvin F. Mickler; Lt. Anthony N. Ricciotti; T/Sgt. Edward L. Bressler; S/Sgt. William J. Ronan; S/Sgt. Roland M. Conrad; S/Sgt. Joe P. Ruiz and Sgt. Norman Jonkman.

Lt. Melody Crew

1st Lt. Charles A. Melody; Lt. Lester H. McAlister; Lt. Robert J. Burk; Lt. Harold F. Couch; Sgt. Edgar O. Tennant; S/Sgt. William A. Finch and Sgt. Napoleon Rousseau.

On The Following Pages, Are Crew By Crew Accounts, Of The Nine Hundred And Fifty Four Bomber Crewmen Of The 465th Bombardment Group (H), Who Became Battle Casualties, While Engaging The Enemy In Combat In The Skies Over Europe, During The Final Year Of World War II, From 5 May 1944 Through 26 April 1945:

29 May 1944: 1st Lt. William L. Vorhies, Pilot, 783rd Squadron, flew a B-24H, #42-52589 named "Moby Dick" to bomb the Atzgersdorf Amme Luther Seck Aircraft Components Factory at Liesing, Austria with crewmembers, Lt. Owen W. Livesay, Co-Pilot; Lt. Daniel J. Ryan, Navigator; Lt. Edward A. Groh, Bombardier; T/Sgt. Hubert P. Johnson, Flight Engineer-Gunner; S/Sgt. Merton P. Pitman, Radio Operator-Gunner; S/Sgt. George J. Payne, Tail Turret Gunner; S/Sgt. Charles G. Yokitis, Gunner; S/Sgt. John J. Luce, Nose Turret Gunner and S/Sgt. Homer L. Ward, Gunner. The weather was clear and their aircraft was seen to crash at Liesing, Austria at 10:31 hours.

Eyewitness, Lt. Ralph L. Pemberton Jr., 782nd Squadron, "Target time as near as I can figure was 10:31 hours and it was just after the bombs went away that the flak got the heaviest and I was busiest. I was flying in Charlie box in number six position and "Moby Dick" was in Able box in number three position. Just after the bombs went away, I happened to glance up and saw one chute already open behind Able box, nothing seemed to be wrong with any of the ships at that time but while I was looking, "Moby Dick" began to lose large quantities of gas. There was no explosion, just as though he had gotten a hole punched in a tank and gas was running out. The ship still held formation and then oil began to come out also. I can't be sure now whether it was a piece of the plane, or a man, but I do remember at the time I said, "There goes another one." No chute opened so if it was one of the crew, he probably made a delayed jump. Only a second or so after that, the ship evidently under some control, peeled up and away from the formation going almost directly over the top of Charlie box and as he passed over I can remember seeing one open chute caught in the open bomb bay. The ship then went out of my line of vision and I became very busy with a runaway prop."

Lt. Vorhies aircraft left the formation over the target 30 to 40 seconds after bombing. All of the crew bailed out except Lt. Ryan and S/Sgt. Luce, who were trapped in the nose and S/Sgt. Payne, who was in the tail turret. Vorhies got an "O.K." check from Payne about half way on the bomb run. After receiving a direct hit on the tail section, on the right vertical stabilizer, while on the bomb run, he could establish no further communication with Payne, who was dead from the flak burst. In Vorhies last conversation with Lt. Ryan, he reported heavy flak coming up as they turned on the bomb run. The bombardier Lt. Groh, who bailed out first through the nose wheel door, said Ryan was putting his chute on and Luce was getting out of the nose turret as the ship was going down and they were apparently uninjured at that time. Sgts. Johnson, Pitman and Yokitis, bailed out of the waist windows. Sgt. Ward and Lts. Livesay and Vorhies, bailed out of the bomb bay. All bailed out within 8 to 10 minutes of target time. The aircraft struck the ground approximately 5 miles southeast of the target. Payne, Luce and Ryan were in the aircraft when it struck the ground. Luce and Ryan were in the nose compartment and Payne was in the tail turret. Payne was dead; Luce and Ryan's condition was unknown. The pilot saw the radio operator Sgt. Pitman, approximately two hours after their capture. He was alive but had flak in his right hand and arm.

A German Officer told the pilot that four bodies were found, but that could not have been possible, as there were only 10 men on the ship and 7 men bailed out and were captured. Crewmembers bailing out of the bomb bay reported that a chute was hung on the nose wheel door and the shroud lines were crossing the bomb bay. Supposition is, Ryan or Luce, opened their chute in the door and hung there, blocking the escape of the other. The catwalk from the bomb bay to the nose was blocked by nose wheel wreckage and fire from a direct hit on the right side of the ship at the nose wheel position.

Lts. Vorhies, Livesay and Groh and Sgts. Johnson, Pitman, Yokitis and Ward were captured and made Prisoners of War until they were liberated in May of 1945. Lt. Ryan and Sgts. Luce and Payne were Killed In Action.

30 May 1944: Lt. George A. Prince, Pilot, 781st Squadron, flew a B-24H, #41 29356, Call Letter Yellow "G" named "Custers Folly" to bomb the Neudorfl Fleugzeufabrik Aircraft Components Factory at Neunkirken, Austria with crewmembers, Lt. Harold D. Holden, Co-Pilot; Lt. Calvin J. Canyock, Navigator; Lt. Murray Septoff, Bombardier; Sgt. Jimmy Patrick, Nose Turret Gunner; Sgt. Abraham Dubinsky, Assistant Engineer-Top Turret Gunner; T/Sgt. Harry M. Smith, Flight Engineer-Left Waist Gunner; T/Sgt. John J. Crowley, Radio Operator-Right Waist Gunner; Sgt. James F. Downs, Ball Turret Gunner and Sgt. Jack C. Williams, Tail Turret Gunner. Visibility was good and their aircraft was seen to crash at 11:37 hours.

Eyewitness, S/Sgt. Harry G. Reifsnyder, 783rd Squadron, "An ME 109 attacked the B-24 from the rear. The plane was hit between number two engine and the fuselage. The wing of the plane burst into flames. Three parachutes were seen to open, with one of them catching fire and burning completely. A few seconds later one more man was seen to jump from the ship. He delayed opening his parachute and fell about 6,000 feet before pulling the ripcord. About four minutes later, two more men jumped from the burning ship and opened their parachutes immediately. The flames in the meantime spread through the bomb bay and back into the waist. Two more men jumped from the plane, which at that moment broke in half. The tail section floated past the two men who had just jumped while the front part of the plane spiraled toward the ground. When the front part of the plane had fallen about 6,000 feet it exploded, throwing the last two remaining men free. The parachutes of the last two men were seen to open, thus making a total of ten men."

Over the target flak hits were scored on the plane and during the return the ship was attacked by 3 ME-109 fighters in the Zagreb area where number 2 engine was set on fire and the gas lines and oxygen lines were badly damaged. Then the electrical system was knocked out. A fire was started at the oxygen tanks and rolled onto the flight deck. Sgt. Smith fought the fire and others prepared to bail out. Sgt. Crowley was wounded in his right shoulder and leg. Lt. Prince was reluctant to abandon ship, but finally when an ammunition box was ablaze and the incendiary shells began to explode, he advised Lt. Holden to go back and see that the crew bailed out (there was no interplane communication). Holden attached his chute and went back. Sgts. Williams, Crowley, Downs and Patrick and Lt. Septoff bailed out. Crowley informed the pilot of his wounds, and that the plane was on fire.

Because of his condition he was the first to bail out of the waist section. He lost consciousness when his chute jerked open and was unable to see what happened to the remainder of the crew. He was in a one-room hospital when he regained consciousness. While in the hospital the Partisans told him that there had been a skirmish between them and the Chetniks, for his possession, when he landed near Troglav. Three days later he was taken by cart to a hospital in the vicinity of Topuske. Holden the co-pilot had returned to the flight deck and took over the controls just as they snapped. The ship lurched into a spin, throwing him out of his seat and pinning him against the side of the flight deck. Because of the terrific physical pressure the spin exerted, he was unable to move and remained pinned in place while the flames rolled around him, burning his hands and face. The airplane suddenly exploded and at that moment 5 men were still in the ship. Holden the co-pilot, Smith the engineer and Dubinsky the assistant engineer, had their parachutes hooked on. They were blown clear of the ship and parachuted to the ground.

The pilot, Lt. Prince, and navigator Lt. Canyock, went down with the dismembered aircraft at 11:37 hours. Holden who was burned severely on both hands and suffered a head wound, landed and was immediately in the care of the Partisans, who attempted to stay the flow of blood from his head. Dubinsky and Smith had parachuted and both were also very badly burned. Dubinsky was picked up by two civilians who gave him water and carried him to a farmhouse where he found Holden and Smith. A Partisan doctor came out and took them to a hospital in a town named Bodemo, located half way between Krupa and Pretovic. Here they were treated by the Partisan doctor. Lt. Septoff got hung up in a tree and a Partisan helped him get down and he was taken to a house about 2 miles away. Sgt. Patrick was brought to him and they were taken to the Majkle Japra area to a hospital. There they met Holden, Smith and Dubinsky. Several days later they were joined by Sgts. Williams and Downs, who had dropped further north.

Smith was too seriously injured to be moved and Dubinsky his intimate friend, who was also severely burned on his face and hands, decided to remain with Smith. An officer, Lt. White remained also to supervise the care of the injured flyers. Holden with both hands severely burned and a head wound was moved on 13 July to a British Mission. Before he left his companions, he viewed the graves of his pilot and navigator, Lt. George A. Prince and Lt. Calvin J. Canyock, who were buried in an Orthodox Catholic Churchyard.

On 14 July Holden left the British Mission for Glamoc, where he joined the large party of Americans who proceeded finally to the point of evacuation. On 12 August 1944 Smith and Dubinsky were moved to a British Mission and then evacuated from an airstrip by a Russian piloted C-47 aircraft on the same night, arriving in Bari, Italy on 13 August 1944. Sgt. Williams had landed west of Slaak, where Peasants picked him up and they went for the woods. They ran into Partisans and he was taken to a house, and about 3 hours later Sgt. Crowley who was very badly wounded, was brought in. They traveled 8 hours toward Petrinja where they met Sgt. Downs. When Downs bailed out an ME-109 made a pass at him, firing a burst and zooming right over his chute. He felt tugs in his shroud lines, as bullets must have hit. When he hit the ground he saw 15 holes in his chute. Williams also saw the holes.

The next day Crowley was taken to a hospital in Daniaj. On 19 June he was moved to an Allied station near a landing strip and evacuated by air later that night. Downs and Williams went to Glina, where they met Sgt. Elders of the 464th Bomb Group. The next day others of Elders group joined them. They traveled from Glina to southwest of Bos Novi, then on south of the area north of Petrovac and stayed in the Japra area of Majkle Japra from about 6 June to 12 July.

Petrovac had been taken by the Germans the latter part of May so the men couldn't be evacuated from there. About 38 American airmen were together and they lived for the first few days, mainly on soup, a greasy water without salt, as food was very scarce. On 12 July, they were told they were going to an airstrip near Glamoc. They headed for Sanleaj, reached Ribnikj then to Rurjahepac over very rough terrain. They were near Glamoc on 17 July and were told the Germans were driving toward the Glamoc airstrip. The evacuation plane did not come that night, as the weather was bad with heavy rain. They moved back northwest a little way, arriving at 3:00 A. M. and at 4:00 A. M., they were roused and told they had to move at once as the Germans were on their way up. They traveled northwest, and reached the hills near Tieavoj and stayed there until 21 July and were evacuated. All crewmembers were evacuated and returned to base, with the exception of Lts. Prince and Canyock who were Killed In Action.

31 May 1944: Lt. Robert M. King, Pilot, 782nd Squadron, flew a B-24H, #42-52543 to bomb the Dacia Roma Oil Refinery at Ploesti, Rumania, with crewmembers, Lt. Frank G. Saxton, Co-Pilot; Lt. Herbert G. Hansen, Navigator; Lt. Warren G. Milum, Bombardier; T/Sgt. Norman B. Huebner, Flight Engineer-Gunner; T/Sgt. Robert D. Walker, Radio Operator-Gunner; S/Sgt. Robert W. June, Gunner; S/Sgt. Eugene C. Long Jr., Gunner; S/Sgt. Joseph L. Landi, Gunner and S/Sgt. George Sherbon, Gunner. The weather was clear and their aircraft was seen to crash in Rumania.

Eyewitness, 1st Lt. Frank J. Teagarden, "The group was flying at about 20,000 feet. I was leading "F" box and was below and to the left of the lead squadron, where the ship was flying, which went down. I saw a small door come off the ship, hit the vertical stabilizer, then float back through the other ships in the formation. As the door flew off the plane, the plane did a wing over to the left and went into a power on spin. I could not see the ship after it went below my ship, but members of my crew said they did not see any parachutes or personnel leave the plane."

Eyewitness, Lt. Robert H. Morrison, "The right rudder and vertical stabilizer of the ship shuddered and tore off, in about three seconds. The ship rolled over on it's back at which time the right half of the horizontal stabilizer also tore off. The airplane proceeded into a vertical dive and slow vertical spin. The inevitable crash was not observed, but an explosion and fire directly below and behind our position was reported to me by the tail gunner. The explosion followed about ninety seconds after the ship left the formation. No fighters or flak were observed prior to the accident. No chutes were seen, nor is it believed possible that any of the crewmembers could have left the ship."

Eyewitness, Sgt. Abraham L. Frank, "I was flying in the lead ship, Major Smith's plane, in "A" box as tail gunner. Lt. King's ship was in number five position of "A" box - a bit to the left and lower than us and about one hundred and fifty feet behind us. At approximately 09:35 hours, I was watching Lt. King's plane and noted a large yellow object fly out of the forward topside of the ship and lodge on the horizontal stabilizers. At first I thought it was an explosion, but within a split second I realized it was the dinghy, which had come loose. The plane pulled up about fifty feet, seemed to stop and quiver in the air, then nosed over and went into a dive, which seemed to be almost vertical. I started to follow the ship down and at the same time called the pilot telling him what had happened. I lost track of the plane for approximately ten seconds and then picked it up again just as it hit the ground. It exploded as it hit and I saw a very large clump of black smoke. I did not see any parachutes come out of the plane. The navigator got the coordinates of where it hit. There was no enemy opposition at the time of the accident."

16

GENDARME LEGION GORJ
Gendarmerie Post Carbunesti

STATEMENT OF CIRCUMSTANCE

This day 31st May in the year one thousand nine hundred forty four, at Tg. Carbunesti.

We Col. Alexandru Niculescu, Chief of 4th Mountain Permanent Division, Commander of Tg. Carbunesti Garrison, Lt. Col. Georgescu Emanoil, Commander of the Gendarme Legion Gorj, Reserve Lt. Mrejoariu Mircea, Chief of the 2nd Bureau of 4th Mountain Permanent Division and Jand. Plot. Major Voicu Coman, Chief of Gendarme Section Tg. Carbunesti, hereby ascertain the following in connection with the crash of an American aircraft on the 31st day of May 1944, 0920 hours, 1500 metres South-East of Tg. Carbunesti, to the left of the Tg. Carbunesti School in the Carbunesti village.

1) During an alert, on the 31st day of May 1944, after a numerous wave of enemy planes was flying from West towards East, it was observed that one of the enemy planes, probably a quadri-motor, had lost control and was leaving behind a trail of smoke.

There could also be observed the efforts that the plane crew were making in order to straighten the plane and then bring her to a normal landing on the ground situated as above mentioned.

However, the manoeuvre did not succeed and the plane crashed in flames on the above mentioned field; her bombs did not explode.

Together with Jand. Plot. Major Voicu Coman, Chief of Gendarme Section Tg. Carbunesti, we applied the required measures.

2) On crashing the plane caught fire which became intense, producing a thick cloud of smoke and causing explosion of automatic weapons on board.

3) Forty five minutes after the crash a small explosion took place followed by a powerful one, when the bombs of the plane exploded, which caused the breaking of some windows in the Tg. Carbunesti dwellings.

This explosion destroyed the plane shattering it to pieces which were scattered over a distance of 5 to 6 hundred metres.

Due to the measures of safety that were taken in time, the civilian population that was imprudently approaching the scene of the crash was driven back, thus avoiding all accidents when the bombs exploded.

After the plane burned out completely, the undersigned went to the spot, in order to apply the legal measures for identifying the corpses, the objects found on them, as well as those parts of the plane that could be identified.

The wrecked plane was a bomber belonging to the United States of North America.

a. The fire and explosion of bombs that were on board destroyed the plane with all the board material, almost completely.

b. Four corpses could be identified by name and serial number and three remained unknown.

Parts of the plane could also be identified, melted by the fire, which constitute another value than that of the raw material and 4 machine guns, partially destroyed.

4) On the corpses identified by name and serial number, or in their vicinity the following were found:

On NORMAN B. HUEBNER, ASN 16241796 T.42-43 A.P., one of the identity tags was left on the body and the other was removed in compliance with instructions No. 201527/1943 of the Ministry for Home Affairs:

-one enameled ring with insignia, series 1940 H.S and underneath R. Blus Island.
-one wedding ring, marked 14 Karats, with no other inscription.
-one wrist watch, antimagnetic, waterproof, with red minute hand, luminous dial, with leather strap.
-one fountain pen with the inscription; Sheaffer's Lifetime Reg. U.S. Pat. Eff. Made in USA 14 K.
-one pencil
-one pocket screw driver
-two embroidered patches, a white star with red in the middle on a blue background, with two yellow wings.
-one insignia, Pilot's wings, marked "Sterling" on the back.
-one first aid kit.
-one note book with personal notes.
-one picture signed Yours Marion.
-one pair fur-lined snow-boots.
-one pair leather boots.
-one pair leather gloves, for airmen.

EUGENE C. LONG, Sgt., airman, age 21, ASN 87692.

- one Special Order No. 1 of January 1944, issued by Airfield Nebraska.
- personal will of Sgt. EUGEN SCRAMMWEL LONG JR.
- 20 French francs issued by the Bank of Algiers
- 10 francs issued by the Bank of France.
- 4 five franc notes issued by the bank of Algiers

WALKER ROBERT D., Sgt. ASN 6567099, 28 August 1944.

- identity card of Machine Gunner's School.
- a leather album with identity card mentioned above and 17 family pictures.
- one Remington pistol, Syracuse USA, 3 clips, 14 cartridges; serial number of pistol 1288793.

HERBERT G. HANSEN 0-691752 C. P.T. 43

5) The following personal objects and plane equipment were found near the unidentified bodies:

- one tire of the landing gear, in good condition.
- one inner tube of the same landing gear wheel, blown out.
- two complete parachutes, in good condition.
- remnants of 6 burned parachutes.
- two rubber oxygen masks, burned.
- two leather coats, burned.
- one parachute case.
- one lantern, destroyed.
- one oxygen mask.
- one knife with leather case.
- one compass with support, damaged.
- five keys, various.
- 12 dollar bank notes, partly burned, amounting to 28 Dollars.
- 6 Italian cent coins.

6)   Objects forwarded by the Gendarme Post Jupanesti to the Section Tg. Carbunesti:

- one double rubberized canvas.
- one air pump, broken.
- 3 oars, detachable, painted blue, one of them broken.
- 1 small hook, for canvas screen.

- one Remington pistol, series 1289558, destroyed.

7)   The following were also found around the wreckage:

- one flare ejector with 3 flares.
- one handle belonging to navigators apparatus, crushed with the lense, damaged.

8) The corpses of the 7 Airmen were removed from the territory of the community Carbunesti Sat to the territory of the Community of Carbunesti Tg., and buried in the Heroes Cemetery, on the 1st day of June 1944 1830 hours, in compliance with instructions No. 201527 of the Ministry for Home Affairs, dated 14 October 1943.
9) The above mentioned objects were forwarded to the 2nd Section of the general Staff, according to the instructions shown under Chapter 3 paragraph b.

Some of the heavy material was retained in the warehouse of the 4th Mountain Permanent Division, at the disposal of superior authorities:

- four plane machine guns, partly destroyed.
- one plane tire.
- one inner tube, blown out.
- 3 oars, detachable, painted blue, one of them broken.

The aluminum and metal parts were gathered and are being guarded; they will be taken to the Gendarme Section Carbunesti Tg., and deposited there till they will be removed.

10) In witness hereof this Statement was drawn up in eight copies, two of which are forwarded to the 2nd Section of the General Staff, two to the Gendarme Legion Gorj, one to the 7th Territorial Corps, one to the 4th Mountain Permanent Division, one to the Gendarme Tg. Carbunesti, while one copy will be retained by the Tg. Carbunesti Garrison.

Commander of the Tg. Carbunesti Garrison
Colonel
/s/ Alexandru Niculescu

Commander of the Gendarme
Legion Gorj
Lt. Col.
/s/ Georgescu Corneliu
Chief of Tg. Carbunesti Section
Plot. Maj.
/s/ Voicu Coman
CHIEF OF BUREAU
Captain
/s/ C. Unga

The following telegram on the fate of Lt. King and his crew reads as follows: Incoming telegram received through the State Department from Bern, Switzerland. Subject: <u>American Interests in Romania</u>. Norman Huebner death not indicated buried Carbunesti, District Gorj. Following killed 31 May; Eugene Long, Robert Walker, Herbert G. Hansen and three unidentified, all buried Carbunesti, District Gorj.

Note: In an Interrogation Statement dated 25 October 1945, signed by Sgt Oscar N. Lebeu ASN. 39415053, he states that S/Sgt. Robert Walker was "killed by German guard while going to latrine in prison compound." Date and place of death: 15 June 1944 at Stalag Luft 4. Official documents indicate Lt. King and his entire crew were Killed In Action.

31 May 1944: Capt. James W. Wray, Pilot, 781st Squadron, flew a B-24H, #42-52558, named "Sacajawea," to bomb the Dacia Roma Oil Refinery at Ploesti, Rumania with crewmembers, Lt. Dale C. Tipton, Co-Pilot; Lt. Vernon L. Burda, Navigator; Lt. Eugene M. Krzyzynski, Bombardier; Sgt. Frank R. Jasicko, Flight Engineer-Waist Gunner; Sgt. Hulitt L. Holcombe, Radio Operator-Waist Gunner; Sgt. Albert D. Ralston Jr., Top Turret Gunner; Sgt. Michael J. Deironimi, Ball Turret Gunner; Sgt. William G. Seteropoulis, Nose Turret Gunner and Sgt. Harold B. Farrar, Tail Turret Gunner. At 12:15 hours the weather was clear.

The final mission for the month of May was flown on the 31st to the Dacia Roma Oil Refinery at Ploesti, Rumania. Because of a smoke screen the primary target was obscured and two targets of opportunity were bombed with fair to good results. One was the pumping station and water separation plant of the Baldesti Oil Field near Ploesti and the other was the Concordia-Vega Oil

Refinery near Ploesti. Flak was intense and a number of ships were damaged. The aircraft of Capt. Wray, who was Squadron Operations Officer and flying with 1st Lt. Dale C. Tipton as his co-pilot, was hit by flak over the target which knocked out number 1 engine and damaged number 2 engine. They were leading Charlie box and were able to keep in formation for about an hour. After number 2 engine went out they were unable to keep up and the pilot reported by radio and ordered the formation to reform, as he would have to fall out of formation over Yugoslavia.

They soon found themselves looking up at the tops of the Dinaric Alps, as they fought to stay aloft long enough to reach friendly Yugoslavian territory held by Partisan forces. They were forced to bail out however and fortunately found themselves in the hands of Broz Tito's troops. Sprained ankles and bruises from landing made it necessary for the crew to stay in the landing area for a couple of days before starting the trip out. Then traveling by foot, horseback and wild truck rides over the mountain roads; they arrived at a British Commando encampment from which 15th Air Force Headquarters was contacted by radio. The next night a C-47 landed by the light of four burning oil drums, picked up the crew and flew them back to Bari, Italy. At Bari they were de-loused and de-briefed, before going to Capri for a week of rest before returning to the Squadron to resume combat operations.

6 June 1944: Lt. Ralph L. Pemberton, 782nd Squadron, Pilot, flew a B-24H, #42-52575, Call Letter Red "K" named "Old Dutch Cleanser" to bomb the Dacia Romano Oil Refinery at Ploesti, Rumania with crewmembers, Lt. Edwin Bernard Boehme, Co-Pilot; F/O William Leppla Jr., Navigator; Lt. William Leonard Claytor Jr., Bombardier; T/Sgt. Walter A. Rolek, Flight Engineer-Gunner; T/Sgt. Thomas R. Whyte, Radio Operator-Gunner; T/Sgt. Sherman Laub, Armorer-Gunner; S/Sgt. Paul Ledney, Gunner; S/Sgt. John R. McGrath, Gunner and S/Sgt. Cecil L. Sammons, Top Turret Gunner. The weather was clear and their aircraft was seen to ditch in the Adriatic Sea at 12:10 hours.

Eyewitness, Lt. Harold J. Smithberger, "The B-24 came over the coast of Yugoslavia at 10,000 feet at 11:46 hours with number two engine feathered. He was holding a fairly good position in formation at that time. Gas was coming off the right wing and out of number four engine. The engineer said he was also losing gas off the left wing directly behind number two engine. Almost immediately after leaving the coast of Yugoslavia he fell behind the formation and started downward. His descent was at 130 to 135 miles per hour and losing approximately 1000 to 1200 feet of altitude per minute. On the descent the crewmembers were throwing things overboard. Ammunition belts were the only things I was able to distinguish for sure, but several other objects were thrown out also. I tried to contact him by radio but could not. At 12:10 hours the plane hit the water. It held together and floated for approximately five minutes. I called Big Fence immediately and gave the position as 42 degrees 11 minutes north and 17 degrees 10 minutes east. Big Fence answered saying they had a fix on the plane just before it hit the water.

I did not see any life rafts come out of the ditched airplane. Another B-24 flew over the ditching position and threw out a life raft. He also dropped smoke flares. The life raft came fairly close to the men in the water. I circled the position until 13:08 hours and a few minutes before leaving I went down on the deck and flew close by the ditching position. I definitely saw four men in the water - three were together and one was by himself. The bombardier thought there were six or seven men in the water. None of them were in the dinghy at that time. I gave Big Fence this information and came on to the field. The other B-24 was still circling when I left."

Seven crewmembers were Killed In Action in the ditching as follows: Lts. Pemberton and Boehme, were killed in the cockpit. Lt. Claytor and Sgts. Laub, Ledney and McGrath, were drowned. Sgt. Whyte was killed, when the top turret broke loose and fell on him. The following three crewmembers were rescued and survived; F/O Leppla, S/Sgt. Sammons and T/Sgt. Rolek. Flight Officer Leppla's injuries were unknown. T/Sgt. Rolek suffered a fractured pelvis in the ditching and S/Sgt. Sammons had severe lacerations on his left leg, right arm and face. All three suffered from hypothermia, after being in the Adriatic Sea for five hours before being rescued.

6 June 1944: 1st Lt. John F. MacFarlane, Pilot, 781st Squadron, flew a B-24H, #42-52505, Call Letter Yellow "K" named "Hell's Belles II" to bomb the Dacia Romano Oil Refinery at Ploesti, Rumania with crewmembers, Lt. Robert L. George, Co-Pilot; Lt. Howard L. Sapenoff, Bombardier; Lt. Sidney Weiss, Navigator; T/Sgt. Albert P. McQuaid Jr., Flight Engineer-Top Turret Gunner; T/Sgt. Thomas R. Jackson Jr., Radio Operator-Gunner; S/Sgt. John R. Duke, Tail Turret Gunner; S/Sgt. Jarmar Jancarik, Gunner; S/Sgt. Hoyt F. Adsit, Gunner; S/Sgt. Ralph C. Finch, Gunner and S/Sgt. Melton L. Crawford, Photographer. The weather was good and their aircraft was last sighted at 11:45 hours. This was an eleven-man crew.

Eyewitness, S/Sgt. Arthur N. Franklin, 781st Squadron, "I saw Yellow "K" hit by flak over the target, apparently number 4 engine was hit as it was feathered. About ten minutes later, some distance from the target the ship peeled off to the right of formation E box and seven men bailed out. The pilot and three other men stayed with the plane and rejoined the formation. The plane stayed with the formation for about fifteen or twenty minutes and then made a bank to the left and went out about ten miles. It is quite possible that the other four men were able to jump safely but I could not see due to clouds and haze. I believe all men should have landed safely."

Over the target the aircraft was hit by flak which knocked out engines number 3 and 4 and the right Tokyo tank sprung a leak. Flak put the controls out momentarily. They dove several thousand feet righting the plane, and joined a new formation. They were then attacked by enemy aircraft causing number 2 engine to run away but number 4 had begun to operate again. They kept losing speed when a gas bubble caused number 4 to stop. At this point seven of the crew, Lts. Sapenoff and Weiss and Sgts. Jackson, Adsit, Crawford, Jancarik and Duke, bailed out in Rumania. They received an ETA from the Group Leader as to when they would reach Partisan territory. At 12:00 hours the remaining four men, Lts. MacFarlane and George and Sgts. McQuaid and Finch, bailed out from 13,000 feet. They claim destroying an ME-109 before bailing out. They landed in the Dornier Mountains and immediately contacted Partisans. They were brought to a nearby house where MacFarlane, McQuaid and Finch all three met and joined forces remaining together for the entire time. Here they also met Lt. George their co-pilot, who was badly wounded. At 16:00 hours a mission came to the house, led by Major Drake.

They told them of a battle at Nikabuja Airdrome. At 22:00 hours they were told to leave due to the enemy coming near. They left there carrying the wounded co-pilot. They walked for three days, with only three hours rest and during this trip one of the Partisan guides was shot when they were attacked by Pro-German Slavs. On the third day they arrived at a Partisan hospital at Buan, but were evacuated immediately due to German activity there. Leaving there they headed for Upper Moraoa in the company of Major Drake's mission.

They spent four hours of the night resting at a farmhouse near Moraoa and then proceeded to Upper Moraoa where they remained the rest of the day. Then they went to Lower Moraoa meeting Major Drake at a monastery, which served as a mission. Here there were other English and American evaders. They spent the night here and left for Kolaoin. They remained one night, then left on 12 June for Barane arriving that afternoon. They remained at Barane for two and one half days and on the night of 15 June they were evacuated for Bari Airdrome.

The seven men who bailed out, Weiss, Sapenoff, Jackson, Crawford, Adsit, Jancarik and Duke, bailed out when someone in the plane, (who is unidentified) gave a bail out signal over the intercom and the men were gone before the pilot could recall them. They bailed out over the Orsova area of Rumania. Sgt. Adsit said, "We landed near the Danube River by a town called Iron Gate, where we were captured by a Rumanian 5th Boundary Guard Company and taken to their jail. We had board benches to sleep on. When I landed I thought I was done because some of the men wanted to shoot us at once.

24

They also said they were going to shoot us a couple of days later while they were asking us questions. We went by horse and cart for about five days and then by rail to Bucharest where we were in prison until our release. The guards made us walk the streets to the camp and on the way the civilians punched and kicked us. We were under air attack many nights and some days. Our food was bread and cheese, a bran coffee, soups and once in a while some meat. It could have been worse. They released us by open gate and some of us went to the countryside because the Germans were bombing the city heavy and also drawing troops out. We had a few close calls from gunfire and fighters coming in at ground level. On 31 August and 1 September 1944, we were returned to Allied controlled territory in Italy."

6 June 1944: Lt. Glenferd E. Funk, Pilot, 782nd Squadron, flew a B-24H, #42-52456, Call Letter White "A" to bomb the Dacia Romano Oil Refinery at Ploesti, Rumania with crewmembers, Lt. Marvin E. Hoffman, Co-Pilot; Lt. Richard C. Kline, Bombardier; Lt. John A. Leins, Navigator; S/Sgt. Otis W. Dunderdale, Nose Turret Gunner; T/Sgt. Elwyn L. Loomis, Flight Engineer-Gunner; S/Sgt. Leroy M. Drane, Radio Operator-Gunner; S/Sgt. Matthew J. Mroczkowski, Armorer-Gunner; S/Sgt. James A. Shaughnessy, Gunner and S/Sgt. Nicholas Stetz, Gunner. Their aircraft was seen to crash in Rumania. Weather was clear.

Eyewitness, S/Sgt. Jesse C. Creech, 782nd Squadron, "At about 09:23 or 09:25 hours I saw Lt. Funk's ship White "A" hit by incendiary flak between number two engine and the fuselage and start to burn back toward the fuselage. The nose wheel door opened and three men appeared, parachuted and fell clear and opened in a free fall. Then five men came from the back of the ship. The ship then went into a spiral and two more parachutes came out making a total of ten. The location was near the Bucharest Airport. I believe the men should have landed safely. I was too busy to watch any longer."

The aircraft left the formation on the rally off the target. All crewmembers bailed out in approximately sixty seconds. Lt. Kline and Sgt. Dunderdale, bailed out through the nose wheel door, Lts. Hoffman, Leins, Funk and Sgt. Loomis, bailed out through the bomb bays. Sgts. Drane, Mroczkowski, Shaughnessy and Stetz, bailed out through the camera hatch. Their aircraft struck the ground 15 miles northwest of Bucharest, Rumania. All crewmembers were captured and made Prisoners of War.

6 June 1944: 1st Lt. Kenneth M. Martin, Pilot, 781st Squadron, flew a B-24H, #42-52449, Call Letter Yellow "E" named "Patches" to bomb the Dacia Romano Oil Refinery at Ploesti, Rumania with crewmembers, Lt. Rex L. Struble,

Co-Pilot; Lt. Robert L. Williamson, Navigator; Lt. Morris E. Finley, Bombardier; Sgt. Wilburn Vorheier, Nose Turret Gunner; S/Sgt. Donald L. Merkel, Flight Engineer-Top Turret Gunner; S/Sgt. Thomas Scalese, Radio Operator-Right Waist Gunner; Sgt. Kenneth G. Foden, Armorer-Ball Turret Gunner; S/Sgt. Gerald J. Simmons, Left Waist Gunner and Sgt. Francis P. Little, Tail Turret Gunner. Weather was clear when this aircraft was last sighted at 09:42 hours.

Eyewitness, Lt. Donald K. Wake, 780th Squadron, "Yellow "E" (Lt. Martin's ship), flying on Godfrey's left wing had two engines on fire, the flight deck and first third of the bomb bay on fire when the first two men bailed out from the waist section. The first man to bail out opened his chute immediately after clearing the plane and apparently broke his neck and suffered other injuries according to observers who saw him falling in a limp position, with his head hanging down. The second man to bail out made a very long delayed drop and apparently landed safely. Two others bailed out shortly afterward and by this time the plane was too far away from ours to observe anything else, except to see the two chutes opening. These four men were all that left the plane. Nobody saw the plane actually hit the ground or explode in the air. There is a possibility that the fire was brought under control and the pilot made a crash landing."

All crewmembers were at their gun positions as their aircraft had been under attack by enemy aircraft. Their aircraft was on fire due to the enemy action. Lt. Martin gave the order to bail out and all crewmembers bailed out within minutes of one another, southwest of Ploesti. Lt. Finley, had asked Sgt. Merkel to check the bomb bay to see if all the bombs had dropped. Lt. Struble and Merkel were both in the bomb bay trying to put out the fire and didn't succeed so they both bailed out through the bomb bay. Lts. Martin, Finley and Williamson and Sgt. Foden bailed out. Williamson was not injured when he bailed out but when he hit the ground he suffered a broken leg. Sgts. Simmons and Scalese bailed out through the left waist window. Sgt. Little bailed out through the rear escape hatch and Sgt. Vorheier, bailed out through the nose wheel door. All of the enlisted men on the crew were on their first mission. They were strangers to the officers and the officers were strangers to them, so they knew very little about each other, although they did become good buddies in Prison Camp.

All of the crewmembers were captured and made Prisoners of War, but were liberated and returned to the States about three months later on 2 September 1944, following the capture of Ploesti on 23 August 1944.

13 June 1944: 1st Lt. Harold A. Hillman, Pilot, 782nd Squadron, flew a B-24H, #42-52495 to bomb the Milbertshofen Ordnance Depot at Munich, Germany with crewmembers, F/O Lloyd B. Satterfield, Co-Pilot; Lt. William D. Thompson, Navigator; Lt. Delbert Little, Bombardier; T/Sgt. Edgar S. Goins,

Radio Operator-Gunner; T/Sgt. Raymond H. Hutson, Flight Engineer-Gunner; S/Sgt. Robert N. Niven, Gunner; S/Sgt. Walter A. Brooker, Gunner; S/Sgt. Harold A. Simpson, Gunner and S/Sgt. John C. Monroe, Gunner. The weather was clear.

The aircraft left the formation between the I.P. and the target. F/O Satterfield gave the order to bail out. Satterfield and Lts. Thompson, Little, Hillman and Sgts. Hutson, Niven, Goins, Brooker, Simpson and Monroe all bailed out in succession as fast as possible. They were all over the Adriatic Sea, off shore from Pirengi, Italy. Their aircraft struck the water just out from Pirengi, Italy. The entire crew was picked up and interned at German Airforce Command 2 at Verona and made Prisoners of War. Sgt. Monroe who was injured was put in the Prisoner of War Hospital #11 at Verone and then transferred to the Prisoner of War Hospital in the district of Freising near Munich, Germany.

30 June 1944: Capt. John R. Dickey, Pilot, 781st Squadron, flew a B-24H, #41-28915, Call Letter Yellow "N" named "Long John Silver" to bomb the Synthetic Oil Refinery at Blechhammer, Germany with crewmembers, Lt. Frank T. Hylla, Co-Pilot; 1st Lt. Jerome F. Jolicoeur, Navigator; 1st Lt. Warren G. Hausold, Bombardier; S/Sgt. Austin C. Davis, Nose Turret Gunner; T/Sgt. Robert H. Carr, Flight Engineer-Top Turret Gunner; T/Sgt. George A. Wilson, Radio Operator-Left Waist Gunner; S/Sgt. Robert H. Hoover, Armorer-Ball Turret Gunner; S/Sgt. Joseph E. Carroll, Right Waist Gunner and S/Sgt. Richard A. Thill, Tail Turret Gunner. This crew experienced extremely cloudy weather on this mission.

Eyewitness, T. D. Cooke, Sgt., 780th Squadron, "When I first noticed Captain Dickey's plane it was approximately 10:04 A.M., coming out of a cloud bank at exactly six o'clock from our plane and just slightly low, about 100 feet. At almost the same instant I saw two fighters attacking him from 7 o'clock lane. As the fighters turned, one chute opened just leaving the camera hatch. The B-24 had a fire coming out of its right rear bomb bay. One of the fighters did not return but the other one made a sharp turn and lined up directly behind the B-24 and fired directly into it until he was no more than 100 feet from it. The fighter then banked sharply to the right and went into a cloud smoking badly. The B-24 continued straight forward for about 30 seconds, the fire getting worse. Then the B-24 banked slightly left with five chutes opening as it turned. After almost completing a 180-degree turn the B-24 exploded. In my opinion, the men who left the plane in chutes had a good chance of reaching the ground alive."

On the way to the target a front over Hungary turned the formation back and it split up in the clouds. On coming into an open place the bombs were salvoed.

Three FW 190's attacked from the rear, knocking out the interphone and the tail turret and started a fire in the waist section. Sgt. Carr was firing at the enemy aircraft from his top turret position just prior to bailing out. Sgts. Thill, Carroll and Wilson, bailed out. Before Sgt. Wilson bailed out he checked on Sgt. Hoover and reported that he was dead. As the aircraft was burning, Lt. Jolicoeur went to get Lt. Hausold and Sgt. Davis out and in doing so, he was severely burned on his hands and face, inhaling flames and suffering a broken right leg. Capt. Dickey was slightly burned and Lt. Hylla was badly burned. Hoover and Davis were in the plane when it blew apart in mid air. Hoover's head was blown off earlier by an enemy anti-aircraft shell. Davis was also killed. Hylla and Jolicoeur were in a civilian hospital together under the care of Jonah Toth, a Hungarian, who did every thing possible for them. Lt. Jolicoeur died from his injuries July 10, 1944 at 4:30 P.M. Lt. Hylla requested to see his grave and was taken there where he is buried at the Soldiers Cemetery, in the southeast corner at Kaposvar, Hungary.

In the Hospital Jolicoeur told Hylla that he was trying to get up front, to tell the bombardier and the nose gunner to bail out and he got stuck and couldn't get out. He claimed he was blown out of the ship because the next thing he knew he was on the ground with his chute lying open beside him. Sgt. Wilson landed about 8 miles from Marcali, Hungary. His left leg was wounded and his right leg was broken by bullets in the plane. He was picked up at once by civilians and police and taken to a local doctor who treated him. He was taken to Marcali, given a shot of morphine by a doctor and then taken to Pecs by ambulance to a hospital. On 27 November, when the Russians were attacking he was taken to Balaton Bogler and stayed there until 10 December. By then the Russians had already taken the place and sent him to Sonagyvar, Kaspovar, Sonbar and Subetzia by truck. Then Partisans took over and he was sent by train on 8 January to Novi Sad and by truck on 10 January to Belgrade and by C-47 to Bari, Italy.

Capt. Dickey, "Three ME-109's, one FW-190 and one fighter not positively identified, took turns shooting us to pieces for several minutes. I was able to do some evasive action since they mistakenly used tracers. At least three bursts hit the armor plate behind my seat. When Jolicoeur came up and told us of our situation, I could not leave a burning airplane in the middle of the group so I worked it out in the clear. Hylla hit the bail out button and we got out. I remember quite clearly how quiet and peaceful the open air felt after leaving the burning B-24. I got a squirt of burning gas in my right ear as I went through the bomb bay and watched our aircraft separate in all directions and finally remembered to pull my rip cord. I felt really good when my chute opened until I discovered my left sleeve on fire. The fire had not reached my chute so I landed in an 80 acre wheat field just in time to see our P-51 escort go over."

Capt. Dickey was awarded the "Silver Star" for his actions during and following the fighter attack. His citation reads in part: "Capt. Dickey maneuvered his plane away from close proximity to any other friendly aircraft and maintained his aircraft in level flight for a sufficient time to permit a maximum number of his crew to escape." Capt. Dickey said later, "I never for a minute thought I did anything on June 30, 1944 to deserve such an award. It was presented to my father while I was a POW and I knew nothing about it until June 1945. Lt. Jerry Jolicoeur was really the one deserving a medal. He could have gotten out safely but he came through our bomb bay fire to tell us on the flight deck that our situation was hopeless and that we'd better get out. In doing so, he received burns that caused his death on the ground ten days later."

Lt. Hylla spent several days in the hospital because of first, second and third degree burns over his head and hands. He was moved on 9 August 1944 to Budapest, where he was interrogated by German SS men and in the process he was beaten on his back and his bandaged hands. He was held in a second floor room with a small window, through which, every day he saw someone being hanged in the yard outside. Hylla and the other surviving crewmembers spent the remainder of the war in German prison camps. They were liberated on 29 April 1945 and evacuated some time thereafter. Lt. Jolicoeur and Sgts. Hoover and Davis, were Killed In Action.

30 June 1944: 1st Lt. Lubie M. Roberson, Pilot, 783rd Squadron, flew a B-24H, #41-28736, named "Shack Queen" to bomb the Synthetic Oil Refinery at Blechhammer, Germany with crewmembers, Lt. William F. Rogers, Co-Pilot; Lt. William B. Downey, Navigator; Lt. Joseph M. Casadevall, Bombardier; S/Sgt. John W. McGuirk, Flight Engineer-Gunner; S/Sgt. Joseph E. Scherger, Radio Operator-Gunner; Sgt. Willard D. Crary, Gunner; Sgt. Donald A. Dumas, Gunner; Sgt. Herbert J. Haskins, Gunner and Sgt. Louis H. Weixelman, Gunner. There aircraft was last sighted at 11:25 hours.

Going towards the target reaching the Lake Balaton area, the formation entered clouds. The aircraft lost number 3 supercharger and about a minute later lost the formation and was alone. Our ship was in clouds for ten minutes, during which time two ships cut into the right just below our nose and two just over our tail. We tried to follow them but again lost them in the clouds. With moderate to severe turbulence and clouds to the north we decided to turn back. We jettisoned our bombs in the northeast end of Lake Balaton and followed the rim of clouds heading generally southwest. We left one bank of clouds to go into another. In the clearing between the cloudbanks, we were jumped by two JU-88's. Sgt. Scherger said, "My God my guns are out," as a JU-88 began the last attack.

The tail guns were knocked out, the engines and the ship were pretty badly shot up and it was getting harder to control. The life raft over the escape hatch was set on fire and the tail gunner crawled back and his chute caught on fire. He got rid of it in the bomb bay but was burned around his face and hands. The bail out order was given when the aircraft was 50 miles past Lake Balaton, Hungary and we bailed out at approximately 22,000 feet. Lt. Downey the navigator, was shot in the back with a 20mm shell and killed in the plane one minute before Sgt. Haskins bailed out. In their last conversation Downey called Haskins for help then collapsed and Haskins left the nose turret to help him. Downey dropped his chute out the nose wheel door after being hit and died in the plane.

Downey was killed outright by the 20mm shell, which exploded in his back and probably hit his heart. At the most he probably lived only ten minutes, at which time the fighter attack was over and Haskins could leave his nose turret to help him. Sgts. Dumas and McGuirk, bailed out with Haskins. Sgt. Weixelman was nearby and Scherger was on the flight deck very badly burned. He was burned so badly that Haskins mistook him for Weixelman, until he saw Weixelman on the ground. Scherger's face was flashburned beyond recognition, but he was waiting to bail out when Haskins left through the right front bomb bay. All except Scherger are accounted for, dead or alive, on the ground. A POW believes he saw Scherger in a Catholic hospital at Pecs but cannot be sure as he was burned about his face and could not talk.

Sgt. Dumas said all was well when Lt. Casadevall the bombardier, made an oxygen check 3 or 4 minutes prior to the bail out order. Dumas saw Sgt. Crary go forward to open the bomb bay door, to help blow out the fire. Crary saved the lives of all the crew by opening the bomb bay doors when the plane caught fire. Casadevall was beaten badly about the head after he landed, which shows the type of people encountered. Dumas saw Crary on the ground and thinks perhaps he was beaten to death. Sgt. Weixelman also saw Sgt. Crary on the ground and said he was in a hell of a shape. Haskins was chased and threatened with pitchforks and knives, but 4 Luftwaffe German soldiers kept any incident with civilians from happening.

This strengthens Dumas and Haskins belief that Crary met with foul play from the civilians. Crary was not believed to have been injured before leaving the plane. The chance that Crary's chute did not open is not very great. If so he would not have been recognizable, due to the 22,000-foot fall. Haskins saw his chute on the ground, open with his initials on the harness at Pecs, Hungary. He seemed to have been beaten about the head according to Dumas, as blood was coming from his mouth, eyes, ears and nose. His body was carried to a barn on a motorcycle and stripped of all clothes and dog tags.

Lts. Roberson the pilot and Rogers the co-pilot, stayed in the plane. Rogers went back to try to fight the fire but was unsuccessful. Ammo boxes started to burn and ammo started to go off and he bailed out just south of Derventa. The ship was pretty much out of control so Roberson bailed out. The plane circled in a steep bank and the prop wash almost upset his chute. He saw the plane burn up when it hit the ground. As Roberson hit the ground there were quite a number of people around him. They were Partisans and they took him into a hill nearby and started to travel southwest. He tried to find out about Rogers and was told that he was being taken down from another direction and he would meet him soon.

He met Rogers that evening. The next day they reached Prajavar and headed for Sanski Most, then for about 7 hours they traveled to a spot where about 39 airmen were. They arrived on 9 July and left on 12 July for a British mission. At Podrueje they got battle jackets, trousers and underwear, food, soup, tea, roast lamb, dark bread and some corned beef. Then headed for Glamoc arriving there in about 4 days on 17 July. They were told that a radio message was sent for an evacuation plane and on the night of 17 July they were taken to an airstrip and started back to a little village arriving at 3:00 A.M. Then at 4:00 A.M. they were aroused and told that the Germans were coming up and had mined the airstrip. The Germans went up further north and then withdrew to Glamoc. They were evacuated on 21 July in the daytime. Sgt. Weixelman was also evacuated by Partisans on 19 January 1945. Lt. Casadevall, and Sgts. McGuirk, Dumas, and Haskins were captured and made Prisoners of War. Lt. Downey and Sgts. Crary and Scherger were Killed In Action.

7 July 1944: Lt. Ralph L. Pilegard, Pilot, 783rd Squadron, flew a B-24H, #42-52419, Call Letter Blue "Z" named "Duration Plus" to bomb the Synthetic Oil Refinery at Blechhammer, Germany with crewmembers, Lt. Frank J. Kanik, Co-Pilot; Lt. James P. Heron, Navigator; Lt. John F. Barnaby, Bombardier; T/Sgt. Durward E. Huebner, Flight Engineer-Gunner; T/Sgt. Fred J. Robinson, Radio Operator-Gunner; Sgt. Rome L. Barker, Gunner; S/Sgt. Kenneth O. Monge, Gunner; Sgt. Jesse L. Henderson, Gunner and Sgt. Bernard A. Wilson, Armorer-Tail Turret Gunner.

The aircraft was under heavy fire from flak and Sgt. Monge heard that there was a fire in the waist, two bursts came, one through the cockpit and one through the nose, wounding Lt. Heron the navigator and Monge. Monge heard Lt. Pilegard the pilot, instruct Sgt. Huebner to shoot the flares of the day. A burst came through the cockpit when Monge was opening the nose wheel door, that cut the hydraulic lines. Monge believes Pilegard was hit and killed at the controls and went down with the ship, as he saw his legs when he went out the nose wheel door. Lts. Heron, Kanik and Barnaby and Sgts. Monge and Robinson, bailed out in the following order. Heron and Monge through the nose wheel door, Robinson, Kanik and Barnaby through the bomb bay door. Heron and Monge were the last men out.

Heron had ordered Sgt. Barker to take a photograph of an enemy airdrome about 20 minutes before the plane went down. They could see three chutes below them in the vicinity of Bodinstadt, Germany. Huebner, Barker and Henderson, were in the waist section and Pilegard, was at the controls when the aircraft struck the ground in a wheat field near a pine forest, near the town of Bodinstadt. Three days later when Robinson was captured, he was taken to Bodinstadt where the people knew of the plane crashing nearby. Heron said that one source stated there were five men found in the wrecked plane, another stated four. Their bodies were mangled.

When the plane was hit, Lt. Barnaby said he saw Barker trying to fight the fire to free the ball gunner. He just motioned me to open the bomb bay doors. I heard that he had gotten the ball gunner out and was in the process of putting on his parachute. I am sure that Barker, in trying to save the ball gunner, was either caught by the fire or was frozen by the spin of the plane in trying to do so and gave his life trying to save that of the ball gunner. If at all possible, I would recommend an award, post-humous, for his action. Kanik stated that as he went out the bomb bays he looked to the rear of the plane and Barker looked at him and waved him out and pointed down. In company with Huebner and Henderson, Barker was fighting a fire in the oxygen system on the half deck in the waist of the plane. They apparently waited too long to bail-out or were killed or severely injured by the burst of enemy fire that Heron heard hit the plane just as he bailed out. Henderson called the pilot on the interphone just after the bailout bell rang.

Heron told Henderson to bail out but there was no response. The interphone was functioning only intermittently. On the interphone Pilegard informed Heron of his intentions of joining a formation ahead of them. Robinson said Pilegard was last seen slumped over the controls in the co-pilot's seat. Heron looked up between the rudder pedals of both seats just before bailing out and saw no one. The co-pilot Kanik stated that the pilot ordered him out of his seat and he took it. Shortly thereafter the pilot waved at Kanik to bail out. Robinson went out just after Kanik and states that Pilegard was hit and fell over the controls while he was climbing from the flight deck onto the bomb bay catwalk and went down with the plane due to wounds received. Heron heard two bursts of fire hit in the cockpit, one before and one after the bail-out bell was rung, so assumption is, Pilegard was killed by one or the other of these. The nose gunner felt the plane drop suddenly, so Pilegard probably was hit and fell forward on the controls sending the plane down in a curve to the right.

Heron was hospitalized for three months, about ten miles from the scene of the crash of their aircraft. During that time through the agency of British POW's who visited him and through friendly members of the German hospital staff, information was obtained regarding the bodies found in the plane. Also he collected information from two different sources stating that on 8 July 1944, a number of military funerals were held at Bodenstadt, Czechoslovakia with either four or five men being buried. The assumption is, these men may have been crewmembers listed as casualties. The best source of information concerning condition of the wrecked plane will be obtained from the citizens of Milbes Dorf, Czechoslovakia. The men who escaped from the plane apparently landed over a five-mile area, east and south of that village and were all captured and made Prisoners of War and questioned at different points in that vicinity. Lt. Pilegard and Sgts. Huebner, Barker, Wilson and Henderson were Killed In Action.

8 July 1944: 1st Lt. Jessie T. Jumper, Pilot, 783rd Squadron, flew a B-24H, #42-52420, Call Letter Blue "L" to bomb the Marshalling Yards at Vienna, Austria with crewmembers, Lt. Royce L. Ward, Co-Pilot; Lt. Ivan J. Kubanis, Navigator; Lt. James D. Mullins, Bombardier; T/Sgt. Eugene Kulczyk, Flight Engineer-Gunner; T/Sgt. Frank C. Sedlak, Radio Operator-Gunner; S/Sgt. Harold Nashalsky, Ball Turret Gunner; S/Sgt. Anthony J. De Lucia, Nose Turret Gunner; S/Sgt. Edward D. Robinson, Gunner and Sgt. Carl D. Moore, Gunner. This was a very heavily defended target.

Eyewitness, John R. Stewart, 2nd Lt., Air Corps, "Lt. Jumper, flying Blue "L" for Love, joined number 7 position in Charlie box just previous to the Initial Point at approximately 10:25 hours. Number 2 and number 4 engines were smoking excessively and he feathered number 2 at the I.P. Proceeding across the target his bombs went away and he gradually lost altitude while lagging behind the formation. It appeared he was trying to join another group formation. At eleven o'clock the airplane was at approximately fourteen thousand feet flying straight and level when five chutes came out all opening, a pause then five more chutes. The airplane apparently was flying on autopilot as it held the wings level as it lost altitude. The crew went out approximately half way between Lake Balaton and the target area. I personally counted ten chutes blossom out of the plane. So far as I know the airplane was not hit and definitely I could not see any fire when the men jumped."

Number 2 and 3 engines were feathered and number 4 ran away and only number 1 was working. The aircraft was losing altitude fast and the right wing was ready to break off. An ME-109 had shot away the feathering switches. Sgt. Kulczyk told Sgt. Nashalsky to try to drop the ball turret out, as it might lighten the ship. The pilot ordered the crew to bail out by bell and interphone. Lts. Jumper, Ward, Kubanis and Mullins and Sgts. Kulczyk and De Lucia, all bailed out of the bomb bay. The rest of the crew bailed out of the escape hatch. De Lucia suffered a badly broken ankle when he hit the ground. When Kulczyk saw De Lucia over the fence in POW Camp, he was limping. Nashalsky was with

Kulczyk in Prison Camp. When they were on the 86-day march Nashalsky complained he couldn't make it, as something was wrong and he couldn't make it. They got separated and Kulczyk hadn't seen him since then. The town they bailed out over, or near, was St. Peters, Hungary. The time was 11:00 hours. The ship went on by itself but lost a lot of altitude and crashed into the mountains. Lt. Jumper said, "If we would have stayed aboard we never would have made it. She was losing close to 1,000 ft per minute." Jumper and his crew were captured, and made Prisoners of War.

12 July 1944: Captain Robert Swanzy, 783rd Squadron, flew a B-24H, #42-52478, named "TS" to bomb the Marshalling Yards at Nimes, France with crewmembers, 1st Lt. William A. Nelson, Co-Pilot; Lt. Robert W. Crabtree, Co-Pilot; 1st Lt. Robert B. Thomas, Navigator; 1st Lt. Ralph J. Smith, Bombardier; S/Sgt. Thomas W. Walsh, Nose Turret Gunner; S/Sgt. Charles A. Cripps, Top Turret Gunner; T/Sgt. Paul H. Hooge, Flight Engineer-Waist Gunner; T/Sgt. Wilber R. Vaughan, Radio Operator-Waist Gunner; S/Sgt. Lupe Montana, Ball Turret Gunner and S/Sgt. Walter P. Wilson, Tail Turret Gunner. This was an eleven-man crew. Their aircraft was last sighted at 11:13 hours.

Eyewitness, 1st Lt. M. H. Stromberg, 780th Squadron, "I was in Easy box 5, when two FW-190's came through the formation. It looked as though they were firing at able 2 and able 1. After the plane was hit, there did not seem to be any smoke or apparent damage. Instead it looked as though the pilot was turning out of the formation. Then he made a gradual turn and went into a shallow spin. The plane appeared to try to level out at about 10,000 feet. Three chutes opened just before this and three opened later near the ground. I did not see the plane actually crash. The men who left the plane in chutes, in my opinion, had a good chance to reach the ground safely."

The plane was flying in No. 2 position of the 1st group when it was attacked by four ME-109's. One of these was shot down but the remaining three returned and attacked again. This time Capt. Swanzy the pilot was killed by a direct hit in the face by 20mm cannon fire and the plane controls including the autopilot and the intercom were shot out. The plane left the formation over the Durance River near Pertuis, France. The order was given for the crew to bail out and nine of the eleven-man crew left the plane. Lt. Nelson who was Assistant Operations Officer and flying as co-pilot, notified Sgt. Walsh the nose gunner of the bail out order and then left the ship, being the first man to bail out. Walsh and Lt. Ralph Smith, the bombardier bailed out. Sgt. Wilson the tail gunner saw Sgt. Montana the ball gunner, lying on the floor in the waist section, struggling to get out of the camera hatch. Capt. Swanzy and Sgt. Montana were in the aircraft when it struck the ground.

Swanzy and Montana were buried by a group of people from the town of La Tour d' Aigues on Bastile day the 14th of July. Members of the underground told Walsh that the people used this as a celebration affair and it was attended by nearly all the village. Montana's body was completely mutilated and burned. Swanzy's body was completely mutilated. Lt. Smith obtained both their dog tags from the town hall and returned them to an Intelligence Officer. All the members of the crew, who jumped, landed safely and were immediately taken by the local population to Maquis Headquarters. Five members of the crew were taken to a small Headquarters in the hills close to where they landed and spent one day and one night there, then were taken by a Frenchman in the British Special Services to a larger group where they met other American airmen including the remainder of their crew, except Walsh, the nose gunner. The party arrived at this Headquarters on 13 July 1944 and remained there for about one month helping the local patriots collect and distribute the contents of the supply parachutes dropped in the area. They also gave instructions on how to handle the guns supplied by the Allies.

On 6 August 1944, contact was made with the ISSU and arrangements were made for a plane to land on a strip some distance north of APT, where they found the last member of the crew, Sgt. Walsh, who was last to bail out as he had difficulty in getting out of the aircraft. As a result of this he was separated from the main party and came down at a point north of Cadanet, where he spent two nights and one day alone in the hills. After this he went to a farmhouse where he was taken in by a small girl and handed over to her brother who was head of the local Maquis.

After one night in this house, he was taken up into the hills again and lived there with a Maquis band until he moved to the Airstrip north of APT. The plane arrived safely on the night of 6 or 7 August 1944, but could only take off twenty of the airmen. This left the members of Capt. Swanzy's crew, so the pilot promised to return the following night. The Maquis, however, were afraid that the Germans knew of the strip and refused to operate the lights that night. The plane came but after circling and finding no lights, went off again. The party waited near the strip for the following two weeks during which time combat teams were dropped in this area, for action further to the northeast, but no more planes landed.

Then the invasion started so the airmen decided to wait in hiding, until the Allied troops arrived in the area. On 23 August 1944, the party set out to reach our lines and met forward elements of the Seventh Army at Forealquier on the same day. They were all sent to Seventh Army Headquarters where they were interrogated for Military Intelligence and the following day they were taken to 12 TAC who flew them to Bari, Italy.

16 July 1944: 1st Lt. Dale C. Tipton, Pilot, 781st Squadron, flew a B-24H, #41-29415, Call Letter Yellow "H" named "Crescent Of The Half Moon" to bomb the Wiener Neudorf Engine Works near Vienna, Austria with crewmembers, Lt. Eugene A. Weiss, Co-Pilot; Lt. Vernon L. Burda, Navigator; Lt. Eugene M. Krzyzynski, Bombardier; T/Sgt. Frank R. Jasicko, Flight Engineer-Gunner; T/Sgt. Hulitt L. Holcombe, Radio Operator-Gunner; S/Sgt. Michael J. Deironimi, Armorer-Gunner; S/Sgt. Harold B. Farrar, Tail Turret Gunner; S/Sgt. Albert D. Ralston Jr., Gunner and S/Sgt. Paul B. Brady, Gunner.

Eyewitness, S/Sgt. Louis J. Sablich, "On the morning of 16 July 1944, at approximately 10:15 hours, north of Lake Balaton near the Austrian Hungarian border, our formation was attacked by enemy aircraft. Immediately after the attack my pilot asked me how many planes were in "E" box. It was then I found that Lt. Tipton's plane was missing. I did not see the plane leave the formation due to the confusion of the moment."

The number 2 engine on Lt. Tipton's aircraft ran out of oil before reaching the target but he managed to hold his position in the formation during the bombing and until they turned away from the target. The plane was hit by ME-109's at 10:15 hours causing damage to number 3 engine and making it impossible to keep up with the formation so they left the formation at Lake Balaton at the Platen Sea. The plane was losing altitude and in the vicinity of Zagreb, Yugoslavia a German fighter appeared and the B-24 was in no condition to defend itself against the fighter so Tipton ordered the crew to bail out. The navigator and the nose gunner went out the nose hatch; co-pilot and top turret gunner went out the bomb bay. Ball gunner, waist gunners, tail gunner and bombardier, went out the rear escape hatch. Tipton was the last to bail out and he went out through the bomb bay. They all landed safely about 30 miles north of Zagreb. Tipton landed about 4 or 5 miles from the rest of his crew but they were all together that same evening and were taken into custody by the Ustachi troops who turned them over to the Luftwaffe the next day. They spent two days in Zagreb being interrogated and then were taken by train to Budapest, Hungary. After about a week at Budapest they entrained for Stalag-Luft III, at Sagan, Germany, where they remained until 27 January 1945. They then were moved to Nuremberg because of the Russian advance and in early April they were moved to Moosberg because of the American and British advance, where they finally were liberated by the Third Army under General George Patton.

19 July 1944: 1st Lt. Archie C. Davis, Pilot, 780th Squadron, flew a B-24H, #42-52466, Call Letter Red "G" named "Jackpine Joe" to bomb the Allach Aircraft Factory at Munich, Germany with crewmembers, Lt. Michael W. Ballbach, Co-Pilot; Lt. Jackson C. Johnson, Navigator; Lt. Nathan Goldenbloom,

Bombardier; S/Sgt. Robert H. Desmond, Nose Turret Gunner; T/Sgt. Theodore L. Weber, Flight Engineer-Waist Gunner; T/Sgt. Alva H. Moss, Radio Operator-Waist Gunner; S/Sgt. Robert A. Wiley, Top Turret Gunner; S/Sgt. Robert P. Guertin, Assistant Engineer-Ball Turret Gunner and S/Sgt. Willie D. Palmer, Tail Turret Gunner. The Weather was cloudy.

Eyewitness, T/Sgt. Robert L. Tate, 780th Squadron, "Approximately three minutes before we reached the I.P., I saw Red "G" which was flying number 2 position, "F" box, drop back in formation, almost dropping on number 5. Red "G" then dropped his bombs, skidded to the right and downward. He then came back behind us. A few minutes later he was lost to my view."

On the way to the target number 3 engine became rough and the prop had to be feathered. Just before the I. P. was reached at 19,000 feet, number 3 was brought in again. At the I. P. number 2 engine was hit by flak and went out. The prop could not be feathered, due to loss of oil, and it was windmilling. The plane immediately lost altitude and the bombs were salvoed. All ammo, guns, flak suits and other equipment were thrown out. The aircraft however, dropped to 10,000 feet before it was out of the flak area. There was a discussion over the interphone as to whether the plane should be landed in Switzerland or Yugoslavia. This was decided for them in favor of Switzerland, as smoke was seen pouring from the left wing. At this point 11 A.M., Lt. Johnson the navigator bailed out near Munich through the nose wheel door, without orders.

Heading for Switzerland the aircraft passed over Friedrichshafen at about 10,000 feet, where flak blew up the oxygen tanks and knocked off the hydraulic reservoir. The number 2 engine propeller then came off. The aircraft lost more altitude and over Lake Constance the pilot gave the order to bail out. The bomb bay doors were jammed, so the following men rolled out of the ship at 12 noon near Lake Constance in Switzerland, across from Friedrichshafen, Germany via the waist camera hatch in the following order, Lts. Davis, Ballbach and Goldenbloom and Sgts. Moss and Weber, (who's foot was cut by flak), Guertin, Desmond, Palmer and Wiley. The pilot reported that Lt. Ballbach was ready to jump from the rear hatch. He was not injured at that time, but he was killed when he failed to pull his ripcord. His chute never opened. He was buried in an American cemetery near Bern. We saw the chute after Swiss people found his body and the cord was not pulled. He must have lost consciousness during the jump. Crewmembers attended his funeral near Bern Switzerland.

The plane immediately went into a dive and crashed into the International Red Cross building where it burned, in the area of Dubendorf. With the wind blowing westward the men landed in Swiss territory, one man only 30 yards from the edge of Lake Constance. Lt. Davis landed 15 miles north of Weinfelden, Switzerland. Three soldiers on the scene ask for his pistol but he had none. He was taken into custody and brought to a small nearby farmhouse. He had a few head wounds and the lady at the house gave him first aid and three other Swiss officers arrived and one, who was a medic, checked and gave him medical attention. He stayed at the farmhouse one hour - got coffee, etc. Then was taken in a car by the Swiss officers to a nearby village. In a small military or police post, 1 officer and 1 civilian tried to interrogate him and asked where he had been and Davis said that he had been on a training mission. They searched him and took a compass out of his escape kit, also a map, a file and concentrated food tablets. They confiscated his parachute, flying boots and Mae West. Davis was sent to an internment camp for officers at Davos, Switzerland. He escaped back to Allied control in October 1944 and was sent back to the U.S.

Sgt. Weber was injured and he spent time in a Swiss hospital and then was sent to Adelboden internment camp. He attempted to escape and was caught and was put in a Swiss camp for discipline. He later escaped to Allied control and was sent back to the States. Sgt. Guertin came down just north of Weinfelden in a flat field. By the time he had walked to a road he was met by four Swiss soldiers who asked him for his gun, map and compass. These he gave to them. He was then taken to a cafe in a small village where he was given a meal and then taken to another village, where he joined the rest of his crew. After one night at Weinfelden, where they were well treated and visited by the American Air Attaché. They went to Dubendorf to fill out Red Cross and Swiss personal details forms. No military information was asked for.

Then they spent about 40 days at Neuchatel. During the first 30 days they were in quarantine, and could not mix with any Swiss personnel. Food was poor and very short, but hotel accommodations were good. Sgts. Guertin, Desmond, Wiley and Moss, left here on 31 August 1944 and traveled by train to Wengen. Internees could travel around the town but were not allowed to travel into the hills unless accompanied by guides. Many took skiing lessons. Accommodations were very poor, food not so good, consisting mainly of soup and potatoes. The men were allowed to visit the local cafes to drink and dance, but were not "officially" allowed to sit with the Swiss women. No cinema was available for the enlisted men, as the sound track was out of order. The "YMCA" obtained musical instruments for a band and arranged for skiing instructions.

On 19 December 1944, Guertin who speaks French went to work for the American Air Attaché in Bern. He remained here until 17 February 1945 and was unrestricted within the city limits. He had to report once weekly to the District Police Station and once monthly to the Swiss Commander in Bern, where he obtained a monthly supply of food and coupons. On 17 February 1945, he joined a repatriation party of about 480 Americans. He traveled with this party to Marseilles where he went into the hospital. He was discharged on 6 April 1945 and traveled via an American Naval L.S.T. to Leghorn, Italy where he remained until 8 April. Thence by "ATS" to Naples on 19 April to a Replacement Battalion at Caserta and on 12 April to Bari, Italy via courier.

19 July 1944: 1st Lt. Thomas W. Greenwood Jr., Pilot, 783rd Squadron, flew a B-24H, # 42-52585, Call Letter Blue "S" named "Section Eight" to bomb the Allach Aircraft Factory, at Munich, Germany with crewmembers, Lt. Francis A. Goplen, Co-Pilot; Lt. William N. Bitterman, Navigator; Lt. Daniel S. Bolinski, Bombardier; T/Sgt. Leonard D. Clutts, Flight Engineer-Gunner; S/Sgt. James W. McCloskey, Radio Operator-Gunner; S/Sgt. Charles E. Griesing, Gunner; S/Sgt. William D. Sams, Gunner; Sgt. William L. Douglas, Gunner and Sgt. Ernest N. Dunnagan, Gunner. The weather was cloudy and their aircraft was last sighted at 11:48 hours over Munich.

Eyewitness, S/Sgt. Steve Schultz, "Lt. Greenwood was flying "Charlie 3." At bombs away his ship "Blue S" got a direct hit in the right wing near the fuselage. He then peeled off to the right away from the formation, losing altitude. Later seeing the ship still flying low at 7:30 and from "C-L" position. I believe it was from Blue "S" that one man bailed out about 30 miles off of the target and the other 9 men bailed out near the Udine area."

After the plane left the formation, Greenwood gave the order to bail out. Lts. Greenwood, Goplin and Bitterman, bailed out of the bomb bay. Greenwood was the last to leave. Lt. Bolinski and the nose gunner bailed out of the nose wheel door, Sgts. Clutts, Sams, McCloskey, Dunnagan, who was injured by flying fragments and Douglas bailed out of the camera hatch. Douglas said to Dunnagan, "See you down stairs." The aircraft struck the ground against a hillside.

Lt. Greenwood stated that all members bailed out at approximately the same time in the vicinity of Wangen. No one was injured seriously. Dunnagan was last seen on a train, enroute from Dulag Luft to Oberursel. Greenwood heard that Dunnagan was executed by SS personnel, near Falig Bosel. (Later, this was definitely proven false by Greenwood). Sgt. Clutts was mistreated, beaten with rifle butts, stabbed through the hand with a bayonet and also made victim of exposure and privation, while on a forced march somewhere in northern Germany. All crewmembers were liberated in May and June of 1945 and returned to the U.S.A.

19 July 1944: 1st Lt. Thomas W. Bonds, Pilot, 783rd Squadron, flew a B-24 #42-52473, Call Letter Blue "A" named "Pith & Moan" to bomb the Allach Aircraft Factory at Munich, Germany with crewmembers, Lt. Guy M. Carter Jr., Co-Pilot; Lt. Richard C. Winston, Navigator; Lt. Ralph Rinard Jr., Bombardier; T/Sgt. Carl S. Adair, Flight Engineer-Gunner; T/Sgt. Jack Albertson Jr., Radio

Operator-Gunner; S/Sgt. Thomas L. Bracey, Armorer-Gunner; S/Sgt. Lloyd F. Dunton, Armorer-Gunner; S/Sgt. Harry G. Reifsnyder, Gunner and S/Sgt. Melvin J. Radebaugh, Gunner. There were cumulus clouds and their aircraft was last sighted at 11:48 hours.

Eyewitness, S/Sgt. Alexander S. Baronoski, "Pith and Moan" was flying number five position in "Charlie" box and apparently left the formation a few minutes before the target was hit and was last seen heading away from the formation in the direction of 9:00 o'clock toward the Swiss border. As I saw Lt. Bonds he was about 1,000 yards from the formation and the plane seemed to be flying steady and under control. There wasn't any smoke or flame seen."

The entire crew bailed out, were captured and made Prisoners of War. The following personal items were taken from Lt. Winston: 1 Pocket Knife; 300 Lira; 1 Mechanical Pencil; 1 Silver Bracelet with name; 1 Woolen Jacket; 1 Pair Gloves; 1 parachute; 1 Flier's Radio (observation); 1 Pad of Notes; 1 Comb; 1 Identification Tag; 1 Pair of Baby Shoes (Talisman); 1 Leather case with Spectacles; 1 Oil Cloth Pocket; 1 Throat Phone; 1 Wrist Watch and 1 Compass.

26 July 1944: 1st Lt. Harry K. Godfrey, Pilot, 780th Squadron, flew a B-24H, #42-52482, Call Letter Red "I" to bomb the Goering Tank Works at Linz, Austria with crewmembers, Lt. William J. Hooper, Co-Pilot; Lt. Donald K. Wake, Navigator; Lt. Norman J. Petitti, Bombardier; T/Sgt. Howard J. Keil, Flight Engineer-Gunner; T/Sgt. Harold M. Printz, Radio Operator-Gunner; S/Sgt. William M. Bradford Jr., Gunner; S/Sgt. Ernest J. Wood, Gunner; S/Sgt. Gerard Martin, Gunner and S/Sgt. Joseph J. Willett, Gunner. The weather was good and their aircraft was last sighted at 11:40 hours.

Eyewitness, T/Sgt. Lawrence H. Brouhard, 780th Squadron, "We were just coming away from the target and had accomplished a distance of approximately ten miles, when Lt. Godfrey's plane started going down, steadily losing altitude. The plane was not spinning nor did it seem to be out of control in any way. No engines appeared to be feathered. There is a possibility that this plane was hit by flak although this is doubtful. I did not see any chutes leave the plane and until lost from my view it apparently was well under control. However, there were enemy fighters around this area."

The aircraft left the formation, just inside Hungary. All crewmembers bailed out, except Lts. Godfrey and Hooper. Lt. Wake the navigator was occupied at the time attempting to give first aid to Hooper who was hit by flak in his side and was dead or unconscious. Godfrey who was not injured gave the command to bail out and indicated that he would try to crash land the plane. Lts. Wake and

Petitti and Sgts. Keil and Wood, bailed out through the bomb bay. Sgts. Printz, Bradford, Martin and Willett bailed out through the camera hatch and all were captured and made Prisoners of War. When Godfrey attempted the crash landing, the plane hit a tree and he was killed. The Hungarians said they found Godfrey dead, face down, in the plane.

They also described him and his ring. Wake saw the ring and heard the description. The Hungarian Commanding Officer told the crew that Hooper, who was killed over the target 10 or 15 minutes before the crash landing, was found outside the plane, without ears. Hungarians buried them about 40 miles south of Shoppron, Hungary in a small town named Shropponvedo, which is near the scene of the crash. Godfrey was very conscientious and would not leave his post of duty until every man had bailed out. There was practically no power available for making a landing, as all four engines were dead.

28 July 1944: Lt. Fred G. Tucker, Pilot, 782nd Squadron, flew a B-24H, #41-29437, Call Letter White "M" to bomb the Astro Romano Oil Refinery at Ploesti, Rumania with crewmembers, Lt. Wilmer Powell, Co-Pilot; Lt. Walter E. Hagen, Bombardier; T/Sgt. Alfred H. Maas, Flight Engineer-Gunner; T/Sgt. Herbert W. Ketron, Radio Operator-Gunner; T/Sgt. Edwin W. Haugh, Nose Turret Gunner; S/Sgt. William N. Evetts, Waist Gunner; S/Sgt. Kenton Waymire, Armorer-Gunner and S/Sgt. Clare M. Musgrove, Gunner. The weather was cloudy and hazy. Their aircraft was last sighted at 12:30 hours over Yugoslavia. This was a nine-man crew.

Eyewitness, Lt. Myron R. Dodd, "When coming off the target at Ploesti, Rumania, Lt. Tucker was reported by my tail gunner to be falling behind. He was still following the formation over Yugoslavian territory, escorted by P-51's. When last seen by the tail gunner he was turning south into Partisan territory."

Our aircraft was hit by flak at Kracuvac on the outbound flight, causing some damage to the aircraft and was again hit by flak at the target, knocking out number 1 and number 4 engines and damaging the controls. We fell out of formation and on the return flight, escorted by P-38's, continued on until it was necessary to feather number 2 engine, then the other two engines went out. At that time the ship was near the Kaponik Mountains and the crew was forced to bail out at 12:00 hours, from 8,000 feet. Sgt. Maas, the engineer saw the other eight chutes as he jumped.

He contacted Sgt. Ketron, the radio operator, upon reaching the ground. They were picked up by a Peasant and taken to a village northeast of the place they landed, where they contacted Lt. Powell the co-pilot. From there the three crewmembers, along with the Peasant guide, walked southwest approximately one mile, to a schoolhouse where these three met three other crewmembers, Lts.

41

Tucker and Hagan and Sgt. Haugh. Maas had walked some distance from the schoolhouse and in his absence, the Germans came and captured the other members of his crew. Maas then met two Chetniks, who guided him through the hills to evade other German patrols. He spent the nights of 29 and 30 July 1944 in a Peasant's home. He traveled with two other Chetniks on the night of 31 July 1944 to the home of another Chetnik.

He remained there 12 days. He then went to a Chetnik camp near Kraljevo. On 13 August 1944 he went to another Chetnik camp in the vicinity. From there he went to Cuca where he remained for approximately one week. On 22 August 1944, he went through Cacak on the way to an airstrip northwest of this town. He arrived at the airstrip on 24 August 1944. An American was at the airstrip. Maas remained there until he was evacuated by plane to Bari Airdrome on 28 August 1944. Sgt. Maas was killed on a later mission. Sgt. Musgrove landed between the towns of Kraiejvo and Raska and contacted Serbian farmers. These people kept him in their home all night. He proceeded in a northwest direction during the next two days, still in the care of Peasants until 31 July when he was turned over to the Chetniks who took custody. They took his name, rank, serial number and home address in order to inform U. S. authorities. Then continued on with him, arriving on 1 August at the town of Cucat, Yugoslavia. He took off again on 2 August arriving in the vicinity of an Airstrip on 3 August. He stayed in the vicinity until he was evacuated on 10 August 1944. Lts. Tucker, Powell and Hagan and Sgts. Ketron, Haugh, Waymire and Evetts were all captured by the Germans and made Prisoners Of War. They were liberated in 1945.

3 August 1944: Capt. Jack M. Faiver, Pilot, 782nd Squadron, flew a B-24G, #42-78322, Call Letter White "P" to bomb the Manzell Aircraft Works at Friedrichshafen, Germany with crewmembers, Lt. James W. Thornton, Co-Pilot; Lt. Richard E. Thomas, Navigator; Lt. Leonard S. Cox, Bombardier; T/Sgt. Ralph P. Sehnert, Flight Engineer-Gunner; T/Sgt. Edwin E. Nolen, Radio Operator-Gunner; S/Sgt. Frank Perrone, Armorer-Gunner; S/Sgt. James R. Adams, Gunner; S/Sgt. William H. Broderick, Gunner and S/Sgt. Henry P. Egerton, Gunner. Their aircraft was last sighted at 11:37 hours.

Eyewitness, 2nd Lt. Peter P. Reder, "Flying in Charlie box position number 5, we were on the wing of Red "R" (Lt. Clarke) which was in number 4 position with White "P" (Capt. Faiver) in number 6 position. The alarm was given that fighters were attacking and I observed White "P" hit in the right rudder and right wing. Flames broke out immediately and White "P" pulled up steeply, out of the formation in a northeasterly direction. I later (2-3 minutes) saw a ship in the distance flying in the same direction, burning furiously but not losing altitude."

Capt. Paul J. Smith, Air Corps, S-2 Officer of the Day, 465th Bomb Group (H), "On the mission of 3 August 1944, on the return trip over Austria-Germany, our group was attacked by enemy aircraft. During the short time the action lasted, the fast action and shifting movements of planes was so confusing that it was impossible for personnel of our formation, to accurately identify our losses in planes as they left the group. Some of the planes were burning and others damaged and dropping out of the formation and down, all in a very few minutes. Parachutes were seen coming from most of the planes but it was not possible to determine the identity of the plane in most cases."

Capt. Faiver's aircraft crashed in Lermoos in the Tirol area and was ninety eight percent burned. The entire crew, Capt. Jack Faiver, Lt. James W. Thornton, Lt. Richard E. Thomas, Lt. Leonard S. Cox, T/Sgt. Ralph P. Sehnert, T/Sgt. Edwin E. Nolen, S/Sgt. Frank Perrone, S/Sgt. James R. Adams, S/Sgt. William H. Broderick and S/Sgt. Henry P. Egerton were all Killed In Action and were buried in Lermoos.

3 August 1944: Lt. Theodore G. Poole, Pilot, 782nd Squadron, flew a B-24J, #44-41017, Call Letter White "I" to bomb the Manzell Aircraft Factory at Friedrichshafen, Germany with crewmembers, Lt. Bernard L. Lowenthal, Co-Pilot; Lt. Benjamin P. Benson Jr., Bombardier; T/Sgt. Conard D. Croston, Flight Engineer-Gunner; S/Sgt. Weldon D. Squyres, Radio Operator-Gunner; Sgt. Robert W. Salmon, Armorer-Gunner; S/Sgt. Arthur F. Reents, Gunner; S/Sgt. Oscar C. Rogers, Ball Turret Gunner and T/Sgt. Albert S. Hill, Tail Turret Gunner. The weather was clear and their aircraft was last sighted at 11:37 hours. This was a nine-man crew.

The pilot ordered Sgt. Rogers to pull up the ball turret, approximately two minutes prior to the loss of the plane. Rogers believes that all crewmembers, except Sgt. Hill the tail gunner, bailed out at Ehrwald, Austria 30 miles Southeast of Friedrichshafen. It is believed that Hill was in the tail turret, unconscious or dead. The Austrian civilians located Lt. Poole's body approximately 1,000 feet above the place where Sgt. Reents, was rescued. Poole's chute did not open. Lts. Benson and Lowenthal and Sgts. Croston, Squyres, Salmon, Reents and Rogers, were all captured and made Prisoners of War and were liberated on 30 January 1945. Lt. Poole and Sgt. Hill were Killed In Action.

3 August 1944: 1st Lt. Howard F. Fiecoat, Pilot, 782nd Squadron, flew a B-24H, #42-95284, Call Letter White "A" named "Polka Dot Gal" to bomb the Manzell Aircraft Factory at Friedrichshafen, Germany with crewmembers, Lt. Robert C. Johnson, Co-Pilot; Lt. Seth C. Babcock Jr., Navigator; Lt. Latham Denning, Bombardier; S/Sgt. Andrew S. Kresnak, Nose Turret Gunner; T/Sgt.

Carl L. Tripp, Flight Engineer-Waist Gunner; T/Sgt. Ralph W. Herrington, Radio Operator-Top Turret Gunner; S/Sgt. Clovis A. Kennedy Jr., Armorer-Ball Turret Gunner; S/Sgt. Francis O. Lee, Waist Gunner and S/Sgt. Francis E. Dyer, Tail Turret Gunner. Weather was clear and their aircraft was last seen at 11:37 hours.

This is a letter to Carl Dugan Tripp, son of T/Sgt. Carl L. Tripp the flight engineer-waist gunner on Lt. Fiecoat's aircraft. This is the account of the fate of Lt. Fiecoat and his crew, as told by a German man named Josef Kranewitter of Nassereith, who found Sgt. Tripp's identification bracelet at the site of the plane crash. He kept it and protected it for 51 years trying unsuccessfully, to return it to the Tripp family. Finally he succeeded in returning it to Carl Dugan Tripp in October of 1995. Mr. Kranewitter witnessed the tragic event when he was only fifteen years old, in August of 1944. His account follows:

"The plane was burning heavily on its right side and then crashed into a steep wood, (Mountain). The crash caused a treeless place of 30 to 40 meters width and 150 to 200 meters in length. In this whole area were parts of the plane spread everywhere. Occupants of the plane and parts of bodies were caught in their parachutes; they hadn't been able to get out of the plane.

Your father must have been on the plane, because the torn bracelet was lying about 20 meters away from the fuselage of the destroyed plane. The corpses and parts of bodies were buried before long at the scene of the crash. All of the bodies were transported to the United States after the war. Over Nassereith and Ehrwald raged heavy air-fights on the day your father died, but all the happenings in Ehrwald have nothing to do with the crash of your father's plane, because the location of the crash is 16 miles western from Ehrwald but near Nassereith. I'm glad to send you the bracelet of your father."

Lts. Fiecoat, Johnson, Babcock and Denning and Sgts. Tripp, Herrington and Kresnak, were Killed In Action. Sgts. Dyer, Kennedy and Lee were captured and made Prisoners of War.

3 August 1944: Lt. Myron R. Dodd, Pilot, 782nd Squadron, flew a B-24J, #44-41011, Call Letter White "Z" to bomb the Manzell Aircraft Factory at Friedrichshafen, Germany with crewmembers, Lt. Leonard W. Matter, Co-Pilot; 1st Lt. Richard F. McDonald, Bombardier; S/Sgt. Willie L. Prince, Armorer-Nose Turret Gunner; Sgt. William R. Campbell, Top Turret Gunner; T/Sgt. William S. Hooper Jr., Flight Engineer-Waist Gunner; S/Sgt. John Kostick, Radio Operator-Waist Gunner; Sgt. John W. Lemley, Ball Turret Gunner and S/Sgt. Ernest R. Zamora, Tail Turret Gunner. Their aircraft was last sighted at 11:37 hours. This was a nine-man crew.

Sgt. Hooper's last conversation with Sgt. Campbell was when he fired a burst from his guns and said, "just testing." Hooper's last conversation with Sgt. Zamora was when he said, "Fighters attacking, they're throwing bombs." Hooper didn't bail out because the plane went down immediately in flames, with all communications shot out and exploded in about 3 or 4 seconds after being hit, blowing him, the pilot and co-pilot out of the aircraft. Hooper believes Lt. McDonald bailed out. He has no knowledge of what happened to the rest of the crew.

The aircraft struck the ground about a mile from Hooper, in the Alps. Lt. Dodd the pilot met him on the ground. Hooper was injured, with splinter wounds in his left hand, left lower leg and burns on his neck. Dodd gave him morphine and first aid and went to get help for him. They were somewhere in the Alps, about seventy-five miles from Munich and about thirty-five miles from Switzerland. A German boy told Hooper that Zamora was dead and brought his ring and gave it to him. Dodd, Matter, McDonald and Hooper were captured and made Prisoners of War. The estimated time for treatment of Hooper's injuries was several weeks. Sgts. Prince, Lemley, Campbell, Kostick and Zamora were Killed In Action. (Sgt. Kostick was wounded by a direct hit of anti-aircraft fire, never the less he parachuted and bled to death).

3 August 1944: 1st Lt. Lloyd N. Clarke, Pilot, 780th Squadron, flew a B-24G, #42-78308, Call Letter Red "R" named "Rum Dum" to bomb the Manzell Aircraft Factory at Friedrichshafen, Germany with crewmembers, 1st Lt. Patrick J. Logan, Co-Pilot; Lt. Edward J. Paluch, Navigator; Lt. DeWitt Garber, Bombardier; S/Sgt. Thurlie D. Cooke, Flight Engineer-Right Waist Gunner; T/Sgt. William C. Burton, Radio Operator-Top Turret Gunner; S/Sgt. Claire J. Allred, Armorer-Ball Turret Gunner; S/Sgt. Victor E. Bullock, Assistant Flight Engineer-Left Waist Gunner; S/Sgt. Albert A. Pearson, Tail Turret Gunner and S/Sgt. Hoyt O. Geohagan, Armorer-Nose Turret Gunner. Weather was cloudy at the point of attack and their aircraft was last sighted at 11:37 hours.

The aircraft left the formation 160 miles northwest of Venice and Lt. Clarke said, "Lts. Logan and Paluch and Sgts. Cooke, Allred and Burton, all bailed out about 15 minutes after target time and just before I went out. A German Officer told me that two men were in the wreckage, but did not say which ones. Whether or not it was my plane I do not know. I saw none of these men after the ship was hit except those named above at time of take-off. I talked to them on the interphone, up until we were hit. I do not know if Lt. Garber, the bombardier bailed out. Just before the attack he went from the nose to the tail of the ship, as was his custom after target time.

The German Officer who captured us told me he was dead. Sgt. Geohagan was uninjured when he bailed out, but the same German Officer told of his coming down in his chute O.K., but he struck the face of a cliff, where his chute collapsed and the fall down the face of the cliff killed him. The last conversation I had with Sgt. Pearson was when he reported fighters coming in at 6:00 o'clock. The top turret gunner reported the tail of the plane was shot to pieces. Pearson could easily have been killed by German fighter fire. I do not know if Sgt. Bullock was injured. The last conversation I had with him was when he called me on the interphone and reported fighters coming in."

When Lt. Paluch bailed out, the interphone was out of order so he did not know when anyone left the plane. He assumed the others bailed out in the same area he did. He believed all members that were in the waist section were dead when the aircraft struck the ground, two miles from Lermoos. Paluch had last contact with Bullock, prior to the enemy fighter attack. Bullock was in the aft or "Waist" of the aircraft and was unable to bail out as he was fatally injured by enemy gunfire. Hearsay is that bodies were found in the wreckage of the plane in the town of Lermoos in Tirol, southwest Austria south of Kaufburen, West of Garmish Peacsh, and the scene of the 1926 Olympics.

The ship received many direct hits and it is assumed that all members in the waist were injured, plus the fact the controls were destroyed, and the plane went into a spin, thereby preventing anyone from bailing out. An Innkeeper - "Gasthaus" in the village adjacent to the town of Lermoos, claimed the bodies were buried on the afternoon of 3 August 1944. Lt. Garber and Sgts. Bullock, Pearson and Geohagan, were Killed In Action. Lts. Clarke, Logan and Paluch, and Sgts. Cooke, Burton and Allred, were captured and made Prisoners of War.

3 August 1944: Capt. Stanley C. Pace, Pilot, 783rd Squadron, flew a B-24H, #42-51137, Call Letter White "C" named "Little Brown Jug" to bomb the Manzell Aircraft Factory at Friedrichshafen, Germany with crewmembers, Lt. John A. Allen, Co-Pilot; Lt. Joseph J. Coote, Navigator; Lt. Ralph D. Eicher, Radar Navigator; 1st Lt. William I. Teller, Bombardier; T/Sgt. Dennis A. Holland, Flight Engineer-Gunner; T/Sgt. Henry S. Bruscinski, Radio Operator-Gunner; S/Sgt. Steve Schultz, Gunner; S/Sgt. Samuel J. Strahan, Gunner; S/Sgt. Cleo H. Jackson, Gunner and S/Sgt. Dwight G. Perkins, Gunner. Weather was cloudy and their aircraft was last sighted at 11:37 hours. This was an eleven-man crew.

Eyewitness, S/Sgt. Lewis D. Levang, 781st Squadron, "On the mission to Germany I definitely saw 12 enemy aircraft, single engine fighters, overtake the second attack unit from six o'clock, slightly high. They attacked in fours, flying right through the formation, two planes of the four splitting to the left and two to the right of each four-plane attack. Each attack was only a second behind the other, and they made only one pass in the described manner. After they had split away, I saw one B-24, Capt. Pace I think, on fire from wing to tail. One B-24 going in a flat spin, another with two engines burning. The first plane to go down was an enemy aircraft, and then I saw another enemy aircraft in a tight spin out of control. I saw a third enemy aircraft, with a huge column of smoke streaming from the left wing. All those were definite. Approximately one minute after this I saw P-51's dive into the fray, four providing high cover. I saw two chutes come out of the B-24 with number one and two engines burning, flying behind and under "B" box."

Capt. Pace's aircraft was near Brenner Pass when they left the formation on the return from the target. His last conversation with Lt. Eicher, the radar navigator, was his verbal order over the interphone for everyone to bail out at approximately 12:00 hours. When the aircraft left the formation, Sgt. Bruscinski the radio operator, was trapped in the radio compartment over the bomb bay. As the crew bailed out, there were four men in the tail section, and seven in the nose section of the plane. Sgts. Schultz, Strahan, Jackson and Bruscinski bailed out of the camera hatch. Sgts. Perkins and Holland, and Lts. Eicher and Allen, and Capt. Pace, bailed out of the bomb bay. Lts. Teller and Coote, bailed out of the nose hatch.

All were quite shaken, and suffered burns. Brusczinski saw Holland at Innsbruck military headquarters. His foot and head were bandaged; also saw Lt. Allen who was in bad condition. He saw Teller, Jackson, Strahan, Schultz and Coote at Dulag Camp in Germany. All suffered from plane or bail out mishaps. He met Perkins and Pace at Lucky Strike camp in France after liberation. Pace had burn scars on his face and hands. Lt. Eicher suffered burns and shock. He was a replacement crew radar navigator. All crewmembers were captured and made Prisoners of War.

The following is Captain Pace's personal account of the mission:
August 3, 1944

On the above date I was a Captain and Flight Leader in the 783rd Bomb Squadron, 465th Bomb Group, 15th Air Force, U. S. Army Air Corps. The target for that day was a factory in Friedrichshafen, Germany, on the banks of Lake Constance, which was on the border between Germany and Switzerland. A Squadron Leader from one of the other three Squadrons of the 465th Group was assigned to lead the 465th Group that day. Similarly I was assigned to lead the "2nd Attack" which was the second half of the Group formation. Specifically, the group was formed of 36 B-24s in six flights of six aircraft each. I was the leader of the last 18 B-24's in three flights of six aircraft each. My crew on that day was my regular crew, except that my co-pilot, Bud Shelor, was on "sick call" and John Allen from Duckworth's crew was assigned as my co-pilot.

After take off and during merging into our formation and during the first third of our trip north, eight of our thirty-six B-24's returned to Pantanella Base because of mechanical problems or other reasons. Upon observing this and in the interest of "tightening up" the formation, I radioed the Group Leader and suggested that our group of 28 B-24's form into four flights of seven aircraft each. This was approved and was done.

During the Intelligence Briefing before take-off our Group Intelligence Officer gave the flight path of the 15th Air Force from southern Italy to Friedrichshafen and return. This included a right turn off the target after bombing. Then he offered his own opinion that such a right turn was a mistake, because it would take us over the heaviest concentration of flak batteries. He suggested that we continue to fly straight ahead after dropping our bombs.

I ignored his "suggestion" and assumed everyone else would because it was counter to the 15th Air Force directive. The flight to the target was normal and dropping our bombs was normal. We had heavy flak over the target and one of the B-24's in my flight of seven lost an engine because it was hit by flak. To my surprise the Group Leader, after the bomb drop, continued to fly straight ahead, while the rest of the 15th Air Force "train" turned right off the target and then turned right again to return to Italy. So for a few minutes our 465th Bomb Group of 28 B-24's was flying straight ahead and the rest of the 15th Air Force was flying in the opposite (180°) direction heading home. Then when the Group Leader turned right and saw that the 15th Air Force was miles ahead of him, he increased speed to try to catch up. Two aircraft flying in 180° opposite directions separate at twice the speed of the aircraft. This maneuver of the Group Leader including his "corrective action" of more speed, turning and descending spread our 28 aircraft into a "looser" than normal formation as well as separating us from the 15th Air Force by miles. Clearly the Germans, with their radar seeing this disorganization, selected our spread, out-of-position group as its target for their fighters.

We were 10 to 20 minutes off the target when the FW-190's attacked. We were flying at about 20,000 feet altitude and there was broken cloud cover below us. The German radar brought the FW-190's up through the broken clouds after the radar had seen our U.S. fighter cover "S" forward over the 15th Air Force "train". The FW-190's were climbing through the broken clouds and attacking in three waves from our rear. Thus the "rate of closure" between the FW-190's and our B-24's was very slow relatively speaking. So, it was a deadly battle. The "slow rate of closure" made both the FW-190's and the B-24's easy targets to hit. We lost eight B-24's out of twenty-eight in about one minute. I read that thirteen FW-190's were shot down in this action.

As the FW-190's attacked us, we called for help from our P-51 fighter cover. They came quickly and attacked the second wave, which was attacking us, and broke up the third wave, which never attacked us. If 13 FW-190's were shot down that day, I don't know how many were shot down by the B-24's or how many by P-51's & P-47's, our fighters. Our B-24 was hit by FW-190 20MM cannon in the aileron, causing it to stick in one position and my co-pilot John Allen and I could not rotate the wheel to activate the ailerons. Both John and I were trying to force it loose by turning the wheel. Finally, it came loose and I looked over to him to signal that I now had control. As I looked at John, he was looking over his left shoulder to the bomb bay and his eyes were wide with amazement. So, I looked over my right shoulder to see what he was looking at. It was a large roaring gasoline fire in the bomb bay.

Upon seeing this fire, my <u>first</u> thought was to "bail out". My <u>second</u> thought was to inform the crew to "bail out". I sat down and called the crew on the intercom instructing them to "bail out". Then I got up and stepped into the flight deck. I immediately saw John Allen spread-eagled on the floor of the flight deck. He must have slipped as the folding door in the floor had closed and had probably caught his parachute harness under him. My <u>first</u> thought was that I should go out the top hatch. My <u>second</u> thought was that I should help him get loose. I grabbed him by the seat of the pants and reached under him to pull the door open. The door came open; John immediately went through the gasoline fire in the bomb bay to the air outside. I followed right on his heels. Both of us were severely burned on the hands and face from the fire. In what I have just described please note the strong natural human nature reaction for self-preservation which came <u>first</u>, while help for others always came <u>second</u>. After clearing the aircraft, I pulled the ripcord of my backpack parachute. It opened and I floated to the ground in this small valley.

As I hung in my parachute the skin from the back of my left hand was flying straight up as I dropped through the air. There were many, many parachutes in the air with me, probably eighty or more. My chute caught on the top of a small fir tree and broke my landing, making it easy and soft. I unbuckled my parachute and the German Army was there. I didn't have an opportunity to run. Also, I was burned sufficiently that I really wanted medical treatment. The soldier took me to a farmhouse where I sat on a bench outside the house. Several citizens came to see. They brought to me one of my gunners. The pain of my burns was increasing. I asked the gunner to open the morphine packet, which we all had, and inject it into me for relief. He tried to do it, but his hands were shaking too much. So, a woman took it from the gunner and injected the morphine into my arm. Pain relief was almost immediate.

After waiting approximately one hour, the soldiers by car or truck took us to a nearby Army Camp and put us in a barracks. My burns were very obvious and they took me to a dispensary where salve was applied and I was bandaged - face and hands. There was some food that evening and the next morning for breakfast. After breakfast, I was taken to a dentist in Innsbruck, who used his dentist drill to cut my West Point ring from my left hand, which was tremendously swollen, in order to avoid loss of blood circulation to my finger. The dentist put the two parts of the ring in a small manila envelope and put the envelope in my left shirt pocket. I kept the ring for the next nine months as a POW. Upon my return to the States I sent the two parts of my ring to Bailey, Banks and Biddle in Philadelphia and they repaired it beautifully. I wear it today.

After the dentist completed his action, I was put on a train with others and taken to a Luftwaffe Hospital in Oberfohring, a suburb of Munich. All members of the crew successfully bailed out. This account was written on July 21, 1995, as I remember the various actions on that day, August 3, 1944. s/ *Stanley C. Pace*

3 August 1944: 1st Lt. Wilbert Elliott, Pilot, 783rd Squadron, flew a B-24H, #41-29377, Call Letter Blue "Y" named "Umbriago" to bomb the Manzell, Aircraft Factory at Friedrichshafen, Germany with crewmembers, Lt. Fay C. Bailey, Co-Pilot; Lt. James L. Connell, Navigator; Lt. Joseph C. Sanford, Bombardier; S/Sgt. Earl R. Cutler, Nose Turret Gunner; S/Sgt. Gilbert D. Kapp, Top Turret Gunner; T/Sgt. Alvin M. Murphy, Flight Engineer-Right Waist Gunner; T/Sgt. Robert J. Griffin, Radio Operator-Left Waist Gunner; S/Sgt. Jack Bernstein, Ball Turret Gunner and S/Sgt. Robert L. Valentine, Tail Turret Gunner. Weather was cloudy and their aircraft was last sighted at 11:37 hours.

Eyewitness, T/Sgt. Arthur P. Haile, "About sixty miles from the target no escort was in sight and we were separated from the Bomb Wing. Suddenly off to the left, flak started popping somewhere on the mountains. Almost at the same time the fighters hit. I saw Lt. Elliott's ship circling and dropping fast. Capt. Pace's ship was going down in flames and chutes were everywhere. Out of the two ships I saw 15 chutes."

Lt. Fay C. Bailey, "I was the co-pilot on Capt. Norman Perry's aircraft named, "Perry And The Pirates", however, on this 3 August 1944 mission I was flying as co-pilot on Lt. Wilbert (Chief) Elliott's crew, whose regular co-pilot was ill. Our target for the day was a ball bearing plant at Friedrichshafen, Germany. We hit our target but unfortunately, on our way home, we were attacked by enemy fighter planes with eight out of twenty eight of our planes being shot down just south of Innsbruck. All of the officers ended up at Stalag Luft III near Sagan, Germany. During the next 10 months and two forced marches, we were released by General George Patton and his Armored Division at a camp near Moosberg, Germany." The enlisted men ended up in Stalag Luft IV.

T/Sgt. Alvin M. Murphy, Flight Engineer-Right Waist Gunner on Lt. Elliott's crew, had the unfortunate experience of making a hard landing high up on a mountain that badly injured his shoulder. He managed to get out of his chute and attempted to partially hide it. Painfully injured he had only managed to travel a short distance, before having to seek cover in some brush before a German Home Guard searching for him, located his chute and gathered it up. Shortly, he flushed him from his hiding place.

As he began marching "Alvy" down the mountain he realized the pain and difficulty in his walking. Coming to a farmhouse the German Home Guard commandeered a wheelbarrow and with the chute as a cushion loaded "Alvy" in and wheeled him down the mountain to the local jail.

The following statements are taken from German documents: On 3 Aug. 1944 at 11:15 o'clock on a precipice (clearing in a forest) a B-24 Liberator was shot down 2 kilometers southeast of Stams/Tirol, 30 kilometers west of Innsbruck. The plane lay scattered in the woods to the extent of 100 meters. It burned and splintered a small number of forest trees. The main part of the aircraft hit a straight narrow clearing in the forest and burned, destroying it ninety five percent. Identification was not found, probably 1293 on right level side. The camera was found in its case. Two additional crewmembers parachuted far from the place of the crash; however, it is questionable that they belonged to a crew that crashed in the vicinity of Mieming plateau and northeast of Telfe. They refused to make a statement. No traces of the dead were found. In all, 32 American fliers were captured in this vicinity, from several machines that did not come very far from the crash. From report of the Gendarmarie in Stems six prisoners proved without a doubt to be members of this airplane.

Supplemental - Apparently both Identification tags were set on fire by the burning crash which were found by Sgt. Schneider of Flier's Communication Innsbruck. In the first inspection of the crashed machine, which was stored for safekeeping. However, there was no trace of any dead near the machine. It is very probable that the tags belonged to a crewmember who parachuted, they had lain in the machine. The aircraft came from the west, apparently was involved in aerial combat with German fighters, burned and flew on and crashed, then after the landing, six persons of the crew were seen.

3 August 1944: 1st Lt. Lawrence R. Crane, Pilot, 780th Squadron, flew a B-24H, #42-52498, Call Letter Red "F" to bomb the Manzell Aircraft Factory at Friedrichshafen, Germany with crewmembers, Lt. Robert R. Kurtz, Co-Pilot; Lt. Joseph Spontak, Navigator; Lt. George H. Britton, Bombardier; S/Sgt. Lawrence J. Hamilton, Nose Turret Gunner; S/Sgt. Anthony J. Jezowski, Top Turret Gunner; S/Sgt. Leeland T. Englehorn, Ball Turret Gunner; S/Sgt. Leonard E. Bracken, Flight Engineer-Left Waist Gunner; S/Sgt. John S. Cooper, Radio Operator-Right Waist Gunner and S/Sgt. Charles F. Sellars, Tail Turret Gunner. Weather was cloudy at point of attack and their aircraft was last sighted at 11:37 hours.

When their aircraft left the formation approximately 80 miles northeast of Bregenz, Switzerland, Sgt. Bracken was tail end "Charlie" at the left waist gun. Eight of the crew bailed out near Innsbruck, Austria. Lt. Britton ran from the waist to the front of the bomb bay and opened the doors and bailed out through the bomb bay followed by, Sgts. Bracken and Englehorn. Lts. Crane and Kurtz, also bailed out through the bomb bay, after helping Sgt. Jezowski put on his chute. Lt. Spontak bailed out through the nose wheel door and Sgt. Cooper, bailed out through the right waist window. Because of an automobile accident several days previously, three gunners of the crew were not available for this mission and three replacement gunners of another crew flew in their place.

One of those replacement gunners was Sgt. Hamilton, nose gunner and the other was, Sgt. Sellars, tail gunner who may have been killed practically instantly in his position as the fighters which shot them down attacked from the rear and the tail was under intense fire. Englehorn saw Sellars on the bomb bay catwalk about two or three minutes after the attack started. Sellars was wounded and his face was burned and his chute had burned up. He was trying to find one of the extra chutes, but there were no extra chutes on board. Engelhorn and Bracken tried to persuade him to ride (piggy-back) but he refused, and returned to the waist compartment, which was burning badly. It is thought that he went down with the ship, due to the fact that Englehorn was the last man out and when he left, Sellars was still searching for a chute. Sgt. Charles F. Sellars was Killed In Action on this, his first mission with this crew.

Spontak was stranded in the nose compartment with Hamilton and bailed out from 19,000 feet. He saw Hamilton a few seconds before bailing out, and he was climbing out of his nose turret and fastening his parachute. About that time, Spontak was struggling to open the nose escape hatch, and fell out when he jumped on it. He saw Hamilton floating down in his parachute, but lost sight of him in the clouds. Taking into consideration that Hamilton was headed for a high mountain peak, he assumed that he met his death upon striking those jagged rocks. Lt. Spontak had heard from Hamilton's mother after the war, that her son's body had not been recovered, and Spontak is firmly convinced that Hamilton's remains are somewhere on those mountains. Sgt. Lawrence J. Hamilton was Killed in Action on this, his first mission with this crew. The remaining eight crewmembers that bailed out were captured and made Prisoners of War.

Following is Lt. Spontak's account of the mission and of his subsequent capture and the hardships he endured as a Prisoner of War:

On August 3, 1944, our target was the Manzell jet airplane assembly plant in Friedrichshafen, Germany. There was an armada of B-24 Liberator Heavy Bombers on this raid with accompanying fighter support. As we approached the target area, the flak was extremely heavy and several planes were lost and others seriously crippled. We were lucky to make it through the flak without taking a hit, dropped our bombs and made our turn for the run home. Although we were not damaged, our pilot, 1st Lt. Lawrence R. Crane, decided to hang back with the crippled planes while the main force of bombers and fighter support continued homeward. I have no idea why he decided to do so and, as it turned out, it was a terrible decision. We were still over enemy territory and subject to attack from nearby enemy fighter bases.

The Germans obviously intercepted communication between the main body of planes and our smaller group, and dispatched fighters from their base at Kaufbeuren. About 150 miles into our return, they were sitting, waiting for us. Wave after wave of Focke-Wulf 190s blazed in, firing their machine guns and 20 mm cannons. The slow moving, crippled bombers were like ducks in a shooting gallery. Disaster followed. Eight bombers, crewed by seventy-nine airmen, were shot down and thirty-one men lost their lives in that singular attack, all in an area near Ehrwald, Austria.

We were hit by the second wave of fighters. I felt the plane rock with a jolt, turn left and begin to descend. From the navigator's window, I could see our right wing on fire. I looked up into the cockpit and, unexpectedly, all I saw were two oxygen masks burning. Lt. Crane and Lt. Robert Kurtz, the co-pilot, had already bailed out. Then someone else jumped out the bomb bay. I immediately opened the door to the nose turret, tapped S/Sgt. Lawrence Hamilton, the gunner, on his shoulder and motioned downward with my finger. He nodded his acknowledgement. I didn't know him very well because this was the first time he had flown with us. I pulled the emergency handle for the nose wheel doors to open, but nothing happened. The plane continued to lose altitude and "G" forces were pinning me against the wall of the plane making it difficult to move. I was finally able to free myself and began jumping frantically on the nose wheel doors, and they finally opened and I fell out. The plane was flying at about 19,000 feet when I left it. When I pulled the ripcord on my chest chute, nothing happened, and while plummeting rapidly, I frantically began to peel the chute out. Luckily, I was able to find the pilot chute and when it came out, the main chute opened.

As I descended, I saw several other parachutes in the air, but I couldn't tell from which plane they were coming. We were over the Alps, and I dropped about nine thousand feet and landed on a mountain peak above the clouds. As I drew close to the mountain, an updraft caught the chute and I landed on a short angle. Meanwhile, some of our fighters had returned and a dogfight was taking place in the sky. I crawled behind a large boulder because bullets began to hit all over the rocks. Since I had landed above the clouds, I knew that I had not been seen from the ground, so as soon as I felt it was safe, I made my way down to the tree line. My plan was to proceed toward Switzerland, which I estimated was about sixty miles away.

My "escape" package was of little value. The rubberized map was useless in the mountain region because it didn't show contours. Had I taken my navigator maps and a few extra K-rations, I could have stayed hidden on the mountain longer and perhaps successfully escaped. Unbeknown to me, the village people had telescopes and they were scanning the mountainside for any sign of movement. As I descended into a wooded valley, I saw a woman who also spotted me. Intelligence had briefed us that we might find friendly civilians in this area. I could have run, but because of the major air battle, the area would soon be crawling with enemy troops and it would only be a matter of time before I was captured. On the other hand, if she was friendly she could assist in my escape. So, I decided to approach her and pretended to be an Italian airman. I don't think my act was very convincing. She pointed to a chalet further down in the valley and said, "Kamerad Schweizer." I interpreted this to mean that there were comrades in the chalet who would help me get to Switzerland so I politely smiled, thanked her, and walked toward the building.

The chalet, I was to learn, was one of a network of luxurious maternity homes throughout the Greater German Reich where selected German women who had conceived a child with an SS officer or another "approved" German male could deliver and raise her child or children in luxury. It was part of the Nazi's Ebensburg (Source of Life) program based on a theory of scientific breeding of a master race of "sacred" German blood. As I approached, the matron of the house and seven or eight very attractive young women, with their tots, gathered and stared at me as if I was some foreign devil. The matron was a very dignified-looking woman who was obviously in charge of the chalet. Around her neck, she wore a two-inch medallion with a swastika in the center. I knew immediately that I was in trouble. She firmly advised that I was a prisoner of the German government, and an elderly gentleman at her side produced a pistol and pointed it at me. With pistol in hand, he escorted me down the mountain and transferred me to a German soldier who took me to the police station in the village of Ehrwald, Austria, where I was jailed. That afternoon they brought in another airman and later that evening two more American airmen were brought in. One was badly injured and I learned later that he had died.

We were turned over to German Mountain troops and taken to Garmisch-Partenkirchen, and a few days later transported by train to the Interrogation Center in Oberursel, a suburb of Frankfort am Main. I was placed in solitary confinement in a soundproof cell with only a wooden table to sleep on. Twice a day, I was given two small pieces of bread and a cup of water, escorted to the bathroom, and not allowed to talk to anyone. They kept me in solitary confinement for four or five days. The scariest thing was the continuous bombing nearby. I feared our own planes would kill me.

Finally I was taken to the interrogation room, which was like an executive suite of a large corporation. The German officer was impeccably dressed and spoke perfect English. He offered me a cigarette but I refused. On a table, he had the organization of the 15th Air Force in several binders. He opened a binder and said, "The 465th Bomb Group is composed of four squadrons but Lt. Spontak is not listed. Can you explain?" I told him that by the rules of the Geneva Convention, of which the German nation is a member, I was only required to give my name, rank and serial number. "Yes, yes, of course," he answered. Then he picked up a piece of white cloth about the size of a handkerchief. "Can you tell me what this is?" he asked. I didn't have the slightest idea but I repeated my name, rank and serial number. I was in the room for a few minutes and then returned to my cell.

The next day, I was taken to a smaller office of a Luftwaffe officer. He too offered me a cigarette then withdrew saying, "I forgot that you only smoke a pipe." This was true and it became immediately clear that they had convinced someone to talk. He handed me a form and explained that if I would fill it out completely, they would turn it over to the International Red Cross who would advise my family of my situation. The form had a number of questions about my squadron, bomb group, personnel, other officers and more. I filled in my name, rank and serial number and handed it to him. He gave it back and said that I had not completed it. I told him that I did not intend to provide any information other than what I had given him. He called for a guard to return me to my cell in solitary. I protested that under the Geneva Convention, I was not to be kept in solitary confinement.

During the night, guards came to my cell and escorted me to one of the barracks. I didn't want to disturb the sleeping men so I slept on the floor. That day I had food other than bread and water for the first time in a week. I even took a shower. Several days later, I was transported in a special prisoner car to Stalag Luft III located in Silesia, near Sagan (now Zagan in Poland), and placed in North Compound with RAF prisoners. Even today, I have no idea why I was placed with the British. Perhaps, because of my belligerent attitude, I was tagged as a troublemaker who needed extra attention.

The "Great Escape" took place from this compound in March 1944. Seventy-six RAF officers escaped but only two made it safely to England. The Gestapo, under Hitler's orders, executed fifty escapees. The remains of forty-six are buried in the British Military Cemetery in Poznan, Poland. After the escape, exceptional security was maintained. Periodically, the Gestapo would come in and make us strip naked and stand outside while they tore the barracks apart looking for evidence of potential escape. Stalag Luft III was composed of five separate compounds. American flying officers were in four of the compounds and RAF officers were in the other. There were a total of about 8,500 men imprisoned there. Life was quite solitary at first. Because of the lack of food and severe cold weather without heat, many prisoners became irritable and withdrawn. Tempers would flare from time to time, but I don't ever recall a fistfight.

Under the circumstances, I felt fortunate to be in the North Compound with the RAF prisoners. Many were graduates of Oxford or Cambridge Universities or the Royal Military Academy at Sandhurst. They conducted courses in college algebra, calculus, German, French, Swahili and other diverse subjects. We even had an all-male theater group that performed classical plays with great expertise. They were good enough for Broadway.

Our food was basically potatoes, cabbage, German bread, mixed with sawdust as a preservative, and barley soup. We received Red Cross parcels once a week that had to be shared among six men. Although minimal, it was helpful. We talked mostly about food, recipes, and the meals we would have when we were free. When your focus is primarily on your next meal, you think of little else. There were seldom conversations about sex and I sensed some men began to lose feelings for their families. Their letters home became cold and uncaring and this likely contributed to a higher than normal divorce rate after they returned home.

We had a very effective counter-intelligence group in Luft III, of which I was a member. Since the Nazi's would infiltrate their prison camps with German-Americans who had returned to their homeland to fight for the Nazi cause, the British POWs were very suspect when an American was placed within their compound. Eventually, I gained their trust and was judged to be a legitimate US Airforce officer and included in their counterintelligence group. I was responsible for Block 106 security. One of our functions was to make certain that German ferrets were not under our building attempting to listen to our conversations, especially when the *Canary* report was given. This report was the latest BBC bulletin on the war's progress obtained by means of a clandestine short-wave receiver in the compound. These reports gave us hope and encouragement and helped keep up our morale.

We became concerned about what the Gestapo might do on Hitler's orders, because a group at our compound had been mistakenly transported to the Buchenwald concentration camp where they had witnessed firsthand the destruction of human dignity and life at this death camp. Now, knowing what the Nazi's were capable of and that the war was going badly for them, we were fearful that one day he would order our execution. We all believed that Hitler was mad and capable of irrational acts. To prepare for this eventuality, we developed a comprehensive survival plan. The British had several intelligence agents deliberately captured knowing they would be sent to our camp. They coordinated the plan within the prison and with people outside. In *The Great Escape* the British dug *Tunnel Harry* from Block 104 to the wooded area on the north side of the camp, which was discovered. Very few prisoners knew about *Tunnel George*, a second tunnel that extended from the camp theater, below the German's armory and into the woods on the east side of the camp. It was never uncovered. Entry was through a theater seat that was put together like a jigsaw puzzle. I served as security during the digging of this tunnel.

As part of the plan, all prisoners were subdivided into squads. Squad leaders were selected and they were privy to only those elements of the plan that they had a need to know. My job was to make copies of area maps obtained from cooperative guards and other sources. I developed a makeshift "ditto machine" made from a large flattened tin can, which contained gelatin from Canadian Red Cross parcels. By tracing the maps on wax paper and using ink, I could make an impression of a map on the gelatin and then transfer the impression from the gelatin to paper. I next color-coated the fields, paths, trees and streams on the reproduced maps. The maps were placed into survival kits for squad leaders' use if a breakout occurred.

A group of Polish RAF officers were to serve as commandos or shock troops and enter through tunnel *George*, dig up into the arsenal and seize the weapons. A pre-arranged signal to the RAF and/or USAF was to be sent via a secret, one-time-use transmitter notifying them that the survival plan was effected. They were expected to drop supplies, weapons and ammunition and, if conditions permitted, paratroopers. The squad leaders were to organize squads and with captured weapons shoot their way out of camp. If we made it out safely, we were to head south toward Czechoslovakia where Czech Partisans would meet us.

The plan was never implemented because when the Soviet armies began approaching from the east, the camp was evacuated. We were moved out in the dead of winter, and traveled about eighty kilometers until we reached a German army tank armory where we were staged for several days. Next, we boarded boxcars and spent three horrendous days locked in these cars without food or water as we traveled west toward Nuremberg.

There, the camp was a bombed-out former Hitler Youth camp near the railroad marshalling yards. Nuremberg was bombed around the clock by American and British bombers. Although we feared for our safety, we were so weakened by the lack of food, we spent most of our time lying on our cots trying to conserve energy. At this camp, I met our pilot Larry Crane and co-pilot Bob Kurtz for the first time since we had been shot down and we had a frank discussion about the raid and the German fighter attack. They explained that when the plane was hit, it obviously lost its communication system and the hydraulic system was on fire. It was a critical situation and there was nothing more they could do. They believed all the crewmen had received the word to bail out. Apparently, I was the last guy who made it out alive.

Besides Crane, Kurtz and me, Bombardier 2nd Lt. George N. Britton, S/Sgt. Leonard E. Bracken, S/Sgt. John S. Cooper, S/Sgt. Leeland T. Englehorn, and S/Sgt. Anthony J. Jezowski made it safely out of the plane. All were captured and became prisoners of war. Gunners, S/Sgt. Charles F. Sellars and S/Sgt. Lawrence J. Hamilton were killed that day.

When Patton's 3rd Army crossed the Rhine River, we were again forced to evacuate our camp and spent the next six weeks walking south toward Stalag VII A at Moosberg, which is located northwest of Munich. Although conditions on this march were deplorable, I felt they were better than what we had at Nuremberg. On the march, we foraged the fields for food stealing whatever we could and when we passed through a village, we would knock on doors and beg for food and often received some. In several larger villages, the German people would set out buckets of fresh water and throw bread into the streets as we passed. Our guards were mostly older men who didn't want to be on this march any more than we did and, on several occasions, we even carried their weapons for them. The war was winding down and the German people were showing acts of kindness to us in the hope that Americans would reciprocate in the future, but we still had our worries. Early in the march, American fighter planes had attacked the tail end of our column, seriously wounding several POWs. They had to believe we were German soldiers on the march. The allies apparently realized their mistake because after that incident, American reconnaissance planes began to track our movements.

The camp at Mooseburg was a sprawling mass of men and chaos with more than 130,000 prisoners strewn all over the fields. Twenty-seven Soviet Generals were imprisoned there along with American, British, French, Australian, Canadians, Sikhs, and others. We were housed in tents and had nothing to do but wait for the war to end.

On April 29, 1945 we could hear shelling and small weapons fire taking place in town and, a few hours later, a battalion of 3rd Army tanks arrived at the camp. I was greatly relieved to know that this terrible war and my personal ordeal were finally over. I no longer had to fear the threat of being executed. Several guards had forewarned us that Hitler had actually issued orders to kill all POWs. We were free of the threat that crazed acts against us might be ordered by the madman.

I had lost 75 pounds and my weight had dropped from 215 to 140 pounds. Much of that weight loss occurred in the final three months of captivity. After I was liberated, I became ill and was taken to a field hospital in Rouen, France, where I spent several days. Following release from the hospital, I went to camp Lucky Strike in northern France to await transport by a ship back to the U.S.

7 August 1944: 1st Lt. Cecil R. Bates, Pilot, 783rd Squadron, flew a B-24H, #42-52403, Call Letter Blue "B" named "Nobodys Baby" to bomb the Synthetic Oil Refinery at Blechhammer, Germany with crewmembers, Lt. Weiser W. Wilson, Co-Pilot; Lt. Charles J. Conlin, Navigator; Lt. Woodrow W. Browning, Bombardier; S/Sgt. Alexander Baronoski, Nose Turret Gunner; T/Sgt. Joe Taylor, Flight Engineer-Top Turret Gunner; S/Sgt. John J. Wilby, Ball Turret Gunner; T/Sgt. Carl H. Main, Radio Operator-Waist Gunner; S/Sgt. Grover J.

Weber, Waist Gunner and S/Sgt. Albert J. Yatkauskas, Tail Turret Gunner. Weather was good and their aircraft was seen to crash at 11:33 hours.

Eyewitness, S/Sgt. Jefferson K. Carpenter, "We were flying Able 2 and Lt. Bates was flying Able 5 which is directly behind us. Lt. Bates was hit by flak over the target, between number 3 engine and number 4 engine. The burst tore part of the leading edge of the wing off. The ship was engulfed in flames. One chute opened immediately after it was hit. He finally got the ship under control and it started into a dive. Six chutes came out then. It exploded when it hit the ground. 7 chutes were all that I saw open."

Our aircraft left the formation right after bombs away over the target and it struck the ground near Bergtodt, Germany. Sgts. Weber, Wilby, Yatkauskas, Baronoski and Main, and Lts. Browning and me, Lt. Conlin, all bailed out. Baronoski was trying to get out of the burning plane in the nose turret. I don't know how he got out, whether he jumped or was blown out as the ship blew up in mid air. There were three men in the plane when it exploded and struck the ground, Lts. Bates and Wilson and Sgt. Taylor. Wilson was wounded severely in the face when a shell exploded in number three engine.

Fire was enveloping him and blood was streaming down his face. I last saw him in the co-pilots seat. The Germans said he was dead in the plane when it crashed. Sgt. Main said, "Taylor was in the top turret and the shell blew up within three feet of the turret knocking the dome off. He was killed at the time the shell blew and if not then, he was burned to death as fire is said to have sucked out of the top turret hole, where the dome had been blown off. Wilson the co-pilot was flying the ship. He was said to have been hit and slumped over the controls. The pilot, Lt. Bates took over the controls of the ship after Wilson was hit and was still with it when it blew. The ship was burning across the bomb bay and right wing. He held the ship level so we could get out, otherwise no one would have gotten out. Wilson died from flak wounds, which came from the shell that hit in number 3 engine setting the gas on fire. When the ship blew up, he couldn't have gotten out. I believe that Lt. Bates was with the ship when it blew, the last to leave the ship was the nose gunner Baronoski, (as close as we can figure). He was on his way out as the ship blew and he said Bates was still at the controls. German soldiers said he was killed when the plane crashed.

Sgt. Yatkauskas bailed out uninjured. He was last seen in Stalag Luft III hospital. I ran into a Captain who claimed to have seen him immediately after he had been shot in the leg, above the knee by German civilians. His left leg had to be amputated, as a result of being shot by the civilians. I believe Bates would not bail out, because he could not get the severely wounded co-pilot out. My last conversation with Bates was when he rung the emergency warning bell, then said over the intercom "let's get out" or something similar, but he stayed at the wheel.

The plane exploded too soon, and he didn't have time to get out. Upon reaching the ground, Weber had broken ribs, Wilby had burns across his eyes and hands and a flak wound in his arm. Baranoski injured his back and had burns and Lt. Conlin had an injured leg."

The seven crewmembers who survived the downing of their aircraft, Lts. Conlin, and Browning, and Sgts. Baronoski, Wilby, Main, Weber and Yatkauskas were captured and made Prisoners of War and were liberated on 29 April 1945. Lts. Bates and Wilson and Sgt. Taylor were Killed In Action. Lt. Bates was awarded the Silver Star posthumously for Gallantry and Dedication to duty.

7 August 1944: Capt. William K. Zewadski, Pilot, 780th Squadron, flew a B-24, to bomb the Oil Refineries at Blechhammer, Germany with crewmembers, 1st Lt. Harry F. Lengvenis, Pilot; 1st Lt. Ralph F. Kissel, Co-Pilot; Lt. Raymond G. Bentrud, Navigator; Lt. Arthur F. Hulesberg Jr., Bombardier; T/Sgt. C. E. Johnson, Flight Engineer-Gunner; S/Sgt. William B. Bowyer, Radio Operator-Gunner; S/Sgt. Tulio P. Jacovinich, Gunner; S/Sgt. Robert T. Maher, Gunner; S/Sgt. Edward L. Yarbrough, Gunner and S/Sgt. Charles B. Sokira, Gunner. This was an eleven-man crew.

Capt. Zewadski and his crew were unable to return to the base but managed to land in Lwow, Poland and returned to Pantanella, Italy Air Base nine days later.

16 August 1944: Capt. Lewis M. Roberts, Pilot, 781st Squadron, flew a B-24H, #41-28904, Call Letter Yellow "P" to bomb the Manzell Aircraft Factory at Friedrichshafen, Germany with crewmembers, Lt. John L. E. Noyer, Co-Pilot; Lt. Elliott B. Sweet, Navigator; Lt. Donald A. Barrett, Navigator; Lt. Richard A. Bergin, Navigator-Bombardier; Lt. James J. Lyons, Bombardier; S/Sgt. Melvin R. Fulkerson, Nose Turret Gunner; T/Sgt. Harold F. Burchards, Flight Engineer-Gunner; T/Sgt. Dowie J. Hymans, Radio Operator-Gunner; S/Sgt. Leonard H. Emmel, Tail Turret Gunner and S/Sgt. Willie M. Golden, Gunner. Weather was cloudy and their aircraft was last sighted at 11:28 hours. This was an eleven-man crew.

Eyewitness, S/Sgt. Edward J. Schreiner, 781st. Squadron, "On the mission to Friedrichshafen on 16 August 1944, I saw Captain Robert's ship peel off from the formation and as far as I know, he had all four engines running. The ship had been hit by flak and gas was leaking. This was just as he rallied right. He cut under the formation and crossed Lake Constance, headed in the direction of Switzerland. Quite a ways down he picked up an escort of four P-51's. The last I saw of him the P-51's were still accompanying him. I saw several bail out. They should all have landed safely."

On the mission to Friedrichshafen, to destroy a V-2 factory, the pilot pulled excess power all the way to the target, to keep in formation. Three minutes before bombs away, flak hit the plane in two gas tanks, and in the bomb bay, destroying the bombsight. Number 1 and 2 engines were gone, including part of the electrical system; also the hydraulic system was damaged. The ship dropped out of formation, and the bombardier salvoed the bombs in the target area. We then started across Lake Constance, and lost 12,000 feet of altitude. The pilot gave the order to bail out. All crewmembers cleared the plane successfully, and the plane crashed in Germany. Lt. Barrett landed near Kuttwileh. Five Swiss military men immediately placed him in a Swiss barracks in town, where he joined four crewmates, one who had a bad shoulder and another with a sprained ankle. After the physician examined them, the group went to Freunfeld to join the other six members of their crew. Only maps were taken from the crew.

The group then went to Dubendorf, where part of their flying clothes and chutes were confiscated. Receipts were not asked for or given. Here the pilot was formally interrogated by a Swiss Captain, while other members were not so quizzed. The Capt. dined with the crew, who were given cigarettes and Red Cross kits. The next day the entire crew, with 10 other Americans proceeded to Adelboden, where they were quarantined at the Beausite Hotel for three weeks. There was an order by an American General posted, to the effect that he "wished" no one to escape. The pilot of the crew took over as executive officer at Adelboden one week before quarantine lifted, and was later under direct orders from the American military attaché in Berne to remain as Commanding officer. One of the crew was later made hotel Commanding Officer, at Beausite hotel, and another was made Supply Officer. Lt. Barrett was made camp Librarian.

About the middle of September the pilot became C.O. when the original C.O. left on an escape attempt. The new C.O. brought about a general improvement in the camp. He got more liberal treatment for the men. Until the time of his escape, Barrett investigated several avenues of escape, buying clothes but he decided against it. An American woman, wife of a Swiss millionaire, sent an invitation for two Americans to the Swiss Commanding Officer. A Swiss Protestant Chaplain managed to get Barrett and another crewmember passes to go, and in the rush to take advantage of the invitations, Barrett got away without having to sign parole and he had passes for himself and the other crew member, who met him at St. Gallen. The crewmember had, a week before, taken a group of enlisted men to Peden, then continued to St. Gallen. Both arrived on the 16th and several parties ensued. On the 20th their hostess offered to help them escape, she offered to buy clothes and place them in a train station at Zurich.

61

Apparently going back to Adelboden, Barrett and his companion detrained at Zurich and went to the consulate building in Zurich, and contacted the American consulate. He had them taken to a friend's house for the night. On the 21st, with consul, they went to the Yugoslav building where they stayed for the night. On the night of the 22nd they, with 21 other men, went to Vevey by truck, where they stayed at Hotel Temperance until the 26th. From Vevey they went to Lausanne, then to Lyon and to 3 kilometers from the border. The group traveled in two different cars. Two Polish and one Italian officer took them across the border to Divonse. They stayed at Hotel Strangers for the night. Next morning, an American Capt. and Sgt. took them to Ansesy, where they received clothes, a bath and food. On the 28th they continued to Lyon, then by Troop Carrier Command to Naples. On the 30th they arrived in Bari.

16 August 1944: Lt. Howard J. Secor, Pilot, 780th Squadron, flew a B-24J, #44-41121, Call Letter Red "F" to bomb the Manzell Aircraft Factory at Friedrichshafen, Germany with crewmembers, Lt. Eugene M. Friedman, Co-Pilot; Lt. George E. Moore, Navigator; Lt. Francis C. Dodd, Bombardier; Sgt. Lawrence C. Meyers, Nose Turret Gunner; Sgt. Robert A. Cook, Top Turret Gunner; Sgt. Munroe E. Shepherd, Flight Engineer-Gunner; Sgt. S. C. Womacks, Ball Turret Gunner; Sgt. Robert F. Johnston, Radio Operator-Gunner and Sgt. John Gidley, Gunner. Weather was cloudy and their aircraft was last sighted at 11:30 hours.

Eyewitness, Lt. Wallace Moore, 780th Squadron, "On 16 August 1944, while participating in an operational combat mission in western Germany, Lt. Secor's plane had number 4 engine out upon leaving the target. Number 1 engine was also giving him trouble, and was believed to be ready to quit. He called the lead ship and informed them of his condition, stating that he could not keep up with the formation. The Colonel told him to get in the formation and he replied by saying he did not think he could make it, and thought he would have to go to Switzerland. The Colonel again told him to make up his mind, and he answered by saying that number 1 engine was finally quitting and that he was going to Switzerland. I watched him turn away from the formation and kept him in sight until he was well over Swiss territory."

Lt. Secor, "We were over the target when we left the formation. The parachute of Lt. Dodd was destroyed by flak, and he refused to take mine so the crew elected to ride the plane down with me. I ordered them into their ditching positions. I yelled to Lt. Friedman my co-pilot, to "cut the switches." We were better off to crash land in Switzerland than to bail out in Germany. Our aircraft struck the ground in Doebendorf, Switzerland. Sgt. Johnston tried to talk to Friedman over the interphone to tell him to press the detonator button on his

I.F.F., but Lt. Moore, the navigator did it. Friedman injured his knee in the crash."

Lts. Secor, Friedman, Moore and Dodd and Sgts. Meyers, Cook, Shepherd, Womacks, Johnston and Gidley, all crash landed with the ship. All crewmembers were interned by the Swiss Military. The officers were sent to Davos, Switzerland and the enlisted men were sent to Wengen, Switzerland. All crewmembers except Dodd and Friedman escaped and returned to base. Dodd and Friedman were repatriated in March of 1945.

24 August 1944: 1st Lt. Harry F. Lengvenis, Pilot, 780th Squadron, flew a B-24J, #42-78538, Call Letter Yellow "G" named "Short Stuff" to bomb the Fanto Oil Refinery at Pardubice, Czechoslovakia with crewmembers, 1st Lt. Ralph F. Kissel, Co-Pilot; Lt. Raymond G. Bentrud, Navigator; 1st Lt. Arthur F. Hulesberg Jr., Bombardier; T/Sgt. C. E. Johnson, Flight Engineer-Gunner; S/Sgt. William B. Bowyer, Radio Operator-Gunner; S/Sgt. Tulio P. Jacovinich, Gunner; S/Sgt. William B. Walker, Gunner; Sgt. Roy C. Conn, Gunner and Sgt. Jesse J. Prince, Gunner. The weather was cloudy and their aircraft was last sighted at 12:50 hours.

Eyewitness, S/Sgt. Kenneth D. Files, 780th Squadron, "Yellow "G" the plane piloted by Lt. Lengvenis was hit and caught fire around the number three engine. The right wing came off, and the fuselage turned over on its side with the left wing in a vertical position, it then fell into a spin. A few seconds after it went out of my view, I heard and felt the concussion from a violent explosion. I saw no chutes. We were flying Lt. Lengvenis wing, in number two position. This was on 24 August at about 12:45, over Czechoslovakia."

The entire crew was Killed In Action. German Documents indicate the following: Liberator shot down by AA fire on 24 August 1944, at 13:00 hours, crashing in Village Kroisboden, Township Haag, Niederdonau. Crew of ten were all dead, buried by Township Haag in Niederdonau. Back part of fuselage and tail assembly 80% wrecked by crash, other Aircraft parts including motors completely destroyed by fire. Propeller model: Hamilton Standard. Armament, 8 machine guns, 2 still serviceable. Other equipment: 1 parachute, 1 rubber boat, and several parts of bomb release apparatus. The above quoted equipment was placed in the adjacent farm (Farm School Haag) and received by Salvage Command on 30 August 1944. Rear section of fuselage including tail assembly lies in a field; the remaining plane parts (fuselage, motors, wings) burned up next to farm field, village Kroisboden, township Haag, N.D. Both places can be approached by trucks. Wreck is guarded by Search Light Unit 5/5 - 29. 2d

Salvage Company, 3d Battalion is in charge of salvage. Probable start of salvage: 30 August 1944. Probable duration of salvage: 2 - 3 days.

24 August 1944: Lt. Leroy O. Buck, Pilot, 780th Squadron, flew a B-24J, #42-51020, Call Letter Red "Q" to bomb the Fanto Oil Refinery at Pardubice, Czechoslovakia with crewmembers, F/O Harry C. Nolen, Co-Pilot; Lt. Lester E. Emery, Navigator; Lt. Robert C. Carlen, Bombardier; Sgt. Irwin R. Gute, Flight Engineer-Gunner; Sgt. Richard F. Lee, Radio Operator-Gunner; Sgt. Walter E. Shanley, Gunner; Sgt. Russell V. Bakes, Gunner; Sgt. George T. Pfeifer, Gunner and Sgt. James P. McParland, Gunner. Weather was cloudy and their aircraft was seen to ditch in the Adriatic Sea at 14:45 hours.

Flight Officer, Harry C. Nolen, "On 24 August 1944, I was flying as co-pilot in Red "Q" piloted by Lt. Buck. We were returning from an operational combat mission over Czechoslovakia. We lost three engines over the Adriatic and the plane was losing altitude. At approximately 14:45 hours, Lt. Buck decided to ditch the aircraft. We notified the Group Flight Commander by radio of our decision. We prepared to ditch, but were at a low altitude and had a very short time in which to get ready. We came in on number 2 engine without the use of flaps, and down wind, the aircraft was under control, however.

The ditching was unsuccessful and the aircraft was completely demolished upon impact. I went out the escape hatch. I had my Mae West on, and I first hung on to an oxygen bottle. I was slightly dazed, but conscious. The entire ship went under water immediately but the front section rose and stayed afloat for about a minute. The water was rough and rather choppy. I was in the water approximately two and a half to three hours. I was picked up by the British Air Sea Rescue unit. I was very tired by this time. There was one life raft afloat, but it was empty. I made a search of the surrounding water, but no one was found. During the time I was in the water, I saw no other boats around. I was taken to the Italian mainland and to a hospital.

s/ *Harry C. Nolen*, F/O, AC.

The entire crew was Killed In Action with the exception of the co-pilot, Flight Officer Harry Clinton Nolen.

24 August 1944: 1st Lt. Robert J. Jones, Pilot, 783rd Squadron, flew a B-24H, #41-29424, Call Letter Blue "E" named "San Souci" to bomb the Fanto Oil Refinery at Pardubice, Czechoslovakia with crewmembers, Capt. Thomas T. Clark Jr., Co-Pilot; 1st. Lt. Russell Christianson, Navigator; Lt. Henry Kardas, Bombardier; 1st Lt. William P. Sheridan, Bombardier; T/Sgt. James T. Sullivan, Flight Engineer-Gunner; Sgt. William D. Stroud, Radio Operator-Gunner; Sgt. Thomas P. Sullivan, Gunner; Sgt. Richard H. Trimingham, Gunner; S/Sgt.

Leonard M. Haustes, Gunner and S/Sgt. Robert L. Lewis, Tail Turret Gunner. Visibility was good and their aircraft was last sighted at 12:40 hours at Jinder Kradec This was an eleven-man crew.

Richard C. Pease, Major, Air Corps, Group S-2 Officer, "On the bombing mission of 24 August 1944, Aircraft #29424, (Blue "E") piloted by 1st Lt. Robert J. Jones, lost one engine over the IP, left our group and joined the 464th Bomb Gp (H). Shortly afterwards that group was attacked by enemy aircraft. Later the 464th Bomb Gp. notified this group that Blue "E" was shot down at 12:40 hours, over Czechoslovakia at approximately 49 degrees 10 minutes north, 15 degrees 10 minutes east. It was believed that five chutes were seen coming from the plane. There are no witnesses from this Group."

The aircraft left the formation 50 miles south of Pardubice, Czechoslovakia. Capt. Thomas Talbot Clark Jr. co-pilot, said in his last conversation with Sgt. Lewis the tail gunner, "He reported a rear attack by seven German FW-190's. He was injured and could have been too badly hurt to have jumped. He was last seen climbing out of the tail turret. Sgt. James T. Sullivan stated that he had been blasted out of his turret by a 20 mm burst. He may have been unable to bail out, but I'm inclined to believe he got it on the ground or possibly died after he bailed out. Sgt. Haustes also could have been too badly hurt to jump. He was last seen in his turret. Sullivan stated that Haustes had also been hit by a 20mm shell. He may have gone down with the plane but I doubt it. I'm sure if he were badly hurt his crewmates in the rear of the plane would have assisted him to bail out, as there was ample time. I believe he got it on the ground."

Lt. Christianson, "The entire crew bailed out. Four other officers on the crew were in prison camp with us, and were okay. Sgt. Trimingham was seen at Port of Embarkation in France. Sgt. James T. Sullivan was last seen at Wetzler, Germany. The last conversation with Sgt. Thomas P. Sullivan was when he reported fighters. The last conversation I had with Sgt. Lewis was when he was reporting fighter planes and the last time I saw him, he was bailing out. The Germans reported that he died of wounds upon reaching the ground. The last conversation I had with Sgt. Haustes was when he was reporting fighter planes and the last time I saw him, he was bailing out. The Germans reported that he too died of wounds upon reaching the ground. Sgt. Stroud was suffering from a concussion of the brain. I was with him at Budjuice, Czechoslovakia; up to the time the Germans took him to a hospital for treatment. That was my last contact with him."

German documents indicate the fate of the crew as follows: S/Sgt. Robert L. Lewis and S/Sgt. Leonard M. Haustes were found dead in the crashed airplane.

They were buried on 26 August 1944 at 07:00 hours at the Community Cemetery in grave section 6, on the Western side of the cemetery, beside the wall at Hosterschlag, Neubistribitz, Nd. in the Lower Danube Region. The dead were Killed In Action during aerial combat in the district of Neubistritz. Before arrival at the Receiving Station, all pockets of the dead man S/Sgt. Lewis, were searched by M/Sgt. Roeschl of Klauenschlag, and found empty. He took one Identification tag, (15328397) and the other remained with the dead man. Before arrival at the Receiving Station, one Identification tag of S/Sgt. Haustes was taken by Secr. Tank of German Kripo (MP's?) in Iglau. One tag remained with the dead man. No personal or military papers were found in the pockets of the dead man according to statement of Mayor of Tieberschlag. The burial was affected without arrangement with Receiving Station, therefore orderly examination could not be carried out and the dates of identification tags of the dead men could not be ascertained. According to statement of Mayor of Tieberschlag, Rudolf Hanzal, the bodies were buried in a badly damaged, blood-soaked parachute.

The following crewmembers were captured and made Prisoners of War: Capt. Clark, Lts. Christianson, Jones, Kardas and Sheridan, and Sgts. Trimingham, Stroud and brothers, Thomas P. Sullivan and James T. Sullivan.

1 September 1944: 1st Lt. Richard Edwin Tout, Pilot, 782nd Squadron, flew a B-24 on a mission to Szolnok, Hungary with crewmembers, Lt. Paul J. Frankhart, Co-Pilot; Lt. Wayne L. Oley, Navigator; Lt. Arthur O. Brenner, Bombardier; Sgt. Arthur E. Bernzott, Flight Engineer-Gunner; Sgt. Arthur W. Goldberg, Armorer-Gunner; Sgt. Joseph A. Lemieux, Radio Operator-Gunner; Sgt. Chestley J. Armstrong, Gunner; Sgt. Joseph R. Grahovec, Gunner and Sgt. John E. Stewart, Gunner.

Lt. Tout's aircraft crashed into the side of a hill and burned, near Lavello, Italy, shortly after take-off on an official combat mission on 1 September 1944. All personnel of the crew were Killed In Action. The cause of the crash is believed to be that an attempt was made to pull into formation a little too quickly for the bomb load and the plane stalled. Due to the fact that the plane was demolished it was impossible to determine whether there was any mechanical failure involved. Identification was made from Identification Tags. The bodies of all members of the crew were taken to Graves Registration, Bari, Italy and were buried in U. S. Cemetery, Bari, Italy, on 2 September 1944.

10 September 1944: 1st Lt. Herbert Parkison, Pilot, 783rd Squadron, flew a B-24H, #41-29360, Call Letter Blue "C" named "Table Stuff" to bomb the Osterreichische Saurwerke-Dieseleng Factory at Vienna, Austria with crewmembers, Lt. Herbert W. Jester Jr., Co-Pilot; F/O James G. Ewer,

Navigator; Lt. Louis U. Dussault, Bombardier; S/Sgt. Richard A. Edmonds, Nose Turret Gunner; Sgt. Orville R. Olsen, Armorer-Top Turret Gunner; Sgt. Douglas F. Miller, Ball Turret Gunner; S/Sgt. Robert E. Riley, Flight Engineer-Waist Gunner; S/Sgt. Vernon H. Buol, Radio Operator-Waist Gunner and Sgt. Lawrence B. Thurston, Tail Turret Gunner. The weather was nine-tenths undercast and their aircraft was last sighted over Hungary at 12:30 hours.

Eyewitness, Lt. Sigmund E. Hausner, 783rd Squadron, "I was flying White "I" for Item and after coming off the target I flew on right wing of Blue "C." It had number four engine feathered and the cowling of number four engine was shot away. Blue "C" started pulling back gradually and when we were around the border of Yugoslavia number two engine went out. Blue "C" fell back rapidly. I called to my tail gunner S/Sgt. Davis to watch and he reported ten parachutes leaving the aircraft, after which it went into a dive to the ground."

When they left the formation, all crewmembers bailed out, F/O Ewer, and Sgt. Edmonds, went out the nose wheel door. Lts. Parkison, Jester, Dussault and Sgts. Olsen and Riley went out the bomb bay door. Sgts. Buol, Thurston and Miller, bailed out through the camera hatch. All bailed out at approximately the same time. Parkison had been hit in the arm by flak. Miller had a sprained back, Buol had a cut on his head and a sprained ankle, and Olsen had a broken leg. The rest were all right. Their aircraft hit the ground southwest of Lake Balaton, Hungary. All ten crewmembers were captured and made Prisoners of War

10 September 1944: Capt. James L. Blackburn, Pilot, 780th Squadron, flew a B-24J, #42-51387, Call Letter Red "W" to bomb the Osterreichische Saurwerke-Dieseleng Factory at Vienna, Austria with crewmembers, 1st Lt. Louis C. Chessmore, Co-Pilot; Lt. Donald E. Hinshaw, Bombardier; Sgt. Kenneth M. Rumble, Flight Engineer-Gunner; Sgt. Edward A. Bitsco, Radio Operator-Gunner; S/Sgt. Roy E. Reynolds, Assistant Flight Engineer-Gunner; S/Sgt. Rex O. Day, Ball Turret Gunner; Sgt. Carl R. Perry, Tail Turret Gunner and Sgt. William T. Hamilton, Gunner. It was 10:50 hours and the weather was undercast over the target when their aircraft was seen to crash. This was a nine-man crew.

Eyewitness, Sgt. William F. Abney Jr., 780th Squadron, "On combat mission of 10 September 1944, Capt. Blackburn's plane (Red "W") was hit in the bomb bays by flak. The plane then started into a climb with the bomb bays burning. While climbing, four chutes came out of the plane and all opened. Suddenly the plane fell off on the right wing and went into a spin with all engines still running. It went on down to the ground, and no more chutes were seen to leave the plane.

I saw a large cloud of black smoke caused by the explosion as the plane crashed among some buildings."

Sgt. Day, "Our aircraft struck the ground 30 miles southwest of Vienna. Sgt. Perry was in the tail near the hatch. He called me and said his oxygen was shot out. The pilot told him to move to the waist section to another oxygen outlet. The pilot was told by crewmembers in the tail section that Perry started to the waist and collapsed before he got there, he was last seen in the tail section just outside the tail turret, apparently lifeless and believed to be dead. The crew received the signal to bail out and with the plane being on fire, they were unable to help Perry. A German showed us his dog tags and said he was dead in the tail section, confirming the above. This was Sgt. Perry's first mission."

Sgt. Bitsco, "Due to flak marring my vision, I hardly found my way out, although I believe I was the last one out of the waist section. Perry was in a crouched position when I left. He was between the belly hatch and the tail position. I saw most all the rest of our crew between hospitals, prison camps, on the march, and after liberation. Directly over the target, just before our plane received its first direct hit, a burst of flak outside my waist position blinded my left eye and partially my right. Just then the ship was hit about 4 or 5 more times knocking it out of formation, gaining altitude fast, putting us who were bailing out in a tough position to open any doors. A couple of the boys were out before I had my flak suit off, and adjusting my chute the best I could, I crawled up to the hatch on the ribs of the ship to help Sgt. Rumble and another of the new crewmembers up with the door. The gravity pull was so great that after the door was opened a little, the wind just sucked those fellows out. I was trying to get the door up just a little more for myself to get out and that is when I saw Perry in a crouched position. I was in no position to help him, lest I would. The force was so strong at that time that when I left the ship the door came down on my feet and ripped my shoe and boot clear off of my foot."

Lt. Hinshaw, "Perry was putting on his chute by the escape hatch. He was suffering from anoxia and a severe case of fright, so he did not have the strength that he should have had, due to the fact the ship was spinning and burning. I do not believe that he had the strength to overcome the centrifugal force to open the escape hatch."

Capt. Blackburn, Lts. Chessmore and Hinshaw and Sgts. Rumble, Bitsco, Reynolds, Hamilton and Day, were captured and made Prisoners of War. Sgt. Perry the tail gunner was Killed In Action.

10 September 1944: 1st Lt. George H. Leggate, Pilot, 781st Squadron, flew a B-24J, #42-51260, to bomb the Osterreichische Saurwerke-Dieseleng Factory at Vienna, Austria with crewmembers, Lt. John A. Nelson, Co-Pilot; Lt. Valmore A. Schilleman, Co-Pilot; Lt. Lewis C. Gordon, Bombardier; Sgt. Paul S. Fisher, Flight Engineer-Gunner; Sgt. Sam J. Ippolito, Radio Operator-Gunner; Sgt. Harry Reuss, Assistant Flight Engineer-Gunner; Sgt. Ray E. Davis, Armorer-Gunner; Sgt. Roger E. Niemann, Gunner and Sgt. Lyle A. Hermanson, Gunner. The weather was undercast over the target and their aircraft was seen to crash at 10:50 hours.

Eyewitness, Sgt. Karl K. Brown, 781st Squadron, "Yellow "H" flown by Lt. Leggate, was hit by flak over the target. Number 3 and number 4 engines caught fire. I saw four chutes open. There was plenty of time for the rest of the crew to get out. I didn't see the plane hit the ground but the ball gunner said it exploded when it hit."

Sgt. Ippolito, "We were approximately 40 miles Southeast of Vienna when we left the formation, Lt. Leggate told Sgt. Niemann that the ship was on fire and gave us the order to bail out. I did not see Lt. Leggate after I bailed out and I don't know if he was injured. I saw him in Budapest later and if he was injured I didn't notice it. Sgt. Davis' right leg was almost completely blown off. I tried to help Davis as he bailed out. I left him in a hospital in Vienna. He was repatriated in January 1945 in exchange for German Prisoners of War. Davis spent some time in an army hospital (Bushnell Gen.) in Utah. In his last letter to me he claimed he was to be discharged as soon as he learned to use his artificial leg.

I also met Capt. Black (Blackburn) and Lt. Chessmore in Budapest. Sgts. Day, Bitsco, Hamilton and Tober all of the 780th Squadron in P.W. Camp. Also Sgt. Vernon Buol of the 783rd Squadron in Camp and Sgt. Leonard Goldstein of the 781st. All these men were from the 465th Bomb Group."

Lt. Leggate, "All of my crew was captured and made Prisoners of War. The officers were sent to Stalag Luft 3 and the enlisted men were sent to Stalag Luft 4. I saw and talked to my co-pilot, Lt. Nelson, at Stalag 7A, Moosberg, Germany six months after we were shot down. He was still at this camp on 31 April 1945 when it was liberated by General Patton's forces. Lt. Gordon and myself were together for five months at Stalag Luft 3 Sagan, Germany. On 28 February 1945, he was moved to a camp near Nuremberg while I went to a camp at Moosberg. For approximately three months I did not know what had happened to him, but on or about 15 April 1945, the Nuremberg prisoners were marched down to Moosberg where I saw and talked with him again. All the rest of the crew was liberated in 1945."

10 September 1944: Lt. Carl V. Dahl, Pilot, 781st Squadron, flew a B-24, to bomb the Osterreichische Saurwerke-Dieseleng Factory at Vienna, Austria with crewmembers, Lt. Warren I. Beeson, Co-Pilot; Lt. Cornelius V. Culhane, Navigator; Lt. William A. Rachow, Bombardier; Sgt. Richard E. Perkins, Nose Turret Gunner; Sgt. Jack C. Pettigrew, Top Turret Gunner; Sgt. John P. Layne, Ball Turret Gunner; Sgt. Franklin B. Martinez, Flight Engineer-Waist Gunner; Sgt. Howard J. Percy, Radio Operator-Waist Gunner and Sgt. Adrian A. Martin, Tail Turret Gunner. It was10:50 hours and the weather was undercast.

Lt. Dahl, "September 10, 1944 started out very much as any other day in the life of young fliers at combat in a deadly war. Crew number 280 of the 781st Squadron of the 465th Bomb Group, trudged half asleep up the hill toward the Headquarters building to be briefed in the early morning hours as had many crews before them, to fly a bombing mission over the Warehouses, Manufacturing Plants and Railroad Marshalling Yards at Vienna, a target well known to them and the rest of the squadrons as a very difficult mission. The pre-flight weather briefing indicated scattered clouds between our base and the target. Fighter escort was expected to pick us up on the way to the target, dropping off before we got to the target and picking us up again on the way home.

Pretty much a standard briefing so far and then the really bad news, "Intelligence" was reporting the heaviest concentration of anti-aircraft guns in all of Europe, was assembled at Vienna on that memorable day. With little inkling of the excitement, tragedy and good fortune that lay ahead, we and the other air crews quickly loaded into the back of the waiting 6X6s and were transported to the flight line where each crewman quickly began a check of his equipment.

That completed, engines were started by the various pilots and ships taxied in order to the flight strip, where they quickly took off to rendezvous in the pre-dawn darkness. As the dawn began to slowly break, we could see the numerous Squadrons and Groups of B-24s stretched out in a long line in front of us and behind us. Somewhat at ease as we gradually climbed for altitude and passed over the beautiful Alps bathed in the early morning light, we shortly after had a suspicion of things to come when we heard the excited chatter on our radio that German fighter planes were attacking some of the other groups ahead, in force. But our group tightened formation and pressed on as we were expected to.

Then before we knew it, Culhane the navigator was calling out the I. P. over the intercom and shortly after, we began the bombing run as planned. The sky was almost solid black and gray as we approached, and over the target the flak was so thick it looked like you could walk on the black and gray smoke from the shell bursts. Bursting shell fragments "thunked" as they pierced the skin of the plane and rattled off like hail stones. Then suddenly from the waist came "were hit" over the intercom. A quick check of the engines disclosed oil pouring from the left outboard engine in a cloud of smoke and fire. Oil pressure on that engine began to drop immediately and I shouted to Beeson the co-pilot so he could hear above the terrible din to "feather" number one and hit the "extinguisher." And while we were trying to get that under control, just an instant later, a huge hole suddenly appeared right in front of me with a loud "chunk" as a German 90 MM shell went right through the ship entering from the bottom and going out the top without exploding and passing right between Rocky the bombardier and Culhane the navigator, without touching either of them while on it's way.

"What was that" Rocky grunted, as he was poised over the bombsight, no response from Neil, then at long last over the intercom the welcome "bombs away" as we held our position in the formation. Not to worry about losing one engine, we knew we could make it back easily on three engines with the bombs gone, and the squadron began to turn right in it's rally off the target. Then from the waist section again, that dreaded shout, "we're hit on the right side too skipper." A quick check again and this time it was a cloud of oil smoke and flame from the right inboard engine and the oil pressure began dropping immediately and again I shouted to Beeson "feather number three and hit the extinguisher." All of a sudden we were sitting up there with two feathered props. Soon the rally was complete, in a short time the fires blew themselves out, the terrible din dropped to a gentle roar and we began to take stock of our situation as the rest of the squadron began pulling away from us, since it was impossible to keep up with only two engines going.

The decision at this point seemed fairly clear since we were slowly losing altitude even though we were carefully conserving every bit of fuel and altitude, to try for the island of Vis. If we had enough fuel and altitude when we got there, we would cross the Adriatic and if not we would set down on the island. There was only one small problem as I asked Culhane for a compass heading for Vis, from the early morning briefing I knew that a large concentration of German fighter planes lay between us and Vis at the Lake Balaton area. Fighter planes I thought, why not call our own since we were all alone, all other bomber formations were out of sight and we were slowly limping along and gradually losing altitude. We knew the Germans might also hear our call but decided it was a calculated risk worth taking and quickly made a distress call to anyone in the area. Almost before we knew it our own fighter escort appeared off our right wing tip and we heaved a big sigh of relief but our relief was short lived.

Before we could get to feeling too secure, from the escort we heard them transmit to us, "good luck guys, we have to leave you now because we are running short of fuel" and our security blanket was gone. The left inboard engine was getting really rough and losing power badly as we skirted the Balaton area and it was beginning to look as if we might not even make it to Vis. Then there was no longer a worry, there they were, German fighters dropping out of the sky, primed for the kill. They could clearly see our two feathered props and considered us a sitting duck.

All of a sudden it was bedlam again but this time fully coordinated as the gunners called out to each other over the intercom, Perkins in the nose turret,

Pettigrew in the top turret, Percy and Martinez at the waist. Even though exhausted from continuous work patching gas and hydraulic lines, holes, bomb bay doors, guns and everything else, these men were ready to fight with a vengeance. Right in the middle of all this, one of them sang out over the intercom, "Don't put your wheels down skipper (the sign of distress and surrender in this theatre at that time), we'll get em' for you." Pass after pass was made by the German fighters from all directions and each was met with a hail of 50-calibre lead.

The first to shout over the interphone was Pettigrew, "I hit him" he said, then it was Layne in the ball turret and Martin in the tail turret, "I hit him" three times in all as the gunners confirmed each others kills, which admittedly, at the time had a great deal more than one gunner firing at it. After some really dramatic air-to-air combat and after losing three of their number, the German fighters apparently decided we weren't long for this world anyway so they broke off but left us with both good and bad news. The good that not one of the crew had been hit in that furious exchange, the bad that the ship had taken its share of hits and the left inboard engine was worse.

We could see the oil flowing out of the engine cowling and the oil pressure was fluctuating, but we kept nursing it along because we knew she wouldn't fly on just one engine. By now I knew we were too low to make it to Vis, so I quickly asked Culhane to give us a heading for the Yugo Partisan territory and call out on the intercom, "I said," as soon as we are there. We may be there now, he said over the intercom and a few minutes later our worst fears were realized as the left inboard engine froze up with such a terrible vibration we thought it would tear itself off the wing. And then the engine was dead but the prop continued to windmill in the air adding a strong drag to our plane, which was already barely flyable.

Now over heavily wooded mountains there was only one choice left as I ordered "prepare to bail out" over the intercom and told Beeson to let me know when everyone was gone, then I would hold it while he went out and I would follow him. Rocky put two 45 slugs into his precious bomb sight as he had been trained to do and I shouted "bail out" and in the space of a few seconds all were gone but Beeson, he wanted to stay and help me get out but was persuaded and jumped after the others. With full power on the remaining right outboard engine it was my intention that the plane spin into the ground at full power and blow up, completely destroying our top secret bomb sight, after I jumped. Standing between the seats I released the wheel to climb down to the bomb bay but the plane immediately lurched violently right, pinning me between the pilot's seat and the bulkhead behind it. Fighting over the seat I grabbed the wheel with both hands and wrenched it left with all my strength, turned and dove out head first through the open bomb bay.

Hitting the air below I was suddenly tumbling head over heels but spreading my arms and legs soon stopped it and a great sense of relief flooded over me at being out of the trap in the plane and floating so freely in the air. What a beautiful landscape below, I thought, and then a small voice inside me said, you better pull the string boy and after what seemed like ages I heard the welcome pop of the chute opening above me. It seemed like I was falling awfully fast but as I neared the ground I could see the forest of giant pines below and also hear the frightening crack of rifles and the whine of bullets from the ground. Now I wasn't going down fast enough, so pulling on the shroud lines I spilled more air from the chute and plummeted right into the very top of one of those giants. As my feet touched the treetop my chute evidently collapsed and from nearly 100 feet I fell crashing from branch to branch as I went. The branches pounded my back, my face, ribs, legs, and every inch of me it seemed like and as the branches got bigger I was mercifully unconscious. Finally waking up to find myself hanging in my parachute harness about two feet off the ground. With a prayer of thanks that I was still alive, I quickly slipped out of the parachute harness, took a fix on directions and headed in the opposite direction from the sound of the shots.

Alternately trotting and walking I soon came to a small stream and began wading upstream as fast as I could. After hiking about twenty minutes in the stream I could suddenly hear the faint sound of voices in the distance ahead and quickly jumped out of the stream and fell to the ground, listening intently as I tried to locate the exact direction the voices were coming from. Cautiously crawling in the direction that seemed most likely, it was only a few minutes until I suddenly saw a clearing ahead that seemed to be under cultivation. Carefully moving forward, I could at last see a group of Peasants gathered together and speaking to someone on the ground in a strange language, at the far side of the field. Decision time again, were they friend or foe. After watching them for a few minutes I decided to take a chance that they were Partisans and stood up.

They were so busy they didn't notice me walking toward them until I had almost reached them. As they turned toward me I kept walking and began saying very loudly American!! American!! and had almost reached them when the group parted and there on the ground with his ankle shattered in eight places was my co-pilot Mike Beeson. After much gesturing and pigeon English we established that the people were indeed Partisans and we started off for their village some three miles away with two of their men taking turns carrying Beeson on their backs. At the small village of about ten homes we were the center of attention as we arrived, and the men carried Beeson into one of the homes and then upstairs with me right behind and my hand on my 45. They slipped Beeson into the bottom of a two tiered bunk and motioned for me to sit down which I refused until I could examine Beeson's ankle very carefully to determine the extent of the damage, it was very bad and he was in a lot of pain.

73

Not long after I finished checking Beeson they brought in a man we hadn't seen before but who had lived in the U. S. for a bit and could speak a fair amount of English - he would it turned out, stay with us the rest of the time we were in Yugo. He told us we were in friendly Partisan hands and that they would notify their Russian zone commander of our presence, and then make arrangements to get us back to Italy - his reference to the Russians had ominous overtones to me and sent cold chills down my back - a feeling that was later to be fully justified.

While I was trying to get oriented to this new and unexpected <u>Russian Factor,</u> we suddenly heard shouts and excitement from outside and I ducked apprehensively near a window. In trooped more Partisans who had rounded up all the rest of the crew, with the exception of Rocky and Frank, and having learned via "jungle telegraph" where we were supposed to be hiding, had brought the others straight to us. After "hoots and back slapping" all around, it was time for bread and soup with our host for dinner and a delicious liqueur made from prunes, as an aperitif. Looking out the window as it began to grow late we saw a man not previously a part of our group, rounding the corner of the building with a horse drawn cart, whereupon our host unceremoniously began to hustle everyone down the stairs with them carrying Beeson, and loading us on to the cart. After a shot of morphine just a few minutes earlier from a first aid kit one of the gunners had presence of mind to bring with him just before the "bail out", Beeson was feeling a little better and was ready to do some traveling. With our interpreter and the driver riding up front and us in the back we took off, and after a couple of hours of riding, we came to another village of about 100 homes.

As we began to enter the village our interpreter, who insisted we call him Fred, and the wagon driver beside him, insisted on taking us to the town square where the "bullet pock marked wall" stood as mute testimony to their tale of the three hundred men, women and children who had been massacred there by the German army just six months before. From the grisly scene of the massacre, we went directly to the office of the Russian Zone Commander, which was upstairs over one of the better houses. The upstairs room had been partitioned and his office appeared to be at the end of the room with the door closed. In just a few minutes Fred knocked at the door and went in at the sound of an intimidating Russian voice, only to emerge a few seconds later - and leaving the door open - to say that the Captain would see us in a little while.

Without being obvious, I could clearly see through the open door the "dour" visage of the uniformed Russian sitting by himself behind a large desk. Clearly, the delay in seeing us was intended as an affront and a slight, so calling our group together in a corner, I explained what was happening and that I would likewise delay, when the Captain finally saw fit to see me which he finally did after about twenty minutes. Then it was my turn to stall, while I talked with the crew for about ten minutes, telling them to stay close to the door when I went in - to come in with their guns ready if I called and <u>not</u> to give up their guns to anyone for any reason. Then, marching into the office in my best military style, I saluted briskly in front of the Captains desk - which he studiously ignored and barked something to Fred in Russian.

Fred then turned to me and said, the Captain wants all your information about your home airfield, your target, your airplane, your bombsight and how many planes took part in your bombing mission. For an instant I was startled by his question, but careful not to let him see this, I said, tell the Captain - and I gave Fred my name rank and serial number - and that is all he is going to get. When he heard this from Fred, he began to color with rage and as he began to rise from his chair, he began to pull his Luger from its holster and at the same time told Fred that I was ordered to hand over my gun and all the weapons of the crew. At this point he was in such a rage that he was shouting at Fred who appeared to be scared to death. Anticipating what was about to happen, I had already pulled my own 45 and cocked it as the Captain had pulled his Luger - so there we stood, face to face, with guns pointed at each others belly and suddenly you could hear a pin drop anywhere in the building.

Tell the Captain I told Fred, he will be dead before his bullet hits me if he pulls that trigger and we want immediately to be returned to Italy according to the U. S./Russian treaty. Poor Fred quickly translated and the Captain saw that we meant business even if he had never heard of such treaties, but then neither had I, - a few seconds more and the stare was over, the Captain holstered his Luger, turned his back, and picking up his field phone began talking to someone presumably in Russian and we were dismissed. Fred quickly motioned for us to follow him, which we were glad to do as we went down the stairs and loaded onto the wagon again with a huge collective sigh of relief.

But, as Fred climbed up beside our driver there was a new look of respect in their eyes as we continued on through the Village. After riding about three miles out of the village our driver quietly detoured down a side road without any explanation and shortly came to a clearing in the trees where colorful lighted lanterns and the sound of music announced that a folk dance was in progress. Everyone was in Peasant clothes and dancing with a lot of enthusiasm and joy on a wooden platform of about fifty square feet, which was raised about six inches off the ground. Nothing would do but to join them in the dancing, so after repeated assurances that we had plenty of time, we all joined in the dancing until about 2 in the morning, with the exception of poor Beeson who could only watch from the cart. About 2 A. M. I insisted we must be on our way, but before leaving, Fred showed us their best-kept secret. Under the dance floor in a huge pit covered by a tarpaulin was their harvest of grain, about two railroad boxcar loads, hidden from the Germans. Resuming our cart ride we returned to the main road such as it was, and had traveled about two hours when we stopped and Fred got down to tell us that we would soon be leaving the forested mountains and had to pass a German check point.

Not good news to us, because at this particular time Beeson was running a high temperature, the morphine was all gone and he was becoming slightly delirious. Passing a German Sentry with this crowd and a sick man seemed ridiculous, so I asked in a somewhat mocking manner, just how our two friends proposed to accomplish this minor miracle. They seemed almost indifferent to the whole matter and said that we must all lay down flat on the bed of the cart while they piled straw on us, and then not to make a sound while they drove through the check point. This was madness, I felt, the Germans would never buy such a simple ruse, but with a lot of misgiving I ordered all the crew to draw and cock their weapons and breath as little as possible when we approached the guard. Then added, that if we were discovered, shoot every guard in sight but not to waste a single shot.

Further, they were to jump into the ditch beside the road after me and begin a retreat as fast as possible, back along the road we had just come down, keeping as low as possible in the ditch as we went. I would take care of Beeson with Neil Culhane helping me. Everyone followed instructions perfectly, the Sentry stopped the horses and cart and then began a lot of conversation while we held our breath, mostly afraid Beeson would begin moaning with the pain he was suffering and give away our hiding place. Peeking through the straw and watching the whole proceeding, after a few minutes we saw the Sentry begin walking toward the cart, we froze like steel springs. Instantly, Fred jumped down from his seat on the cart right in front of the Sentry, - from the intensity and tone of the conversation that ensued, I'm sure Fred was putting his life on the line for us at that very moment, but he finally prevailed. The Sentry waved us on as Fred got back into his seat on the cart and our journey was resumed once more.

Our travel was over a fairly flat plain now, compared to what we had grown accustomed to, and not long after we came to a fairly large town, large enough to have paved streets and lighted street lights. This came as a real surprise to us, no way did we ever expect to be riding around a lighted town somewhere in the middle of Yugo, and let me tell you, the sound of horses feet on the paved street at 5 A. M. sounded like cannon shots, because there was not another sound in that entire town. Expecting to be pounced on at any second, we traveled only a few blocks when our cart stopped in front of a little one story white house that was totally dark. Our two guides quietly slipped down from their seats and hustled us all inside with Neil and I carrying Beeson, and once inside, the place was a blaze of light which was effectively shut off to the outside by heavy blackout curtains. We shortly learned from Fred that we would go the rest of the way by truck, which I could not believe - but within about ten minutes, a short burly, mustachioed man was admitted quietly to the house, and we were informed that he would be our driver. At Fred's signal we all quietly slipped outside, and surprised again, we see and hear the German Lorry waiting for us. Carefully, Neil and I wrestled Beeson into the cab with us while the others crawled into the back. I'm sure all of us were thinking at that moment, this was too easy, and wondered if this last leg of our trip was to be our final betrayal. The stocky driver crawled in and the Lorry started out with hardly a whisper and the driver soon guided it out of town with consummate skill and totally without lights.

Once outside the town he began rolling along the deserted road about 40 miles an hour, still without lights and I swear that I could hardly see the end of the Lorry's hood. We traveled about 50 minutes in total silence; the driver apparently spoke no English. Then the driver slowed up as he swung the Lorry off the road to the right and we began to bump across an open field. After a few minutes of bumping and groans from Beeson who was in terrible pain by this time, we began to see a large light about three quarters of a mile away. As we got closer our hearts raced, we could see it was the lighted interior of a C-47 aircraft with its cargo hatch open, just waiting for us. Safety at last, the crew jumped out of the back of the truck and scrambled into the waiting C-47 like it was their mother.

Culhane and I began getting Beeson out of the cab and into the C-47 and just about had him loaded when our Lorry driver suddenly began shouting Go! Go! Go! And as I turned to see what the problem was I could see headlights of a car coming from the direction we had come, men in the car started shouting and some shots were fired. Nothing needed to be said, Culhane and I jumped into the C-47 and both shouted to the pilot, who already had his engines running, Go! Go! Go! We were all sure that it was Germans after us. Without further ado, the pilot advanced full throttle while we finished pulling Beeson in and the plane crew closed the hatch. The C-47 was airborne in seconds and as the pilot banked left, we could see in the light of the planes landing lights, our Lorry heading for the far side of the field with the car in hot pursuit, was it a car full of German soldiers?

We never found out but we were sure many of those Partisans had risked their lives to save ours. Once in the air, several of the crew immediately went sound asleep and never stirred until we put down in Italy. At the request of the pilot, ambulances were waiting to take us to the hospital when we landed, at the hospital we all were de-loused, fed and put to sleep for all of us were near the point of exhaustion. And so our September 10 mission ended the afternoon of the next day. After the doctors examined Beeson they immediately sent him back to the U. S., two days later the rest of us were sent back to our squadron to resume flying again."

12 September 1944: Lt. Thomas G. Depp, Pilot, 780th Squadron, flew a B-24H, #41-29406, Call Letter Red "L" named "Whiskey Jim" to bomb the Wasserburg Jet Propelled Aircraft Factory at Wasserburg, Germany with crewmembers, Lt. William I. Bowen, Co-Pilot; Lt. Alfred R. Mock, Bombardier;

Sgt. Carmine M. Durante, Flight Engineer-Gunner; Sgt. Ernest W. Carter, Radio Operator-Gunner; Sgt. Robert L. McCurley, Gunner; Sgt. Howard A. Sabin, Gunner; Sgt. Brian H. Cleworth, Gunner and Sgt. James V. Borrelli, Gunner. The weather was clear and their aircraft was last sighted at 14:30 hours near the Italian, Adriatic coast. This was a nine-man crew.

Eyewitness, Sgt. William F. Abney, Jr., 780th Squadron, "Before we reached the target on the combat mission of 12 September 1944, Lt. Depp's plane had number 4 engine smoking, but he continued to the target OK. After we had passed over the target, just before passing Trieste, the plane began losing altitude and air speed rapidly. It dropped down and was following the valley of the mountains below the peaks. When the plane passed out of my range of vision, it was flying in a southeasterly direction, and appeared to be holding altitude which was approximately five thousand to seven thousand feet."

The aircraft left the formation on the way back from Wasserberg, Germany. Lt. Bowen told the pilot they were losing altitude fast - "try and get together on the ground, we'll have a better chance." The entire crew bailed out over the German Alps, south of Wasserberg. Lts. Depp, Mock and Bowen, and Sgts. Durante, McCurley and Sabin, went out through the bomb bays. Sgts. Carter, Cleworth and Borrelli went out the back hatch. Lt. Depp was the last man out. This crew had not flown together until the day they went down.

Lt. Depp, "Our aircraft hit a big house near the place where we were captured. I don't remember the name of the town. I saw the rest of the crew near Balzano, Italy in a jailhouse and they were all in good condition. Lt. Bowen was next to the last to bail out, he told me that he was going and he saw that all the rest of the crew was out. Later, he told me he had a rough chute landing. I saw the following members of the crew at Camp Lucky Strike, France after our release from P.W. Camp, Lts. Bowen and Mock and Sgts. Durante, Sabin, Borelli, Carter, Cleworth and McCurley. Bowen, Durante, Borrelli, Sabin and McCurley indicated that they had sustained various degrees of injury from the bailout or at the hands of the enemy. Only two of the men stated that they had injuries they thought serious."

12 September 1944: Lt. Sigmund E. Hausner, Pilot, 783rd Squadron, flew a B-24, to bomb the Wasserburg Jet Propelled Aircraft Factory at Wasserburg, Germany with crewmembers, Lt. William D. Wine, Co-Pilot; F/O John R. Smith, Navigator; Lt. Orville J. Deegan, Bombardier; S/Sgt. Owrie V. Brown, Flight Engineer-Gunner; Sgt. Harold W. Saalfeld, Radio Operator-Gunner; Sgt. David D. Bradford, Armorer-Gunner; Sgt. Benjamin J. Davis, Armorer-Gunner; S/Sgt.

Allen A. Honey, Armorer-Gunner and Sgt. Donald M. Ruffalo, Armorer-Gunner. The weather was clear and their aircraft was last sighted at Manfredonia, Italy.

Lt. Wine, "On 12 September 1944, we were returning from a combat mission and were over the Adriatic when we noticed that our fuel supply was getting low. We had already transferred our fuel from the Tokyo tanks and were running on the four main tanks. We continued our flight toward the base in formation with our squadron until the fuel pressure on number 2 engine dropped. We then put all the switches on tank to engine cross-feed. When we sighted land we broke the formation and continued to the closest place on shore hoping to find some place where we might make a landing if necessary.

There were low clouds present and the terrain was mountainous. We called Big Fence and they told us that our position at present was over the town of Viesta and we should continue along the coastline. We called Big Fence again trying to find out where the nearest landing field was. They told us to steer a course of 245 degrees and that there was a field 28 miles away. The crew was alerted and told to get ready to bail out. We continued a little further and when we looked around, we noticed that the crew had already bailed out along the coast near the town of Manfredonia.

Big Fence was notified that eight men had bailed out. I noticed that the altitude at present was 3,500 feet. We immediately decided to try and land the ship after sighting a field just around the side of the mountain. Big Fence was called again immediately after landing and told that the pilot, co-pilot and ship were all right. I stayed with the ship while Lt. Hausner went into town to the Air-Sea-Rescue to see if they had found any of the crew. I was told that there were a couple of ships out looking for them and that they had picked up two of the crew.

I also noticed that there was a Catalina searching, too. I waited for the boat to dock and found that they had picked up three of our men. Sgts. Brown, Ruffalo and Saalfeld, who was apparently drowned. Brown said that when they picked up Saalfeld his parachute harness was still fastened and his Mae West was inflated and he believed that Saalfeld was suffocated by his own Mae West because his upper parachute strap was fastened and his Mae West was inflated. We were informed that Sgt. Honey had been picked up by the Catalina. A Capt. from the Medical Corps assisted us in trying to get some boats out in the vicinity and by this time we left for the 61st General Hospital at Foggia. We were told that there were 14 boats in the searching party. At the time the wind was strong, coming from the north-west and the sea was pretty rough."

F/O Smith and Lt. Deegan and Sgts. Saalfeld, Davis and Bradford were Killed In Action. Lts. Hausner, and Wine and Sgts. Brown, Ruffalo and Honey were rescued.

13 September 1944: Lt. Allen D. Fischbach, Pilot, 783rd Squadron, flew a B-24H, #41-28977, to bomb the Synthetic Oil Refinery at Oswiecem, Poland with crewmembers, Lt. John S. Biddle, Co-Pilot; Lt. Samuel Bier, Bombardier-Navigator; Sgt. Orval E. Griffin, Flight Engineer-Gunner; Sgt. Edmund J. Miosky, Radio Operator-Gunner; Sgt. William S. Coburn, Gunner; Sgt. William J. Wightman, Armorer-Gunner; Sgt. Joseph E. Harrison, Gunner and Sgt. Robert H. Arnold, Gunner. Visibility was good and their aircraft was last sighted at 13:20 hours over Yugoslavia. This was a nine-man crew.

Eyewitness, 1st Lt. George W. Williams, "Lt. Fischbach flew Able 7 on the mission of 13 September 1944. He remained in formation until Able box was broken up over the target. Nothing was seen of him until sometime after the group had reformed after coming off the target. He was seen several times over the reformed group but he did not seem able to get into formation. He was flying across the top of the formation. He was last seen a few miles east of the Yugoslav border in apparent control of the ship, but his ship was still not in formation. Nothing further was seen of his ship after the group crossed into Yugoslavia."

After bombs away, engines number 1 and 3 were hit by flak. Number 1 went out straight away, and the pilot headed for the Island of Vis. After an hour number 3 went out. Sgt. Miosky tried to contact their base on the emergency frequency but could not get through. All guns, ammo and kits were thrown overboard as the plane was losing altitude rapidly. Over Yugoslavia, number 4 engine ran away and at about 4,000 feet, the pilot gave the order to bail out. All the crew bailed out successfully with Sgts. Harrison, Miosky, Arnold, Griffin and Coburn bailing out the back escape hatch. Lts. Fischbach, Biddle and Bier, and Sgt. Wightman bailing out of the bomb bay. Wightman said he preferred to jump, rather than crash land.

Harrison heard that Wightman was in good health and on the ground safe, but he disappeared after the first day. Harrison saw Lt. Bier on the ground as they landed in parachutes within 100 feet of each other. About 30 minutes before the crew bailed out, Sgt. Arnold talked to Wightman and he was not injured. Arnold saw him about a mile from him coming down in his chute. Wightman's chute was one of the two chutes that floated across the Danube. The Partisans reported that of the nine crewmembers, the Germans captured six and three escaped. The Partisans had Arnold and Harrison and one was unaccounted for. Miosky joined them later so they assumed that Wightman was the one unaccounted for. Arnold had no idea what may have happened to Wightman, other than being captured. Harrison told Arnold that he saw Bier taken prisoner by men dressed as German soldiers. Wightman was last seen in prison camp by Sgt. Coburn. They were separated when the Germans marched them out of prison camp in the face of advancing Russians. Griffin saw Wightman while on the march from Luft number 4 and westward and his feet were giving him trouble.

The ship crashed in the area of Smederevo and blew up. As Miosky's chute opened, some of the shroud lines broke and he drifted away from the others and landed between Belgrade and Smederevo, hitting the ground very hard in a clearing so that he was knocked out. He regained consciousness to find himself surrounded by a group of soldiers dressed in mixed German uniforms, some of whom were kicking him. The language they spoke was Serbian.

He was questioned in Serbian, and asked if he spoke German. All his clothes, dog tags and possessions were then removed leaving him in his shirt, underpants and shoes. These men then took him a short distance to a German truck, tied his hands behind his back and drove about an hour and a half towards Smederevo. Machine gun fire was heard ahead of the truck, which pulled off the road by a deserted house, and he and his captors went inside. He was put in a bare room with straw on the floor. With his hands still tied, he managed to escape the same night by jumping through a hole in the wall, which was not barred. As he ran away he heard shots. He ran for some distance through the woods, and after about four miles he laid down in a cornfield where he tried to sleep. (13 September 44').

The following morning he managed to untie his hands, but was forced to remain hidden in the corn until the morning of 16 September, as he saw guard parties looking for him in the area. On the morning of 16 September he contacted some Yugoslav civilians (with Chetnik tendencies). Miosky, who is able to speak Serbian, Lithuanian and Polish, conversed in the former language and told these people he was an American. Here he obtained some civilian clothes and food, but he was feeling very sick, after his two nights of exposure and was suffering from a severe skin rash and boils. After living with these people for about three days, in the area of Smederevo, Miosky who was then semi-conscious was taken to the outskirts of a village in an area near Sopave. He entered the village, and found it was Partisan held. The Partisans were very suspicious of him. When he asked for a British Mission, he was kept at this compound, in a room with some straw to sleep on, and was given a little food, the first he had since leaving the Yugoslav helpers.

After one day at Partisan Headquarters he was taken via Sopave, Arenolelavno, Slenovice to Ljig, under Partisan guards. He told the Partisans, in Serbian that he was an American, but was obviously not believed. At Ljig, he was put into a guardhouse, in soaking wet clothes, with only straw to sleep on. He was refused any food or cigarettes. The following morning, a Partisan officer put him on a train, in a boxcar, with eight Chetnik prisoners.

He protested and said he was an American, but the Partisan officer merely shrugged his shoulders, and he was told by Partisan guards that he was thought to be a Chetnik, and not an American. In the boxcar, he signaled to a British

Captain he saw in the station, but was quickly pushed into a corner and told to keep quiet. The doors and windows of the boxcar were then closed. Soon afterwards, however, a British Major arrived with another Partisan officer's interpreter (known as "The Professor"), they questioned him and had him released at once.

The Partisans were then full of apologies and told him to "forget the whole thing as it had been a bad mistake." He learned afterwards that the eight Chetniks who had been with him were to be shot, and that he would have been shot with them. He was released on or about 1 October and joined the British Mission in this area, where there were two other members of his crew, Sgts. Harrison and Arnold. The whole incident was reported to the British Mission and the Major threatened the Partisans that he would have all supplies immediately cut off, if he heard that one other American was being held prisoner by them. The opinion of the Major was that the Partisans had been given information that Miosky was a Chetnik spy. He lived with the British Mission for about five days, until he was evacuated on 7 October 1944 by C-47, piloted by Russians. Lts. Fischbach, Biddle and Bier, and Sgts. Griffin, Coburn and Wightman were captured and made Prisoners of War. Sgts. Harrison, Miosky and Arnold were evacuated by the Partisans.

13 September 1944: Col. Charles A. Clark, Jr., Pilot, 783rd Squadron, flew a B-24 to bomb the Synthetic Oil Refinery at Oswiecem, Poland with crewmembers, 1st Lt. Milton H. Duckworth, Co-Pilot; 1st Lt. Aloys Frank, Navigator; Lt. Herbert V. Burkhardt, Navigator; Capt. John V. Knaus, Bombardier; T/Sgt. Victor Cohen, Flight Engineer-Gunner; S/Sgt. Jack A. Walters, Radio Operator-Gunner; S/Sgt. Edward M. Reagan, Gunner; S/Sgt. Weyland B. Feely, Gunner and T/Sgt. Leroy J. Crenshaw, Gunner.

This is an account of the mission as told by S/Sgt. Weyland Feely:
"At the briefing on September 13, 1944, we were told our target would be an oil refinery in Oswiecem, Poland; that the flak would be heavy and fighter opposition was unknown. The target was 75 miles from the German-Russian lines. We had a map to the target but no maps from there on.

All went well to the target. Our fighter escort was with us all the way to the target and we had no fighter opposition. We made our bomb run through heavy flak and had just dropped our bombs when all "Hell" broke loose. Our right engine was hit by flak and was on fire. We started down at a very steep angle with the flames from the engine reaching past the tail turret where I was sitting. My parachute was laying about halfway between my turret and the camera hatch. Just as I reached for my "chute" the plane leveled off, the engine was "feathered" and the flames went out. The pilots did a wonderful job controlling the plane.

I don't know how much time passed as all of this was happening, but it didn't seem very long to me. And as I looked out, we weren't very far from the ground either. I looked up and could see the rest of the boys going home. We called our escort but they told us we were on our own, as they could not leave the Group. So we manned our guns, lowered landing gear, and headed for the Russian lines. If we passed over the front lines, and I'm sure that we did, we couldn't tell it, as we saw no activity. It seemed to me we flew along at about 1,000 feet, but it could have been more. We skirted around a couple of large airfields, because we didn't know where we were. We weren't looking for any more flak or fighters!

We finally spotted three or four fighters in a small field, which we later discovered was a potato patch. We strained our eyes looking for a red star. Then we saw them on the fighters. We shot some flares and braced ourselves for a landing. It was a small clearing with a small irrigation ditch across the middle. Again the pilots came through and made a walkaway landing. They shut the engines off, and we waited for further orders. It dawned on me that I was low on cigarettes - not counting on a one way flight. We started digging up every butt we could find in the corrugated flooring.

We had quite a reception from men and women military personnel on a big flatbed model truck. Only one Russian driver could speak English. We boarded the truck, and were driven about five miles to a small village or farm. There were not many buildings. We were taken to a two-story house; upstairs we were shown very coarse straw mattresses about a foot thick where we would sleep. We were told that we would eat at 6:00 PM. At that time we were taken to a small family house where two tables were set up with benches on each side. On each table were cold cuts of meats and cheeses, also fresh vegetables, and all the Vodka you wanted. Then came a big bowl of potato soup, followed by fried goose. After we had finished dinner we went back to our quarters. Later in the evening they had a dance for us downstairs. There was an accordion player. The Russians showed us their dances, and we showed them how to jitterbug. Before it was over, everyone was jitterbugging.

The next day (September 14) we walked around the area, sightseeing and taking pictures. Jack Walters and I found this soldier who had a motorcycle with a sidecar. It looked like one they used in World War I. It ran pretty good until Jack tried to go between two trees and didn't make it - too much Vodka I think! That night we went to an outdoor movie - *Chicago* with Alice Faye - in Russian. Sometime during the movie all the lights went out. We could hear a plane overhead. They told us it was a German plane.

The next morning (September 15) they sent five of us out to cover the plane with camouflage netting. We had the same truck that had brought us in, but I do believe the driver was taking his first solo. We were off the road more than we were on it. Three of us were standing in the back wrestling 55-gallon drums. We looked back and could see the plane behind us. We banged on top of the truck until we got the driver's attention. We showed him the plane and convinced him that it was our destination. He spoke no English, and we later found out he was taking us to the front lines! We covered the plane and were taken back to our quarters.

The next day (September 16) we were picked up in a C-47 transport. We were flown right on top of the ground for 600 miles to Poltava, Russia, which was the shuttle base for the Eighth Air Force. Poltava was not a big town, but all of the stores and restaurants were closed or off limits to us. There was a large park where the old and the young met to pass the time of day or night.

We were given a B-17 to get us back to Italy. At first it was rumored that we would go back by way of Cairo and spend the forty-eight dollars in our escape kit. But later word came down that we would wait for the Eighth Air Force shuttle run. We would join them and fly a mission coming back. On September 19th we joined the Eighth Air Force and hit a target in Szony, Hungary, on the way back to Italy. We must have flown over every anti-aircraft gun between Russia and Italy, and by the grace of God I made it!"

13 September 1944: Lt. Robert A. Coahran, Pilot, 782nd Squadron, flew a B-24J, #42-51320, Call Letter White "L" to bomb the Synthetic Oil Refinery at Oswiecem, Poland with crewmembers, Lt. John M. Hill, Co-Pilot; Lt. Edward F. Fairbrother, Navigator; Lt. William L. Cassel, Bombardier; Sgt. Lemuel L. Whitman, Flight Engineer-Gunner; Sgt. Argonne F. Campbell, Radio Operator-Gunner; Sgt. Richard L. Beaubien, Armorer-Ball Turret Gunner; Sgt. James S. Bugg Jr., Gunner; Sgt. Lawson D. Stoneham, Gunner and Sgt. William G. Petrole, Gunner. Visibility was clear and their aircraft was last sighted at 13:20 hours over Yugoslavia.

Eyewitness, Lt. Alfred R. Frick, "When the formation had more or less recovered after the break-up following Colonel Clark's difficulty, Baker box flew in the Charlie box position. Lt. Coahran, flying (White L), then took up a Baker 6 position flying off our left wing, we being Baker 4. He seemed to be in no serious trouble; all four engines were turning over. About five minutes before reaching the Yugoslav coast, I heard him call Baker 1, stating his number 3 engine was cutting out and thought he might be running low on gas and was heading for Vis. He appeared to have half flaps down all the way back. I did not see him leave the formation but he was still with us up until approximately five minutes before reaching the Yugoslav coast."

Crewmembers stated, "We had trouble with number 3 engine on our way to the target. We went over the target with one engine feathered. After the target we had surging superchargers and were low on gas so we headed for Vis. Soon after

84

passing the Yugoslav border number 1 engine caught fire and then number 2 and number 4 quit. The order was given to bail out. Sgt. Beaubien went out at the tail hatch. All crewmembers got out, but the chute of Sgt. Campbell didn't open and he was killed. Beaubien landed on a rock pile, on an island off the coast, breaking his leg. About 5 minutes later the Partisans came.

They took him to a hospital on the island and put a crude splint on his leg. He stayed in this vicinity for seven days moving from one island to another. The British came and evacuated him by boat to Vis. He stayed at Vis about four days and then was evacuated to Bari by air, arriving on or about 24 September 1944. Sgts. Petrole, and Stoneham were captured and made Prisoners of War. Sgt. Whitman landed, hitting his head on the rocks and he died at a hospital on the Island. Partisan information indicates that, Sgt. Argonne F. Campbell was buried on 13 September 1944 in Preminvo, Yugoslavia and Sgt. Lemuel L. Whitman's body was picked up in the sea and was taken to a Partisan First Aid Station and he was also buried on the same small island on 15 September 1944. The rest of the crewmembers were returned to Italy."

13 September 1944: Lt. James Ayres, Pilot, 782nd Squadron, flew a B-24, to bomb the Synthetic Oil Refinery at Oswiecem, Poland with crewmembers, Lt. James B. Harper, Co-Pilot; Lt. Edward Gehrki, Navigator; Lt. Thomas E. Vinophal, Bombardier; Sgt. Richard F. Klein, Nose Turret Gunner; Sgt. Richard A. Keenan, Ball Turret Gunner; S/Sgt. James Hoard, Flight Engineer-Gunner; Sgt. Joseph Tardiglione, Radio Operator-Gunner; Sgt. Forrest Morgan, Waist Gunner and Sgt. Perry Bailey, Tail Turret Gunner. Weather was clear at 13:20 hours.

Lt. Harper, "I was flying as co-pilot in a B-24 piloted by Lt. Ayres on a mission to Oswiecem Poland, in the Gracac area. Over the target there was heavy flak and after bombs away, number 2 engine was hit by flak and went out. Number 1 engine lost power and number 3 was set on fire. The ship was badly holed by flak, the ailerons were smashed, the hydraulic system was knocked out and the petrol tanks opened up. Only 75 gallons of fuel remained in the tanks. The plane was headed for the Russian lines. Over the area of Osbica at about 7,000 feet, a Russian "Yak" aircraft attacked the plane with cannon fire, setting it on fire. Orders were given to bail out and all the crew left the plane safely. The plane crashed on the Russian lines and was completely wrecked. We were never in the hands of the enemy. While in our chutes all members of the crew were machine gunned by Russian troops. Although our chutes were holed, none of us were hit. I landed in an open field about a half-mile behind the Russian lines and was picked up by Russian troops before I had time to remove my chute.

The Russians at first thought that I was a German. They had been expecting a German airborne attack and thought we were the attacking German force. I was taken to a Russian Company Headquarters, where all of my possessions, watch, rings, dog tags, camera, escape purse, etc., were all removed. I gathered that I was to be shot, but was saved by the timely arrival of a Russian who could speak English. Once the Russians realized that I was an American, I was well treated. All my belongings, except the camera and pistol were returned to me.

My pilot was brought in and we were both taken to a field hospital where we stayed for seven days. While at this hospital in the area of Ropaczyea, I met the remainder of my crew. Three crewmembers were injured, Sgt. Tordiglione had a broken ankle, Sgt. Bailey was badly injured in the face by a 20mm shell and Sgt. Keenan had fragment injuries to his face. Treatment in the hospital was as good as possible and we were given complete freedom to walk around the countryside. As there was a battle going on in the area, I never walked very far. An American film was shown my crew and me and the Russians did all they could to make recompense for shooting at us on our parachute descent. I was well fed, mainly on German rations. On about 25 September 1944, my crew and I, with the exception of Sgt. Bailey, were taken to an airfield at Jesczow, and flown to Poltava in a Russian piloted "C-47."

Thence two days later in an ATC "C-46" to Cairo, thence in ATC "C-47" via Benghazi to Bari, arriving 27 September 1944. Sgt. Richard A. Keenan, the ball turret gunner, was left in the hospital in Poltava and rejoined the others at group in Bari, Italy on 28 September. Some Polish civilians spoke English and had relatives in America. They were not particularly Anti-German. Russian "Yak" planes are armed with a 37mm cannon, firing through its propeller, with two 20mm cannons in each wing. Most also have some 30-38 caliber machine guns. Russians appeared to be using obsolete aircraft on the front line. They have little mechanical equipment and use horse drawn ambulances. I saw some new low built tanks with medium barrels. 1936 Ford V8s are used as command cars and trucks."

Sgt. Bailey landed near a Russian Army Headquarters and does not remember the name of the town. Russians picked him up and brought him to a First Aid Station. He had difficulty at first convincing them that he was an American but finally they searched him and found an American Bible with the address, Mitchell Field, N.Y. From that moment on the Russians treated him very well. He was then taken to a hospital where he met Sgt. Klein and where he stayed for two hours. He was then taken to another hospital where he stayed for 24 hours. From there he was moved to a private house near another hospital where he found eight other members of his crew.

Bailey received medical attention here and stayed for 4 days. An American Doctor attached to an American air base found them here and took Bailey to a Russian hospital at the American Base. He stayed here for six days and was then evacuated to the 19th Station Hospital where he stayed for 76 days. He was then taken to the 113th General Hospital where he stayed for 10 days. Sgt. Bailey was discharged from the hospital and sent to Teheran where he stayed for 4 days and then flown to Cairo where he stayed 4 days and was then flown to Naples arriving 29 December 1944.

From the diary of Sgt. Richard A. Keenan, Ball Turret Gunner on Lt. Ayres Crew:

Today was our fatal day. Thank the good Lord above that he watched over us and protected us all. This morning in briefing we were told that we were going to bomb the Synthetic Oil Plant at Oswiecem, which is west of the city of Krakow. They told us the flak would be moderate, but they sure were wrong. Well we got to our target, and went over it in flak, and dropped our bombs and then it happened. We got hit by flak that we were told would be inaccurate. The flak knocked out one engine and we had a runaway prop. Our oil lines were knocked out and so were our fuel lines. We were losing altitude fast and our pilot said, "lets head for Russia," because it was only about 200 miles away and we might be able to make it. We never could have made it back to Italy.

Big Ed (Ed Gehrki our navigator) got on the ball and started figuring out our heading. There was a couple of fields he had on his map that we could land at if our gas held out. Well, we got about a couple of miles over the front lines, with the pilot and co-pilot nursing the ship along all the way. All of a sudden there was a crashing and banging in the waist. I was out of the ball turret and had it retracted because with it down there was too much drag on 3 engines. I thought the whole ship was blowing up. The half deck was on fire and I thought, "Jesus" you better get out of here before the whole plane goes, so I went out the waist window.

I pulled the ripcord and felt my chute open. The jerk pulled my helmet and oxygen mask off, but I didn't care much then, all I knew was that I was out of that ship. There were clouds all around me and I could hear a lot of machine-gun fire and I thought it was the ammo in the ship exploding. I saw two other chutes below me and I thought that only three of us got out. I was in the clouds for quite a while; I guess I had bailed out at about 5,000 feet. (I must have pulled my chute right away.) When I came out of the clouds I felt a stinging around my mouth and head. I put my hand up to my face and when I looked at it, it was covered with blood. Boy, I was scared stiff, I thought my face was half blown off. (But as it was, I just got wounded a little.)

I was getting nearer the ground now and I was beginning to figure where I was going to land. Pretty soon I heard bullets zinging by me and at first I didn't know they were shooting at me, but then I saw some tracers whiz by me and I got scared more than ever. I put my hands together and started to pray, but then I thought I better get my hands in the air. I thought I was landing in Germany. I tried to slip my chute and got it swinging back and forth so I wouldn't be a good target. Then the ground started coming up fast. I could see two farmhouses near together, and I knew I was going to land near them. Then I saw I was headed for some electric light wires so I slipped my chute and just missed them. As it was, my chute fouled against a pole as I landed.

As soon as I hit the ground, a lot of guys rushed at me with tommy guns. I saw the star on their cap and the sickle and hammer and I knew they were Russians. They asked me if I was German and I held my hands in the air and yelled "American! American!" Pretty soon an officer came and took me to a house. I waited there for about an hour and then they came and got me in a jeep. They took me to another house that seemed to be a Field Headquarters. Then I met Sgt. Forrest Morgan, our waist gunner and I was sure glad to see him. I had my head bandaged up and I guess I looked pretty rough. We thought, we and one other fellow was the only ones to get out. We thought all the rest of the crew were killed because Morgan saw the ship crash.

Pretty soon they piled us in a jeep and drove us around and into a field, there we saw Sgt. Joe Tardiglione, our Radio Operator; riding in a wagon. We were sure glad to see him. He told us that J.C. got out but he didn't know about Lt. Ayres or Harper. He had a busted foot so we got him into the jeep and we drove to another house and we walked in and there was Harper and Ayres, and we were sure glad to see them. They fed us there and fixed Joe and I up. Then they took us to another place and there we met Big Ed and our bombardier, Lt. Vinophal and Sgt. Hoard, our Flight Engineer. Vinophal was not our original bombardier. (Our original bombardier was going to school in Bari, Italy.) There was eight of us there altogether and the Russians said that one of the chutes didn't open and one caught on fire when the guy bailed out so we thought Sgt. Klein, the nose gunner and Sgt. Bailey the tail gunner were dead and we felt pretty bad. The Russians had an interpreter there for us. That night we had borsch and rice and Vodka for supper and that's about all we had every day, the same thing.

On September the 14th the Russians took Joe and me over to the hospital and bandaged us up again. They treat us pretty good here, now that they know we are Americans. Morgan and I found out from Lt. Ayres yesterday, that it was a German ME 109 that finished us off over the front. This information was wrong, as it was a Russian Yak -9 that finished us off. I guess that's what all the firing was that I heard. We landed two miles behind the Russian lines and they took us back to the field hospital and now we are five miles behind their lines. Yesterday (Friday September 15) at the hospital the Russians shaved all my hair off my head. They bandaged my head up and put Joe's foot in a cast.

They brought Bailey in tonight and we were sure glad to see him. His face is all swollen up and he had a bandage on it. He can't eat and he looks pretty bad. He said he saw Klein and he is O.K. and that makes 10 of us. Boy, I'm sure glad we all got down safe. Saturday, September 16, we have just been hanging around and we want to get out of here. We are all jumpy. The fellows built a horseshoe set and have been playing all day. Bailey looks pretty bad. I wish we could get him to an American doctor. We went out to see what was left of our ship. The engines were buried right into the ground and the tail was broken right off and was about 500 feet from the rest of the ship. I got a couple of hunks of it for souvenirs.

Sunday September 17, we all went to church today. There was a little stone church up on a hill. It was about 2 miles from where we were. Joe went up on crutches. It was a Catholic church, but I didn't care, I prayed in my own way and thanked God for saving us all. We hung around the yard until about 4 PM when a Lt. Col. from Poltava came and said he was looking for us, and had been for two days. We left with him and rode around for about 2 hours in a Model A Ford. When we got to the air field, Klein was there waiting for us. He had a pretty good time I guess, he stayed with a Russian Lt. and had his picture taken with him and everything.

They flew us back to Poltava (about 600 miles) in a C-47. We were all pretty nervous after what we had been through. When we got to Poltava, they put Joe, me, and Bailey in the hospital and fixed our wounds. Monday, September 18. I slept most all day today and ate. It felt good to get some American food once more. At about 6 A.M. I got sick. I guess the G.I.'s. They wake me up and keep giving me medicine. God, I was sick. Tuesday, September 19. I was sick all day today. The other fellows are leaving tonight. I hope I am well enough to go with them. I still feel pretty weak though. Wednesday, September 20. Well the fellows left last night at about 12 o'clock. They woke me up and told me I could go too if I felt well enough. I got up and tried to stand but I fell back on the bed. I tried to get my shoes on but I couldn't even see them, I was so dizzy. So Joe went instead. I wanted to go with them awful bad. I feel better today. Thursday, September 21. I am still in the hospital. They changed my bandage today. They have been feeding Bailey through the arm. He still can't eat. I smoked two packs of cigarettes today; I got to cut that out. Friday, September 22. Still in the hospital but I got up today. I am feeling a lot better. Smoked two more packs of cigarettes again today. God, but I am nervous. Hope they let me out of here soon. The doctor said I would be O.K. in a couple of days. Bailey feels better today. They have some nice nurses here.

Saturday, September 23. I feel O.K. now. I keep watching for an A.T.C. plane to come in so I can get started back to Italy. The doctor said he thought Bailey would go home. He says he will never fly again in combat. I guess we all feel the same way. Bailey is coming along good; he can eat a little now. They brought me some extra clothes today; mine were all dirty and ragged. Sunday, September 24. I went to church today and again thanked God for saving my life. They discharged me today but they are letting me stay at the hospital. I hope I leave tomorrow. I think I will because a ship came in tonight. Wednesday, September 27. I got into Cairo about 9 P.M. last night. I thought I would lay over but I had to leave at 12 o'clock midnight. I met Lt. Ayres at the snack bar. I was sure glad to see him. He told me that the rest of the crew left yesterday but he missed the plane. Lt. Ayres and I flew all night, and got into Bari, Italy about 11 o'clock this morning, September 28. Ayres called up for a plane and about 3 P.M. a B-24 from our Squadron came up and got us. Ayres and I put on our chutes the first thing. When we got back we saw Johnny, the Crew Chief of the plane we were flying when we went down. He was damn glad to see us.

22 September 1944: Lt. Roger L. Kraft, Pilot, 783rd Squadron, flew a B-24H, #42-50404, Call Letter Blue "B" named "Flying (Out-House With Wings")") to bomb the industrial area at Munich, Germany with crewmembers, Lt. John N. Coleman, Co-Pilot; Lt. Earl O'Brien, Navigator; F/O John Bistarkey, Bombardier; Sgt. John Sangas, Flight Engineer-Gunner; Sgt. Brooks K. Truitt, Radio Operator-Gunner; Sgt. William H. Curry, Gunner; Sgt. Robert E. Goldman, Gunner; Sgt. Joseph R. Horne, Gunner and Sgt. Leonard T. Rosen, Gunner. Weather was cloudy and their aircraft was last sighted at 12:22 hours, over the German Alps.

Eyewitness, S/Sgt. Joseph J. Korf, 783rd Squadron, "Blue "B" pulled out of formation before hitting the I. P. and fell below us to the left. No engines were feathered and I don't believe they were close to any flak."

Lt. Kraft, "We were assigned to the 8th Air Force and were transferred to the 783rd Squadron of the 15th Air Force. We were assigned to a proud old lady whose name was only a picture, "The Flying Outhouse." When we took off for Munich, Germany the crew reported an oil leak developing from our number 3 engine which did not deter us from our mission. As we turned on our Initial Point (I. P.) and proceeded to the target area, the oil pressure dropped off and required that engine to be feathered. With only three engines we were unable to maintain our place in the formation due to loss of speed and altitude. As we had 700 bombers in our formation with 699 of them above us about to drop their bombs back on us, we were forced to turn out to the side of the group. By the time the bombs were dropping we were well below and to the rear of the group.

We were escorted by two P-38 fighters for a short distance but they were forced to return home. As we were near the Swiss border we set our hopes of making it to that neutral country. On our way we encountered a cloud cover with mountain peaks protruding above the clouds. The last chance to get below the clouds was a small hole about as big as our plane, so down through the hole we went and no sooner had we leveled-off under the clouds at about 4,000 feet above ground when the anti-aircraft guns found us. Two more of our engines were hit as well as several parts of our plane. Somehow we were able to get out of the range of the enemy guns and struggled on to the Swiss border at Lake Constance and the Rhine River. A small patch of green grass was the only level place to be seen so I elected to land (without any other choice). On our approach we were surprised to find our hydraulic system had been shot out and with no power to delay our landing, we were forced to belly in as we were way too low to get the crew to bail out. Fortunately we survived and were unhurt.

We were interned in that country until February of 1945. Our co-pilot and bombardier escaped in January of 1945 and made it home about 30 days before the rest of us. The Swiss treated us well and did as good as they could under the circumstances, as the Germans kept a close look at us with a legation stationed across the street from our hotel. We were required to be present at 11:00 P. M. for bed check and from 8:00 A. M. to 11:00 P. M. we were allowed to mingle with the town people freely and enjoy snow sports. At the end of 1945 we were released and taken by train to Marseille, France and returned to Italy. From there we were returned to New York."

22 September 1944: 1st Lt. George W. Williams, Pilot, 783rd Squadron, flew a B-24J, #44-41137, Call Letter Blue "O" named "Porky" to bomb the industrial area at Munich, Germany with crewmembers, Lt. Gordon A. Grieble, Co-Pilot; F/O Harry Falkoff, Navigator; Lt. Chin I. Ngoon, Bombardier; S/Sgt. Robert W. Ferroll, Flight Engineer-Gunner; T/Sgt. Ralph W. McElyea, Radio Operator-Gunner; S/Sgt. Perry J. Capps, Gunner; S/Sgt. Austin F. Enzor, Gunner; S/Sgt. Donald F. Lafata, Gunner and M/Sgt. James F. Thompson, Gunner. Weather was cloudy and their aircraft was last sighted at 12:00 hours over the German Alps.

Eyewitness, S/Sgt. Zane D. Hoyle 783rd Squadron, "Blue "O", the airplane which Lt. Williams was flying was hit in the number one engine just at "bombs away." He peeled off to the left and feathered number one engine at once. I watched him until he cleared the flak and then seven P-38's joined him. The plane seemed under control and no chutes were seen."

This aircraft left the formation about a minute past the target. Lt. Williams, who had slight wounds to his face and hands, gave the order to bail out. Lts. Grieble and Williams both wished each other good luck before bailing out. All crewmembers bailed out about the same time and all were seen on the ground by Sgt. Thompson. They were all captured and made Prisoners of War. The enlisted men were in Stalag-Luft 4 and the officers were in Stalag-Luft 1. Their aircraft struck the ground 35 miles south of Munich, near a farmhouse.

4 October 1944: 1st Lt. William A. Miller, Pilot, 783rd Squadron, flew a B-24J, #44-41012, Call Letter Blue "Z" to bomb the Main Marshalling Yard at Munich, Germany with crewmembers, Lt. George A. Wynn, Co-Pilot; Lt. Kenneth R. Bassler, Navigator; Lt. George W. Hayman, Bombardier; Sgt. Alvin

I. Musch, Flight Engineer-Gunner; Sgt. Harold N. Graham, Radio Operator-Gunner; Sgt. Robert S. Denny, Gunner; Sgt. George E. Taylor, Gunner; Sgt. George F. Jaeger, Gunner and Sgt. Thomas J. Mooney Jr., Gunner. Visibility was forty miles and their aircraft was last seen at 12:02 hours over Germany.

Eyewitness, Sgt. Orbin E. Rutledge, 783rd Squadron, "I was flying in dog 5 as nose gunner in Blue "A." Blue "Z" was flying in dog 2, just above and in front of us about 150 or 200 feet. Just after we hit the I. P. and started the bomb run, Blue "Z" had just opened its bomb bay doors and about one minute before the target, it was hit before dropping its bombs. It seemed to be a direct hit right next to the right side of the fuselage in the fuel tanks. The wing broke off at the same time that the plane exploded. It happened so fast that I didn't see any chutes get out. Neither did the waist gunner."

Eyewitness, Lt. Vern L. Larson, Pilot, 780th Squadron, "On mission of 4 October 1944, enroute to Munich, Germany to bomb Marshalling Yards, B-24 Blue "Z" flying in dog box, appeared to have had a direct hit by flak in the bomb bay causing the plane to immediately explode. The waist gunner Sgt. York, saw one parachute blown out of the explosion and it opened immediately, but it is my opinion that the force of the explosion opened the chute as the man appeared to be dangling from the chute in a lifeless position."

Eyewitness, Lt. Otis M. Scott, Jr., 782nd Squadron, "We were just making our turn at the IP when I noticed a big explosion in the flak over the target. I saw what I thought to be one parachute but could not be certain because we were approximately 23 miles away. As we passed over the scene of the accident I asked the ball gunner if he could see any parachutes and he reported there were none."

Lts. Miller, Wynn, Bassler and Hayman and Sgts. Musch, Graham, Denny, Taylor, Jaeger, and Mooney, were Killed In Action.

11 October 1944: Lt. Richard C. Klug, Pilot, 780th Squadron, flew a B-24J, #44-41296, Call Letter Red "F" to bomb the Diesel Plant at Vienna, Austria with crewmembers, Lt. Walton L. Huey, Co-Pilot; Lt. Robert P. Jackson, Navigator; Lt. George E. Jurenec, Bombardier; Sgt. Billy B. King, Nose Turret Gunner; Sgt. William R. Ratliff, Flight Engineer-Gunner; Sgt. Bert D. Arzt, Radio Operator-Gunner; Sgt. Victor S. Ziklo, Ball Turret Gunner; Sgt. Bobbie T. Robertson, Waist Gunner and Sgt. James T. Giblin, Tail Turret Gunner. The weather was undercast and overcast. Their aircraft was last sighted at 11:44 hours over Vienna.

Eyewitness, Sgt. Robert F. Hazeleaf, 780th Squadron, "On combat mission of 11 October 1944, I was standing in the left waist window when I saw Lt. Klug's plane (Red "F") hit by flak. However, this was before we came into the most intense flak area. As the pilot pulled the plane away from the formation, flame was coming out of the bomb bays. He seemed to be holding the plane carefully in order to give his crew a chance to get out. First I saw two men come out, then two more came out, and next one man came out alone. A second later four men left the plane all at once. Only one of these men opened his chute before hitting the under-cast. The others were probably making delayed jumps. After this, the plane simply fell to pieces. First the tail dropped off and then the whole ship just seemed to disintegrate."

Lt. Klug, "We left the formation approximately one minute after bombs away rallying to the right. The ship was on fire and I gave the order to bail out and ordered the co-pilot Lt. Huey to leave the ship. He went aft immediately and was making an attempt to bail out. To my knowledge he was not injured. I glanced back once and saw him shielding his face against the fire. Lt. Jerunec, saw Sgt. King coming out of his turret. Lt. Jackson was uninjured and seen by Jurenec, crouched at the escape hatch ready to bail out.

Jackson saw that Jurenec was ready and in position so he said: "Go ahead, I'll follow you." I do not know if Sgt. Ziklo the ball turret gunner got out or not, from indications, we received a shell hit near the rear bomb bay just before a hit was received in the forward bomb bay. This hit may have some bearing on the fate of those crewmembers in the waist and tail. I do not know if Sgt. Robertson got out, as there was no acknowledgment of the bailout order received from the waist or tail. Over the interphone Sgt. Giblin was heard to say, "We're on fire, Lets get outta here." There was no reply from Sgt. Robertson, who was replacing a gunner of my original crew. Sgt. Arzt was seen by Sgt. Ratliff milling around in front of the fire. Due to the intensity of the fire in the forward bomb bay and rear of the flight deck there is or was, a great possibility that he was unable to make his way through to the open bomb bay.

I adjusted the autopilot to hold the ship and became trapped by the fire. About 45 seconds later the ship went into a dive and blew up throwing me clear. Ratliff was attempting to put out the fire after the bail out order was given and he was blown out. To my knowledge the only other man to bail out was Lt. Jurenec. On the first order of bail out the bombardier buckled on his chute, opened the hatch and was given a nod by Lt. Jackson to go. The bombardier stated that the navigator was ready to follow him and he saw the nose gunner backing out of his turret.

After being blown clear of the plane I saw only small pieces of the aircraft in the air. After hitting the ground I saw a chute high in the air being carried by the wind about five miles to the northwest of me. I didn't go to investigate as I assumed the chute had been spotted. In that direction, I found that I could see signs of habitation. I struck out to the southeast from where I landed and came across a large piece of the right wing and part of one engine. The engine was smouldering and the smoke could be seen from quite a distance. As I proceeded south-east I would find small pieces of the plane such as an air-scoop, a piece of twisted metal and also found parts of burned GI blankets that we carried in the plane. I found no trace of any of the crew. I can't state the exact location where I landed. I remember that it took me twelve hours to reach the Danube River on a heading of southeast. Before I reached the Danube I swam across a small river about sixty feet wide and flowing in a southeasterly direction. I followed the Danube downstream and hid out in an abandoned boat or rather a small houseboat.

From the point where I hit the Danube to the houseboat took about one and one half hours of walking. This may be of some help in determining the location where evidence of my crew may be found. A letter from Ratliff to me after we returned to the states said that the Austrians showed him the metal cover of a small Bible that Sgt. King always carried with him. Ratliff recognized the cover as Sgt. Kings. The Austrians stated that he was dead but the letter didn't state how. Ratliff stated in his letter that he felt the Austrians right here made a false statement to him in an attempt to break him down. But after no further word was received on Sgt. King, I believe that the Austrians were telling the truth about him being dead.

Lt. Jurenec opened the nose wheel doors and bailed out. He was knocked unconscious upon leaving the plane by a near burst of flak or the explosion of the plane. He fell to about 5,000 feet and opened his chute and lost consciousness again. He came to in a shack surrounded by German Guards. They told him they had found him lying in a nearby field. Being unconscious he had seen no other chutes or none of the members of his crew. He was shown a backpack type chute by Austrian soldiers at an airport southeast of Vienna, and was told that I, the pilot was dead.

After Jurenec and I met we assumed that the chute was Lt. Huey's, as the pilot and co-pilot were the only ones wearing back pack type chutes and Jurenec said he saw Huey who was burned, trying to reach the bomb bays but the flight deck was ablaze with burning oil and gasoline. He didn't get out as he could not get through the flames to the bomb bay. It is believed that he died in the flames on the flight deck. The German Guards told me all the rest of our crew was dead. Jurenec was in a Vienna jail with me suffering a sprained ankle and temporary shell shock. He claimed that he was shot at by flak on the way down and was knocked unconscious twice. He also lost consciousness on hitting the ground. He developed a bad case of jitters after the first night in jail when the British were night bombing the city of Vienna, Austria."

Lts. Huey and Jackson and Sgts. Arzt, King, Giblin, Ziklo and Robertson were Killed In Action. Lts. Klug and Jurenec and Sgt. Ratliff, were captured and made Prisoners of War.

11 October 1944: Lt. Russell I. Hongola, Pilot, 782nd Squadron, flew a B24G, #42-78391, Call Letter White "I" named "Quanto Costa" to bomb the Diesel Plant at Vienna, Austria with crewmembers, Lt. Charles H. Metzger, Co-Pilot; Lt. Ernest V. Grabowski, Navigator; Lt. Charles A. Beckman, Bombardier; S/Sgt. Robert L. Glos, Flight Engineer-Gunner; S/Sgt. Jesus Q. Geurrero, Radio Operator-Gunner; Sgt. Arla L. Thomas, Armorer-Gunner; Sgt. Wallace G. Jabben, Gunner; Sgt. Earl L. Eckhardt, Gunner and Sgt. Francis A. Crane, Gunner. Their aircraft was last sighted over the target at 11:44 hours. Weather was undercast and overcast.

Eyewitness, Lt. W. D. Kirby, 782nd Squadron, "A few minutes after "bombs away" I saw White "I" (Lt. Hongola) pull up over the lead ship with fire in the bomb bay. After a few seconds the ship peeled off and went into a dive. I did not see any chutes leave the plane while it remained within my vision. One of my gunners reported after landing that he watched the ship disappear into the cloud layer below without seeing parachutes leave the burning plane."

Captured German documents indicate that Lts. Ernest V. Grabowski and Allen Beckman and Sgts. Wallace G. Jabben, Earl L. Eckhardt and Francis A. Crane, were Killed In Action. Lts. Russell I. Hongola and Charles H. Metzger, and Sgts. Robert L. Glos, Arla L. Thomas, and Jesus Q. Geurrero, were captured and made Prisoners of War.

13 October 1944: 1st Lt. Alexander Lovey, Pilot, 781st Squadron, flew a B-24J, #42-51628, Call Letter Yellow "L" named "Lovey's Dovies" to bomb the Blechhammer South Synthetic Oil Refinery at Blechhammer, Germany with crewmembers, Lt. Raymond F. Morse, Co-Pilot; Lt. Donald E. Toomey, Navigator; S/Sgt. Walter Clausen, Nose Turret Gunner; S/Sgt. C. D. Hudson, Top Turret Gunner; T/Sgt. Lowell M. Lunn, Flight Engineer-Waist Gunner; Sgt. Leonard J. Goldstein, Radio Operator-Waist Gunner; Sgt. Harold W. Grant, Ball Turret Gunner and Sgt. Pierre J. J. Kennedy, Tail Turret Gunner. Visibility was good and their aircraft was last sighted over Blechhammer at 11:21 hours. This was a nine-man crew.

Eyewitness, S/Sgt. Charles N. Fry, 781st Squadron, "Yellow "L" flown by Lt. Lovey, was hit by flak over the target on 13 October 1944. The number 3 engine caught fire and the ship started down rather rapidly. It seemed to be under control when I last saw it. There were no fighters. I saw three men abandon the ship and their chutes opened. When I last saw the plane it seemed to be under control but was burning. The three men who bailed out should have gotten down safely unless they were hit by flak."

Eyewitness, Sgt. Eugene C. Deal, 781st Squadron, "Yellow "L" flown by Lt. Lovey, was hit by flak over the target. When hit, the plane pulled up from the other planes and then started sliding down sideways. The No. 3 engine was hit and started burning. The plane was going down slowly and the pilot seemed to be trying to pull out. I don't know whether it was contacted by radio or not. There was heavy flak over the target and no fighters. Right after the ship was hit, two men bailed out and their chutes opened. Another man abandoned the ship as it was going down. He fell quite a way before the chute opened. These three men should have gotten down safely. The plane disappeared from view right over the target. I did not see it crash."

The aircraft left the formation at the target and Sgt. Clausen bailed out, as did other crewmembers. Clausen said, "I believe that Lts. Lovey and Morse were in the aircraft when it struck the ground. The last conversation I heard from Morse was an oxygen check. Sgt. Hudson said that Morse was all right and putting on his parachute. Then he was going to take the controls while Lovey put his chute on. When Hudson left, Lovey was still at the controls. If Lovey did bail out it would have been over "The Blechhammer Oil Refinery." If he did not bail out it was because the plane blew up before he could. It is my belief that the plane did blow up before Lovey and Morse could bail out, because the report I had from the squadron stated that the plane was on fire and on its back. I also think Lovey was trying to keep the plane level so the rest of us could jump.

I saw all the other crewmembers in the prisoner of war camp in November of 1944. They were alright, except Sgt. Grant who had a swollen ankle."

Sgt. Kennedy said, "I saw Sgt. Lunn jump from the camera hatch. No one else was in the waist when I left. I think that the plane either exploded, as the right wing was on fire when I left, thus killing the pilots, or that they did jump but were killed by the Germans."

Lt. Toomey said that Sgt. Hudson's last conversation with Lovey was when he called the pilot and the co-pilot said, "Looks like no flak today." The co-pilot was standing behind the seats with his chute in his hand and he told Hudson to get out. Lts. Lovey and Morse were Killed In Action on this mission.

13 October 1944: 1st Lt. George Gaines Jr., Pilot, 781st Squadron, flew a B-24G, #42-78352, Call Letter Yellow "N" named "Easy Maid" to bomb the Blechhammer South Synthetic Oil Refinery at Blechhammer, Germany with crewmembers, F/O Murray Knowles, Co-Pilot; Lt. Francis R. Clark, Navigator; Sgt. Lawrence J. Tiehen, Nose Turret Gunner; T/Sgt. Louis J. Deslatte, Flight Engineer-Top Turret Gunner; Sgt. Charles R. Murray, Ball Turret Gunner; T/Sgt. Karl K. Brown, Radio Operator-Left Waist Gunner; S/Sgt. Edward J. F. Chapin, Right Waist Gunner and Sgt. Thomas R. C. McNew, Tail Turret Gunner. Visibility was good and their aircraft was last sighted over Blechhammer at 11:21 hours. This was a nine-man crew.

Eyewitness, 1st Lt. Richard L. Crutcher, Jr., 781st Squadron, "Yellow "N"" flown by Lt. Gaines on 13 October 1944, was hit by flak over the target. At the rally my gunners reported that Lt. Gaines had number 3 engine feathered and had a bad gas leak in number 2. He dropped out of formation with his plane under control. No one was seen to bail out."

Eyewitness, Lt. Arthur L. Zalk, 781st Squadron, "Yellow "N"" flown by Lt. Gaines, was hit by flak over the target. One engine was knocked out. The ship seemed to be under control and was last seen joining another formation about two groups back. This was about 11:45 hours. No one was seen to abandon ship. There were no fighters. It is possible that Lt. Gaines might have gone to Russia to avoid coming back across another flak area that had to be crossed with his damaged ship."

The aircraft reached the target at approximately 11:25 hours when it was severely damaged by flak. Bombs were immediately jettisoned, approximately 30 seconds before "bombs away" of the group. Number 3 engine was hit and the propeller was feathered, number 1 was severely damaged, the regulator was gone and racing, and the aircraft was losing altitude rapidly. Sgt. Chapin was seriously wounded in his right arm and right leg by flak, breaking the bone in his arm. Lt. Gaines continued on course for about 10 minutes, then changed course for Russia.

Unable to maintain altitude, number 1 engine caught fire, so at about 12:00 hours the pilot gave the order to bail out at approximately 2,500 feet. All left the ship safely as nine parachutes were seen in the air. The crew landed about 2 kilometers from Tuchow, Poland. Lt. Clark suffered a broken left ankle in landing. While in the air, he saw the aircraft crash nearby and explode. F/O Knowles was injured when he landed in trees after parachuting. F/O Knowles and Sgts. Deslatte, McNew, Murray, and Brown and Lt. Gaines were captured by the Germans. Sgt. Tiehen was brought to a Doctor at a Camp in Tarcow, Poland suffering from Diphtheria.

Clark and Chapin were surrounded by German soldiers on landing and taken to Tuchow where they were joined next day by four other crewmembers. Clark and Chapin were questioned briefly by Army Officers and on the following day they were turned over to the Air Corps for questioning. After a very cursory interrogation they were shipped to a Russian Officers camp in Lodz. On the following day, Lt. Clark and Sgt. Chapin were taken to a hospital in Wollstein, Poland. The hospital was overrun by the Russian offensive on 25 January. They remained there under Russian guard until 20 February when they departed through a hole in the wire and made their way to Odessa and were evacuated.

The Polish Red Cross at Krotuscin, Ostrow and the YMCA at Lodz was always especially helpful. They provided meals and bedding during the evacuation from Wollstein to Odessa. A Polish Capt. Jabosky, a Doctor at Wollstein and Polish Lt. Grimtasky, a Doctor at Wollstein, gave services to American POW's, beyond their call of duty, from October 1944 to February 1945. A Polish Doctor, Lesnavotich, at Wollstein, took charge of 200 Red Cross parcels, British and American, while there were no American and British in camp. The Germans endeavored to obtain these parcels. Russian POW's of which there were about 500 in Wollstein, were very underfed by the Germans. The Russians had an average daily mortality rate of three. Typhus, "T. B." amputations and malnutrition were mainly responsible. Many of the Russians had all their clothing removed by the Germans and in October and in November 1944 they were forced to go about wrapped in sheets. This was punishment for attempting a tunnel escape.

Reserve Lazarette, Wollstein, (lately known as "21C"). Reserve hospital for Schubin POW Camp (Oflag 64). This camp was situated on the edge of the small town of Wollstein, having about 5,000 inhabitants. It consisted of a group of wooden barracks divided into two compounds. Compound Number 1, housing about 500 Russian POW's and Compound Number 2, housing never more than 28 American POW officers and enlisted men and about 35 Italian POW's 2 Dutch and 1 Norwegian Naval Officers. Men were only sent to this camp when sick, and numbers were always small. The men slept on single tier bunks, with two blankets, one Red Cross comforter and straw filled mattresses. Outside latrines were provided. An adequate supply of water was available and a supply of hot water could be drawn twice daily. Hot showers were available once weekly. De-lousing equipment was available. There was ersatz coffee once daily, cabbage soup, 3 slices of black bread and a small ration of sugar.

Twice weekly some type of meat was issued, but was discontinued in November 1944 and nothing issued to replace this. Either British or American Red Cross parcels were issued. The contents had to be used daily and orders were issued that anything left in the cupboards would be confiscated. No one was allowed to store any food. No more than 3 packs of cigarettes could be held by one individual at any one time. POW's lived on the contents of these parcels and without them many would have starved. Due to this being a hospital camp there were no parades and discipline was slack. A count in barracks was made twice daily by the Germans. Two letters and four postcards per month could be sent home by enlisted men. Three letters and four postcards per month could be sent home by officers.

The Camp Staff was a German Commandant, (Major Medical Corps), his name is unknown. He was not a party man and was fair in his treatment of American POW's. Pvt. Schmidt and Pvt. Hartley were the Camp guards. They had stolen many Red Cross parcels captured by the Russians. An Austrian Capt. was the Security officer, his name was also unknown. He was not troublesome in any way and he was a very frightened man. There were over 100 guards and 80 of these were Polish. Many of the German guards were friendly. The only name remembered is Cpl. Lice, a German who was anxious for the war to end, definitely not a party man. He would assist us in supplies, etc. The American Camp Staff was 1st Lt. Jas. Godfrey a Medical Corps Doctor, captured in Africa and he was in charge of the hospital. In December 1944 an American Lt. Col. Shields or Schel arrived in camp and became Senior Officer. There was no Escape Committee. American War department orders from Oflag 64 forbade escape without approval of an escape committee. There were no escapes made from this camp. A crystal receiving set had been constructed from parts sent in by families of POW's. We were in this camp from 18 October 1944 until 20 February 1945.

F/O Knowles and Sgts. Deslatte, McNew and Murray, were all last seen in a Russian Officer POW Flying Camp in Lodz, Poland, on 17 October 1944, Lt. Clark left this camp for a hospital. He probably was moved to a German Air Force Camp in Germany. 14 Americans were left in the Wollstein Camp when we were evacuated 20 February 1945. They are under Russian care and will be evacuated soon. 1st Lt. J. Godfrey was in charge. Two men were bed patients; others were more or less fit.

13 October 1944: Lt. Homer W. Lane, Pilot, 783rd Squadron, flew a B-24J, #42-78516, Call Letter White "D" to bomb the Blechhammer South Synthetic Oil Refinery at Blechhammer, Germany with crewmembers, Lt. Marvin Tannenbaum, Co-Pilot; F/O Marvin Guiffre, Navigator; Lt. Eric W. Volkman, Bombardier; Sgt. Stanley A. Phillips, Flight Engineer-Gunner; Sgt. William C. Prouty, Radio Operator-Gunner; Sgt. William W. Wilson, Gunner; Sgt. John R. Harlin Jr., Gunner; Sgt. Michael H. Zacharias, Gunner and Sgt. Harry A. Betz, Gunner. Weather was scattered cumulus clouds and their aircraft was last sighted at 11:21 hours over Blechhammer.

Eyewitness, Sgt. John H. Chapman 782nd Squadron, "On the mission of 13 October 1944, I last saw White "D" when it went down directly over the target area. It was spiraling down and I saw 6 or 7 chutes open. That is all I had the chance to see."

13 Oct 1944 we were on a B-24 mission to Blechhammer, South. Target time was 11:21 hours. We dropped our bombs and good results were observed. Smoke from the target was observed up to approximately 12,000 feet. Flak was heavy, intense and accurate for 8 minutes. We rallied off the target and set our return course. Flak was encountered at Komaron. In the Lake Balaton area the engineer started a fuel transfer. At this point number 2 engine fuel pressure dropped to 3 pounds, and manifold pressure went down to 24 inches R.P.M. Lt. Lane believed a vapor lock to be present or flak damage to the lines at Komaron. He feathered and unfeathered number 2 engine, which brought it back to full power. The engineer checked the fuel on the north Yugoslavian border and discovered 180 gallons of gas was left. All boosters were off (tank to engine) the right auxiliary to both was on. Fuel pressure again dropped on number 2 engine and only minimum power was obtained from it. It was impossible to transfer fuel. Number 3 engine cut out. The pilot gave the order to bail out. Number 4 engine cut out after bailout. All ten chutes were seen to have opened.

We landed in the vicinity of Car Snica and all members of the crew were fired upon by machine gun, rifle and small arms fire until we ran a considerable distance from the point at which we landed. Lt. Tannenbaum, and Sgts. Phillips and Harlin were captured and made Prisoners of War. The rest of the crew was collected together in this town within twelve hours. We were fed and quartered at Partisan Headquarters. We stayed here until the morning of 15 October 1944 at which time we were taken by cart to Samarica. On 18 October we were taken by cart to Mikleus, where we were interrogated as to name, rank, birthplace and profession. No questions of military nature were asked. After the interrogation, we then walked to a British Mission. We remained there until 21 October. On 22 October, we left, escorted by a Brigade of Partisans for Sumetuca and arrived that night. On 23 October we left Sumetuca for Corsovica and stayed there until 28 October.

The night of the 28th, we left there because of enemy activity in the vicinity, retreating to Bratyanacs, where we remained for three days. Southwest of Kutina, Partisans mined railroad tracks and blew up a German armored train from Zagreb. (Partisan information stated that, Pro-Nazi Cossack troops were reported in the area of the rail line from Belgrade to Zagreb, with an estimated strength of 8,000. They are said to be more ferocious and fanatical fighters than either the Ustachi or Partisan troops. Two American Officers from a B-17 crew were reported to have been captured by Ustachi troops. The body of one was found with 200 bullet holes in it.)

We then started on foot for a mission area. The night of 1 November was spent in the town of Borcjavice. On 3 November, we were carried by cart to a mission area. While here we were cared for by Partisans under British supervision and treated very well in general. On 19 November, we departed for an airdrome located at a point approximately 80 miles south-southwest of a mission where we remained all night, departing 20 November for Obrovac. We spent two nights at Obrovac, leaving for Zara on 22 November arriving at Zara on the same date and taken aboard a British light cruiser. Embarked from Zara on 24 November for Ancona aboard a British motor launch.

13 October 1944: 1st Lt. John T. McWhorter, Pilot, 780th Squadron, flew a B-24J, #42-51330, Call Letter Yellow "O" to bomb the Blechhammer South Synthetic Oil Refinery at Blechhammer, Germany with crewmembers, Lt. Howard W. Meute, Co-Pilot; Lt. James Jensen, Navigator; F/O Robert McCullagh, Bombardier; S/Sgt. Thomas Napody, Flight Engineer-Gunner; S/Sgt. Mask W. Harwood, Radio Operator-Gunner; Sgt. Charles Mayo, Gunner; S/Sgt. Edwin H. Nowak, Gunner; Sgt. Edwin J. Rostedt, Gunner and Sgt. William A. Meehan Jr., Gunner. Their aircraft was last sighted at 11:30 hours over Blechhammer.

Eyewitness, S/Sgt. Sidney M. Rothman, 780th Squadron, "While participating in combat mission of 13 October 1944, I saw Yellow "O", piloted by Lt. McWhorter, pass under us which indicated that it was lagging behind the formation. Number 4 engine was smoking. This plane remained on course parallel to ours for approximately ten minutes after the target, and then I noticed that its number 1 engine was smoking slightly. With number 1 engine smoking slightly and number 4 engine smoking severely, the pilot turned the plane left in the general direction of Russia. No one bailed out. The plane was definitely under control and was maintaining its altitude. Then the plane passed out of my range of vision, no engines were feathered. It is my opinion that Lt. McWhorter was able to get to Russia safely."

Crewmembers said, "We reached the target and dropped our bombs. Number 4 engine was hit and number 3 engine ran away. We lost our place in formation but managed to feather number 4. Then number 1 supercharger went out. We started toward friendly territory and flew into another flak area, I think it was Oswiecem. Our radio had also gone out. We ran into a third flak area in Cracow. We landed at Lwow, Poland. No one was hurt in the landing and we were never in the hands of the enemy. The pilot left our crew at the airplane and went looking for the Russian commandant at the field. We were interviewed by a General in command of the area.

We began to repair our plane and stayed at Lwow for nine days. We left our ship at Lwow and flew to Poltava in an American C-47 and stayed in Poltava about 5 days and then five of our crewmembers went to Lwow and flew our ship to Poltava. When we got back, four members of our crew left by A.T.C. to Teheran and stayed overnight, thence to Cairo where they stayed two hours and then to Bari arriving on 31 October 1944. The other six crewmembers flew our ship back over the same route as above and arrived on 7 November 1944."

20 October 1944: Lt. Dean P. Evans, Pilot, 783rd Squadron, flew a B-24H, #42-52464, Call Letter Blue "X" named "Ruff N' Ready" to bomb the Marshalling Yards at Prien, Germany with crewmembers, Lt. Gordon L. Edwards, Co-Pilot; Lt. Wilson M. Hatch, Navigator; Lt. Melvin O. Roberts, Bombardier; Sgt. Thomas A. Nunn Jr., Flight Engineer-Gunner; Sgt. Wilford J. Corn, Radio Operator-Gunner; Sgt. Robert A. Fenski, Armorer-Gunner; Sgt. George B. Rhinevault, Gunner; Sgt. Charles L. Austin, Gunner and Sgt. Victor E. Pohlman, Gunner.

Eyewitness, Lt. R. J. Hess, 782nd Squadron, "On 20 October 1944, at approximately 11:15 hours, I saw airplane Blue "X" fall out of formation. Apparently the pilot was having trouble, as the plane seemed to be out of control. He then made a normal turn and headed toward Yugoslavia."

Lt. Evans and his crew were captured and made Prisoners of War.

20 October 1944: Lt. Delbert E. Forsberg, Pilot, 783rd Squadron, flew a B-24J, #42-51298, Call Letter Blue "U" named "Puss" to bomb the Marshalling Yards at Prien, Germany with crewmembers, F/O James R. Curtis, Co-Pilot; F/O Gorden H. F. Fowlie, Navigator; Lt. Lyle H. Long, Bombardier; S/Sgt. Richard K. Rutgers, Flight Engineer-Gunner; S/Sgt. Charles A. Mangan, Radio Operator-Gunner; S/Sgt. Royal E. Edmark, Tail Turret Gunner; S/Sgt. William A. Marsh, Nose Turret Gunner; S/Sgt. Gerald L. Harris, Gunner and Sgt. Earl J. Werner, Ball Turret Gunner. The weather was clear and their aircraft was last sighted over Yugoslavia at 10:40 hours.

Lt. Forsberg, "On my first mission scheduled to the industrial area of Munich, we were shot down while climbing to target altitude over Yugoslavia. The enemy had brought in 80 M.M. guns mounted on Railway flat cars. As we climbed to our altitude they would literally blacken the sky with flak. We suffered a hit to our number 4 engine which caused a fire. I couldn't put the fire out since the prop feathering device and fire extinguisher were knocked out. I knew we only had seven minutes before the fire would burn through the firewall and be in the wing tanks, then a massive explosion. We were close to the Adriatic Sea at that moment so I went out over water and salvoed the bombs and 50 Caliber guns on board, then turned sharply inland to clear the mountains along the coast so we could bail out on level ground.

I got the crew on the intercom and told them as they parachuted down which way to run when on the ground so they might not be captured by the Chetniks.

Our morning headquarters briefing laid out the sections as to the expected areas occupied by Chetniks or Partisan troops. I had trimmed the plane in a big circle descent hoping it would blow up before it hit the mountains and fortunately it did. My navigator and three gunners were captured by the Chetniks. The rest of the crew followed me on the ground. We ran into some Partisan soldiers who helped us escape. They took us to the closest headquarters. Tito had the country set up in 100 different zones we were told. We were greeted by a young man by the name of Vinko Kuzina who was the leader. He arranged our return. We walked at night and hid out during the day until we reached the coast.

From there we went in a small 12 foot rowboat to the Island of Vis which was only a small runway sticking up out of the ocean. Vinko's people contacted our headquarters by short wave radio and arranged for a pick up by plane back to our squadron."

Flight Officer Fowlie, and Sgts. Marsh, Werner, and Edmark, were captured by the Chetniks, turned over to the Germans and made Prisoners of War. Lts. Forsberg and Long, Flight Officer Curtis, and Sgts. Rutgers, Mangan and Harris, were picked up by the Partisans and evacuated to Italy.

6 November 1944: Lt. Robert T. Stinson, Pilot, 782nd Squadron, flew a B-24J, #42-78287, Call Letter White "E" named "Joker" to bomb a target in Vienna, Austria with crewmembers, Lt. Bruce Harriman, Co-Pilot; Lt. Robert J. Randle Jr., Navigator; F/O Irwin Schwarz, Bombardier; S/Sgt. John W. Hawn Jr., Nose Turret Gunner; Sgt. Harley T. Ferrel, Top Turret Gunner; Sgt. Charles P. Kovar, Flight Engineer-Waist Gunner; Sgt. Roy C. Swan, Radio Operator-Waist Gunner; Sgt. Karl J. Hamann, Ball Turret Gunner and Sgt. Karl A. Kubitz, Tail Turret Gunner. Weather was completely undercast and their aircraft was last sighted at the southwest tip of Lake Balaton at 12:00 hours.

Eyewitness, 1st Lt. William D. Kirby, Pilot, "On the bombing mission of 6 November 1944 to the Vienna area, I was flying number one position of Able box, and Lt. Stinson was flying number four position. About ten minutes after leaving the target area and in the region of Lake Balaton, Lt. Stinson, flying White "E" left the formation. A few seconds later I saw him flying below our formation with one engine feathered. He was in view for only a few seconds and was not seen again by any member of my crew."

Lt. Harriman heard many rumors in Yugoslavia that the Partisan group of the Ustachi captured aircrews torturing and killing them. Some of the men so killed were buried by the Partisan groups. These rumors centered around the vicinity of Zagreb, Yugoslavia. From the Russians, Harriman was informed on or about the latter part of December 1944, a B-24 crew bailed out over the Danube and all members of the crew were drowned. The reliability of Harriman's statements are unquestioned.

On the way to the target all engines had to pull excessive power to keep in formation. Number 2 engine had an oil leak and after the "I P" had to be feathered. The ship lost the formation, but remained in radio contact and joined the tail end of another formation. While following this other formation, oil pressure of number 1 engine dropped to 40 pounds. The pilot ordered the bombs to be salvoed in the area of Varazdin and following the formation headed for Vis.

Soon after the oil pressure on number 1 engine dropped to 20 pounds and the ship was lightened by throwing out guns and some other equipment. Three P-51 planes, with yellow tail markings were contacted and gave top cover. Oil pressure was fluctuating on number 4 engine so the pilot decided to look for a briefed emergency landing field at Vocin. He circled the Vocin area at 4,500 feet but could find no suitable landing ground. At 2,500 feet he headed southeast and ordered the crew to bail out.

The crew started to bail out in the area of Daruvar and all left the ship except the pilot, co-pilot and engineer who bailed out at 1,500 feet in the area of Hum, north of Vocin. The crew was never in enemy hands. Sgt. Hawn was the third man out of the ship and landed in some woods where he was picked up by some Peasants who took him to their field Headquarters 15 miles from Dulavel where he was looked after until the morning of 7 November when the Partisans took him to Dulavec by cart. Here Hawn met F/O Schwarz, and Lt. Randle. Schwarz and Randle landed about 6 kilometers west of Dulavec. Schwarz had landed in a farmyard and was assisted by Peasants, then taken towards Dulavec. Randle who came down in a field, met some Peasants who gave him wine and then started to walk towards the aircraft, meeting Schwarz on the way, then Hawn, Schwarz and Randle were taken by Partisan youth to Dulavec where Schwarz received Medical aid for his sprained ankle. Here they were joined by Sgts. Swan and Kubitz, who had landed among some rushes where they were contacted by Peasants who took them into Dulavec.

Harriman came down on a hillside, close to where the plane had blown up in the Vocin area. Partisans and Peasants contacted him as he landed and as he spoke some French he had difficulty in proving that he was an American but the 15th AF patch which he wore convinced them he was indeed, an American. They took him to a nearby house and fed him and he was then picked up by the Partisan Commandant of the Vocin aerodrome. He was then taken several hundred yards to another house where he joined Sgts. Hamann, Ferrel and Kovar. Harriman then made an inspection of the aircraft, which was completely demolished. He then returned to the Partisan house and was taken the next day to an Allied Mission "Geisha" joining Lt. Stinson, Hamann, Ferrel and Kovar at a Partisan station on the way.

Stinson had landed about 1 mile north of the crashed aircraft. He rolled up his chute and about 20 minutes later saw some Partisans whom he contacted. He was taken to a house in this area and thence by a Partisan, to a Partisan telephone exchange where he joined Harriman. All traveled the next day to an Allied Mission "Geisha". Hawn, Schwarz, Randle, Swan and Kubitz after staying at Partisan Headquarters in Dulavec where they received good treatment, were taken on 9 November 1944 to Mission "Geisha" where they joined the rest of their crew. They remained 42 days at "Geisha". All food and clothing supplies were very short, but the personnel did their best for them. They all lived in log houses under crowded conditions and slept on board beds with no mattresses. During the last three days, seven parachutes were given them to use as bedding. German troops in the valley were expected to make an attack and they were necessarily very restricted in their movements. At this mission they joined the crew of Lt. Bodycomb, from another Group. A week later one member of a B-17 crew arrived and later another four men from another B-17. About 12 December 1944 another 25 men arrived, some of them were from Lt. Parkison's ship from the 783rd Squadron. By the time the evacuation took place there were about 52 American airmen at this station.

On 16 December 1944 two trucks arrived and took all the Americans to Barcs, where Russian troops took charge of the party - under Maj. Quinette - and billeted them on the Hungarian population. The Russians did the best they could for the Americans, but food and other comforts were provided by the people housing the parties. They all remained here until 18 December and were again moved by truck to Kaposvar. They were all billeted in the "Korand" Russian hotel, and were well treated and ate the same meals as the Russians. On 21 December they were all moved by bus to Pecs, then by truck to Subotica where they remained from 23-24 December, again billeted on civilians. They all moved by truck to Timosoara where they entrained in an unheated coach and spent a very miserable Xmas. Rations provided by the Russians consisted of salt pork and black bread.

After a four-day journey in this train via Caransebes, Turnu/Severin, Craiova, and Pitesti, the party reached Bucharest on 29 December 1944. One night during the journey was spent at Caransebes billeted on civilians, but the rest of the time was spent under very unpleasant conditions on the train. At Bucharest they were all looked after by American personnel (O.S.S.) at the "ACC" Headquarters. The Americans who lived in a school were not allowed out after 16:30 hours. Otherwise they were well fed and looked after and had clean clothing issued. On 14 January 1945, they were evacuated from the Bucharest airfield, in a "C-47" plane, carrying 26 men in all. The other aircraft left at the same time and landed at Bari, Italy on 14 January 1945.

16 November 1944: Capt. Irving R. Stringham, Pilot, 783rd Squadron, flew a B-24J, #42-51996, Call Letter Blue "L" to bomb the West Marshalling Yard at Munich, Germany with crewmembers, Lt. Delbert C. Brimhall, Co-Pilot; Lt. Eugene M. Kipp, Navigator; Lt. Edward J. Latimer, Bombardier; Sgt. James A. Ferguson, Nose Turret Gunner; S/Sgt. Natale E. Greco, Flight Engineer-Gunner; S/Sgt. Pasquale A. Gialo, Radio Operator-Gunner; Sgt. Egbert E. Mead, Armorer-Gunner; Sgt. Albert J. Gibhart, Gunner and Sgt. Albert Dyrda, Gunner. The weather was undercast and their aircraft was last sighted at 13:00 hours over Munich, Germany.

Eyewitness, S/Sgt. Otto L. Marcucci, 783rd Squadron, "Going in on the bomb run just a few seconds before "bombs away" I observed Blue "L" suffer a direct hit in the left wing. The ship began to burn immediately. The right wing was torn off and the plane went into a half spin. At this time the plane was past my observation and drifted toward the rear of our plane where the tail gunner said he saw it disintegrate into a fireball of flame. No chutes were seen coming from the plane."

The aircraft left the formation directly over the western outskirts of Munich. Capt. Stringham and Lt. Brimhall had stood and released their flak suits just prior to the explosion. When the aircraft exploded it blew Brimhall out. Lt. Kipp was also blown out by the explosion. Brimhall believes that Stringham was killed instantly by the explosion or rendered unconscious by the blast and was unable to use his parachute. He was wearing a back-type chute. After Brimhall drifted through the undercast he saw someone in a parachute some distance away but was unable to contact or recognize him. Lts. Brimhall, Kipp and Latimer and Sgts. Greco, Gialo, Mead, Ferguson, Gibhart and Dyrda, were captured and made Prisoners of War. Brimhall last saw Kipp in a prison camp hospital at Wetzlar, Germany. Capt. Stringham was Killed In Action and buried on 17 November 1944 in Braunthel near Munich, Germany.

16 November 1944: Lt. Emil E. Wayman, Pilot, 783rd Squadron, flew a B-24H, #42-51172, Call Letter Blue "K" to bomb the West Marshalling Yard at Munich, Germany with crewmembers, F/O John G. Knous Jr., Co-Pilot; Lt. George R. Cross, Navigator; Lt. Collie E. Sheets, Bombardier; Sgt. Hollis E. Payson, Nose Turret Gunner; Sgt. Francis A. Kraemer, Armorer-Top Turret Gunner; Sgt. Joseph C. Forbes, Ball Turret Gunner; Sgt. Dale D. Miles, Flight Engineer-Waist Gunner; Sgt. Vernon L. Smith, Radio Operator-Waist Gunner and Sgt. Roy D. Fisher, Tail Turret Gunner. Weather was undercast and their aircraft was last sighted at 13:05 hours over Munich.

Eyewitness, Sgt. Aaron Wolfson, 781st Squadron, "On the mission on 16 November 1944, Blue "K" was flying level with the ship I was in. Suddenly it dropped down through the clouds very fast and disappeared from sight. Number 1 engine had been smoking and something must have happened to another engine. This was just before we came out of the flak at the target. I did not see any fighters. I saw no one abandon the ship. The pilot was trying to keep it under control. The crewmembers should have had plenty of time to bail out."

Sgt. Francis A. Kraemer, the top turret gunner said, "The target was reached around 13:30 hours and bombed from about 27,000 feet. Number 1 engine was shot out over the target and the prop was feathered. Soon afterwards number 2 engine ran away and that prop was feathered. Later number 3 engine ran away and caught fire. Lt. Wayman tried to reach an emergency field in Switzerland but on finding he could not get over the mountains he changed course toward Udine. By this time the aircraft had only 12,000 feet of altitude and soon afterward the pilot gave the order to bail out. At that time the aircraft was over land at 10,000 feet somewhere between Udine and Fiume. I was the fourth man out and went out the bomb bay."

All parachutes opened and all of the crew except the pilot reached the ground more or less uninjured in spite of heavy small arms fire directed against them by German troops. Sgts. Kraemer and Forbes landed in some brush near the wreck of the plane. They heard shots close by and ran off into the bushes. In several minutes they came upon a woman and two girls who led them to Sgts. Miles, Payson, Fisher and Smith, and Lt. Sheets, all of whom were gathered about half a mile from the wreck. Partisans appeared and led Miles, Payson and Kraemer to a nearby farmhouse and the others to a farm further on. Miles, Payson and Kraemer and two Partisans crowded together in a tiny tunnel beneath the house for 3 days, and were not able to talk most of the time and could often hear Germans about them. On the night of 19 November, guides took them four hours across country to a village where they rejoined the other four members of their crew and they also met Lts. Knous, and Cross and a man nicknamed "Rabbit" who was a Radio Operator on another crew.

They spent the 20th in the village because Knous had a fractured ankle. At 21:00 hours on the 21st three Partisans took them several miles across country to a house where they met the pilot and the bombardier of "Rabbits" crew. Then they walked on till 06:00 hours of the 22nd, and hid in a woods near a farmhouse till dark. In the afternoon the farmer, who would not put them up for fear of the Germans, brought them some food and sometime later they set off across a railroad track and walked till 03:00 hours of the 23rd, when they reached a farm and received shelter in a barn. They were just getting to sleep when they heard shots. There upon their guards hurried them off to a covered pit in the middle of a field where they hid for three hours. Then they were led to another farm where they slept all day in a barn. They always had guides who changed at each place to which they came. They skirted all towns in occupied territory and very seldom used roads.

Since there was snow on the ground they were usually wet, tired, cold and footsore. Kraemer wore only the inserts of his flying boots. The night of the 23rd they walked to another farm where they had a good meal, then went on, up and down mountains and across flooded valleys, finally coming to a village where they met Lt. Reynolds, a bombardier from another group. They dried their clothes there and then left, reaching a Partisan garrison sometime on the morning of the 24th and had just got to sleep on the floor when the Germans turned up and they had to take to their heels again. In three hours they reached a Partisan hut in some woods and they were just going to be given some food at noon on 25 November, when there was more shooting. Again, with the help of their guides they evaded the Germans and walked all that afternoon and night, doubling on their trail to confuse the enemy, who were busy lighting up the landscape with flares and they eventually returned to the village where they had met their co-pilot, navigator and four other members of their crew and "Rabbits" nose gunner and bombardier.

They dried their clothes and went to a shed where they slept for 2 hours and then went on through the woods to a settlement where a Yugoslav who spoke English gave them some food and let them sleep in his barn for a few hours. At 18:00 hours on the 26th they started again, walking till 02:00 hours on the 27th, where they slept briefly in some woods near Fiume. Later they found a Partisan station and slept there the next night and that day, leaving on the 28th, when they learned that the Germans were coming to destroy the building. They found a rocky pocket in some woods where they stayed seven days. For three days they had no food or water, then a Partisan brought them some potatoes and they had boiled potatoes once a day for the next four days.

Meanwhile on the night of the 30th and 31st, while some of the Partisans were going to get supplies there had been another encounter with the Germans and during the confusion, Cross, Payson, Smith and Sheets disappeared and did not return. It was learned later that they had reached safety and had been repatriated. About the 4th of December they went to a village where there were a number of Partisans. One subjected them to questioning and they confined their answers to name, rank, and serial number. They were fed here and at 14:00 hours they started off again and skirting Fiume they took off their shoes to cross a railroad bridge behind the town. They reached another small Partisan station at 03:00 hours the next morning. For several days thereafter they hid by day and walked by night till they reached Gerovo, the first free village in Yugoslavia. Here they had a good meal, slept on beds and were able to buy some apples.

The next day they reached Delnice, where they received food and shelter. The day after that they came to Mrkopalj. They had been taken there because it had been confused with the Mission itself. By this time Fisher and Kraemer's feet were in very bad shape. The Walky-Talky operator at Mrkopalj contacted a Major at the Mission and was able to bring Fisher and Kraemer to the British Mission by jeep. There the Yugoslav doctor told Kraemer, Knous, Fisher and Lt. Reynolds that they would have to remain there for at least 12 days to rest their feet. Meanwhile the rest of the party went on.

On 27 December, a Captain from the Mission received a dropping, which enabled him to supply Kraemer, Knous, Fisher and Reynolds with a few items of equipment. Meanwhile some other Americans had arrived. They were Cpl. Franklin Young, Lt. Kernahan, F/O Nels, Lt. Kemper, Cpls. Roth, Kirby, Swanson, Dennis and Behn. On December 29th, Kraemer and his companions and all of the above except Young and Kernahan started for Vrbovsko. By the time they reached Moravice, Kraemer and Reynolds were in such bad shape that they telephoned the mission and were told to return. This they did on a cart while the others went on to Brbovsko and Slunj. Kraemer and Reynolds stayed in Skrad for another 10 to 14 days. On the second day after their return they were joined by Cpls. Maclean and Ferguson and F/O Hague. On 10 January, Kernahan started for Sloreala by ox cart while Kraemer, Young, Reynolds, Maclean, Ferguson and Hague walked to Vrbovsko, where they spent two nights and a day. On the 12th they went on to a village where they stayed with a Russian who was the minister of the Greek Orthodox Church there. On 14 January they reached Periodica an exceptionally filthy village where they were able to telephone the American mission, where the Major promised to send a jeep to pick up Reynolds in a village some 20 miles further on. Reynolds, who had been wounded in the arm, had a high fever. They all reached the village the next day and the jeep came for Reynolds.

The day after that Kraemer and his companions reached Slunj where they stayed two weeks waiting for transport, which was delayed by the heavy snow. F/O Hague became ill and was taken to Topusko, in the Major's jeep. On 5 February they left Slunj by truck together with 5 RAF men who had recently turned up there, and reached Gorlanza that evening. There at a British Mission they had their first good meal. On 6 February the Major's weapons carrier brought them to Zara where they had a bath on a British Cruiser. On 7 February they embarked on the HMS Wilton, a destroyer that brought them to Bari, Italy at 09:30 hours on 8 February. Lt. Wayman was captured and made a Prisoner of War.

16 November 1944: 1st Lt. Harvey D. Wright, Pilot, 783rd Squadron, flew a B-24H, #42-51842, Call Letter Blue "W" to bomb the West Marshalling Yard at Munich, Germany with crewmembers, 1st Lt. William Mitchell, Co-Pilot; 1st Lt.

John K. Hartman, Bombardier; T/Sgt. John F. McNamee, Flight Engineer-Gunner; T/Sgt. Robert H. Messinger, Radio Operator-Gunner; S/Sgt. William T. Rutan, Gunner; S/Sgt. Zane D. Hoyle, Gunner; S/Sgt. Joseph J. Korf, Gunner and Sgt. Louis A. Rebottaro, Gunner. Weather was undercast and their aircraft was last sighted at 13:05 hours over the German Alps. This was a nine-man crew.

Eyewitness, T/Sgt. Oscar E. Baumgardner, Jr., 783rd Squadron, "On the mission of 16 November 1944 over Munich, Germany, I was flying number four position and was in a position to observe Blue "W" as we left the target. Making our rally to the right off the target Blue "W" fell behind the formation and seemed to be having trouble with number 3 engine. I watched them as long as I could and the last time I saw their plane they were coming over the Alps and back toward the formation. All four engines were still running and they had sufficient altitude to clear the mountains. No chutes were seen from their plane and the last report was that they were still airborne and headed for home."

Sgt. McNamee, "Our aircraft left the formation over the target. We bailed out one hour after leaving the target and just before we bailed out, our pilot Lt. Wright said to me, "Mac, no use, we will have to bail out." He was holding the plane so the crew could get out. To my knowledge he was not injured. The Germans told us he did not get out of the aircraft and was killed. I saw his flying clothes and parachute, which was open. Lt. Mitchell our co-pilot was uninjured and he asked what was wrong with the aircraft when the bail out bell rang. Lt. Hartman our bombardier was uninjured and I told him that the bail out bell had rung and to bail out. After we had bailed out and were taken prisoner Sgt. Rutan and I talked about Lt. Wright. Sgt. Rutan was also uninjured."

German Documents indicate: 1st Lt. Harvey D. Wright, was Killed In Action and was buried at St. Martin, near Lefer on 17 November 1944.

The following crewmembers were captured and made Prisoners of War: Lts. Mitchell and Hartman and Sgts. McNamee, Messinger, Korf, Hoyle, Rutan and Rebottaro.

20 November 1944: Lt. Col. Clarence J. (Jack) Lokker, Pilot, 783rd Squadron, flew a B-24H, #41-28853, Call Letter Blue "I" to bomb the Blechhammer South Synthetic Oil Refinery at Blechhammer, Germany with crewmembers, Capt. Milton H. Duckworth, Co-Pilot; 1st Lt. Joseph P. Kutger, Navigator; Lt. Joseph S. Whelan, Radar Navigator; 1st Lt. Grosvenor W. Rice, Navigator; 1st Lt. Robert M. Hockman, Bombardier; Sgt. James A. Bourne, Nose Turret Gunner; Sgt. Jack Rabkin, Top Turret Gunner; T/Sgt. Lee R. Billings, Flight Engineer-Waist Gunner; S/Sgt. Edmund J. Miosky, Radio Operator-Waist

Gunner and Sgt. Paul Flynn Jr., Tail Turret Gunner. There were scattered clouds and their aircraft was last sighted at 12:25 hours. This was an eleven-man crew.

Eyewitness, Sgt. John W. Bartlett, "I was flying as waist gunner in B-24 Blue "R" Baker 3 position on 20 November 1944, when about forty seconds before "Bombs Away" I saw Blue "I" burst into flames due apparently to a direct hit in the bomb bay by flak. Immediately two bombs could be seen falling from the plane and the right wing came off. I did not see any of the crew leave the plane and doubt if anyone survived."

Lt. Kutger, "Lt. Whelan was sitting two feet to the left of me and directly behind Capt. Duckworth. He was conferring with Lt. Hockman concerning Mickey operations near the target prior to the time the bombardier decided on a visual bomb run. It is possible that Whelan was injured or killed when the aircraft sustained a flak hit. As I motioned to him to bail out his eyes appeared to register nothing. The ship was mortally wounded with a wing blown off and it is my belief that unless a man left the ship within 2 or 3 seconds after the hit he didn't have a chance. I had this feeling at the moment of impact and I left the ship immediately, grasping my parachute in my right hand as I pulled the bomb release handle with my left. I attached my chute while falling towards the ground, and I was almost certain no one else left the ship and thought Whelan would follow me out of the bomb bays, but this would have been impossible as the ship rolled over on its back as I slipped out.

Before we were hit, Col. Lokker had been talking to the bombardier concerning the bomb run and the target. The last time I saw Lokker he was fighting the controls of the ship, at about 23,000 feet over Blechhammer, Germany. He appeared to be uninjured. My last contact with him was when he was conversing with the bombardier and me concerning the bomb run, target, smoke screens, etc. Lt. Rice the bombardier was trapped in the nose turret and didn't bail out. The need for immediate exit from the stricken aircraft made it impossible for anyone in the turrets to extricate themselves from those turrets and then bail out. Capt. Duckworth tried to get out of the side window but could not because of the spin of the plane. He then went for the top hatch and pulled himself out by grabbing the gun barrels from the top turret sticking out over the hatch. He told me that Col. Lokker bailed out of the top escape hatch prior to him and that they were both captured together on the ground. While held in a farmhouse both attempted to escape and Duckworth said that as he was recaptured, the last he saw of Lokker, he was running towards nearby woods with German guards firing at him.

I believe Sgt. Miosky the radio operator, was last seen in the waist of the aircraft throwing radar chaff out the waist window and is believed to have been unable to bail out due to the centrifugal force of the spin and he burned to death in the aircraft. Sgt. Rabkin, asked me to fill his oxygen bottles about twenty minutes before the target. I last saw him as I bailed out and he was sliding out of the top turret after he had released the drop seat. It is believed that Rabkin never succeeded in sliding out of the top turret as the ship immediately flipped on its back and spun in and he was thus thrown back into the turret. Sgt. Flynn the tail gunner didn't have a chance to bail out. The last known interphone conversation of his was with Col. Lokker, to whom he relayed formation appearance prior to the bomb run. He was in the waist of the airplane when last seen and I don't know if he was injured.

Sgt. Bourne told me that immediately after the ship was hit, flaming 100-octane gasoline swept in a waist window and enveloped Flynn. Bourne said that he switched on the inter-phone and told him to get out of his turret. When Bourne last saw Flynn, he was in the tail turret and he was on fire and burning. Bourne helped Miosky adjust his chute directly over the escape hatch where he stood at the time we went across the target. He was not injured at the time of last contact, but he was last seen standing over the escape hatch and he apparently caught fire when flames whipped into the waist window.

Hockman said that according to the information given to him by Duckworth, Col. Lokker did bail out. Lokker's face was lacerated and seriously burned. Sgt. Billings said that he was blown out, or fell free. Duckworth and Hockman bailed out after the ship was in a spin. Bourne was blown out, or fell free as Billings was. The German guards at the Hospital told Billings that seven men were still in the burned plane. The German interrogator told him that Rice, Duckworth and Hockman were also prisoners, Bourne and Billings were together. Billings had no record of Col. Lokker. The interrogator thought Lokker had bailed out and was still not captured. He told Billings the rest of the crew was finished, meaning they went down with the ship."

German documents indicate that Col. Lokker was Killed In Action and was buried on 22 November 1944 in the cemetery at Langenlieben. Those documents also indicate that Lts. Rice and Whelan, and Sgts. Flynn, Miosky and Rabkin were Killed In Action. Capt. Duckworth, Lts. Kutger and Hockman and Sgts. Billings, and Bourne were all captured and made Prisoners of War. Sgt. Bourne was put in a Hospital in Cosel, Germany

20 November 1944: Lt. Ernest R. Taft, Pilot, 783rd Squadron, flew a B-24J, #42-51402, Call Letter Blue "E" to bomb the Blechhammer South Synthetic Oil Refinery at Blechhammer, Germany with crewmembers, F/O Thomas Pope, Co-Pilot; F/O Erwin J. Cole, Navigator; F/O Michael Kolago, Bombardier; Sgt. Robert H. Lowman, Nose Turret Gunner; Sgt. Jack E. Cassady, Top Turret Gunner; Sgt. Richard H. Goldsworthy, Ball Turret Gunner; Sgt. Charlie C. Ritch, Flight Engineer-Waist Gunner; Sgt. Charles F. Burda, Radio Operator-Waist

Gunner and Sgt. Richard M. Balke, Tail Turret Gunner. There were scattered clouds and their aircraft was last sighted at 12:25 hours over Germany.

Eyewitness, Sgt. Fred Simpson, Jr., 783rd Squadron, "I saw Blue "E" get a direct hit believing it to be in the bomb bay. The ship did not explode right away but it was flaming a good deal from the bomb bay. The ship continued to fly straight and level for approximately thirty seconds, in which time I saw one man jump, I believe from the escape hatch in the back of the ship. The ship then rose a little and started into a downward plunge out of my visibility."

Lt. Taft's ship received a direct hit by flak in the nose and he left the formation between the I. P. (Initial Point) and the target. Taft said, "Immediately after being hit I told Flight Officer Pope the co-pilot, to bail out. He was last seen going through the fire on the flight deck. After I received first aid the Germans told me that they would take me to a hospital as soon as transportation could be arranged and we would pick up Pope on the way. They said they had found Pope after the air raid without me mentioning his name so it was apparently the truth. The next day after the raid I was taken to a hospital but we failed to pick up Pope as they had said they would. I believe he must have been injured to the extent that he died before we came to pick him up. I was taken to a hospital for treatment of my burns the following day after being shot down. The hospital was located in Kosel Germany, which was operated, by Catholic Sisters and one German Army Doctor.

I was under the care of a Sister named Unjuard who belonged to the Catholic Order of Sisters of Mercy. If she could be found I believe she would be very cooperative in giving information which might lead to the uncovering of the fate of my crew. She did an awful lot for the Americans who were brought to her for treatment. I believe Flight Officer Kolago the bombardier, must have been killed instantly. Sgt. Burda the radio operator was at the waist position and I believe he must have been able to bail out but I have heard nothing from him since being hit. I believe Sgt. Balke the tail gunner, must have been able to bail out as the fire was contained to the forward part of the plane and I believe there was no damage in the tail or waist section, but I have no idea what happened to him if he did not get out. Sgt. Lowman was in the nose turret and I believe he must have been killed instantly.

I had no contact with Sgt. Goldsworthy the ball gunner after we were hit. I was unable to get back to him myself. A week after being shot down a German soldier brought Goldsworthy's billfold to me and said they had found it but had no trace of him. The billfold showed no signs of being damaged. It was full of snap shots and had he dropped it or had it fallen out when he jumped, the pictures would have fallen out. I believe he must have fallen into the hands of civilians and was killed by them. Had he not bailed out of the plane his billfold could not have been found in such good shape for the plane was on fire and the bombs were still in the racks. The last time Sgt. Cassady the top turret gunner was seen he was getting out of his turret. A German soldier told me that they found Cassady dead when he landed. The navigator helped him out of the turret and I believe that he either jumped without his parachute to get out of the fire or his chute failed to open."

German documents indicate that Lts. Taft and Cole were Prisoners of War. F/O's Pope and Kolago and Sgts. Ritch, Burda, Balke, Lowman, Goldsworthy and Cassady were Killed In Action.

20 November 1944: 1st Lt. Joe Norman Jr., Pilot, 780th Squadron, flew a B-24, to bomb the South Oil Refinery at Blechhammer, Germany with crewmembers, 1st Lt. Robert F. Wills, Co-Pilot; Lt. Robert Kaiser, Navigator; S/Sgt. Frank D. Love, Nose Turret Gunner; S/Sgt. Richard D. Block, Top Turret Gunner; S/Sgt. Robert E. Crist, Armorer-Ball Turret Gunner; T/Sgt. Thurman Atkinson, Flight Engineer-Waist Gunner; S/Sgt. Theodore Deitsch, Radio Operator-Waist Gunner and S/Sgt. Mike Urda, Tail Turret Gunner. This was a nine-man crew.

Lt. Norman's aircraft reached the IP, and on the bomb run the ship directly ahead blew up, throwing Norman's plane off to the right. Flak struck number 2 engine, causing a runaway prop. The left wing received severe dents from wreckage of the other plane. The gas lines on number 3 and 4 engines and the manifold were shot out. Number 4 engine went out, possibly from lack of gas. Number 2 propeller froze when the pilot stalled it out. Bombs were dropped on the target and the pilot took a heading to the rally point, being slightly ahead of the formation. At the time the pilot intended to rejoin the formation, not knowing the extent of the gas shortage. Sgt. Atkinson informed the pilot of the loss of fuel and the pilot decided to try for Russian lines, so Lt. Kaiser the navigator gave the heading to the east. The plane was difficult to control because of aileron damage.

Continuously losing altitude, the plane passed over Crocow twenty minutes later at 13,000 feet, where flak again hit the plane. The pilot rallied left, and then resumed his original heading. The navigator could not pin point their position because of the lack of maps. Number 3 and number 4 engines conked out completely, causing the plane to drop to 7,000 feet. As the plane was falling, officer crewmembers, discussed the possible wisdom of bailing out, where upon Sgts. Crist and Urda left the ship successfully. Number 3 engine recovered at 8,000 feet and the pilot leveled out at 9,000 feet. About five minutes later the crew spotted a landing field, circled it, and came in wheels down for an excellent landing with no injuries. The aircraft had 175 flak holes in it.

Friendly Russians met the plane and escorted the crew to Headquarters at Zamoac where a Russian Officer interrogated them by sign language and promised to notify American authorities of their safety. Then the crew was taken to a Polish civilian house where they remained, under guard, for 20 days. On 21 November they were joined by Crist and Urda. Crist landed near Gorgkow where Polish soldiers (serving with the Russians) surrounded him and carried him to a nearby house. They searched him and found his escape kit with maps. He experienced much difficulty convincing them he was not a German Spy. He slept under guard that night. The following morning two Russian soldiers in a Studebaker truck came to the house, ordered him to drive it and this he did, to their satisfaction and pleasure. Polish soldiers escorted him to a large schoolhouse near Parlow where he joined Urda who had also landed near Gorgkow, four miles from the spot where Crist landed. Removing his boots and parachute harness, he ran into nearby woods to avoid soldiers whom he could not identify.

From this vantage point he watched the soldiers (who later proved to be Polish) chase the civilians who were making off with his boots and chute. He soon contacted some civilians who called the soldiers. After an argument between members of "Company 6" and "Company 4" as to who would have the honor of "Capturing" the "Suspect," Company 6 won out. They escorted him under heavy guard to Polish headquarters in Gorgkow where he ate and slept. A Polish Lieutenant who knew a few English words tried unsuccessfully to quiz him. All articles, except his watch and money were confiscated. Next morning he joined Crist at Parlow. Crist and Urda were introduced to a Polish Major at the Schoolhouse, who after some discussions took them to Lublin by jeep, turning them over to the Polish Secret Police. Two interpreters interrogated them as to the number of men on the crew, altitude and characteristics of the plane. They refused to answer and the Poles became angry and sent them to a Russian Major who informed them the remainder of their crew was in Zamoac. The following morning they joined the rest of their crew.

During the crews stay in Zamoac their rooms and belongings were searched many times when the members were absent. An intelligence officer, a Major, lived with the group at all times. He and Urda, conversed in Polish on general subjects, but the Major would not give the crew any information whatsoever. On 10 December, a Russian piloted C-47 carried them to Poltava, an American base, where the group was deloused and thoroughly interrogated by an American Captain. On the 12th they left by an American piloted, Russian navigated, C-46, for Teheran but because of bad weather the A. T. O. plane landed at Makhah Kale on the Caspian Sea, where the party remained two days. Teheran was the next stop, on the 14th. Here the crewmembers discovered $50.00 worth of their personal clothing had been stolen from the plane but had no idea at which locale the theft occurred. The next day they journeyed to Cairo and were quartered at camp Muckstep. Forced down at Luka airport, near Velatla, Malta on 17 December, then eventually flew to Naples, arriving in Bari, Italy on 20 December 1944.

20 November 1944: 1st Lt. Ord A. Campbell, Pilot, 780th Squadron, flew a B-24, Call Letter Red "S" to bomb the Synthetic Oil Refinery at Blechhammer, Germany with crewmembers, Lt. Arthur H. Bernstein; Lt. Anthony J. Stage; F/O Edward M. Ryan, Navigator; Sgt. C. M. Thompson Gunner; Sgt. Irving Cohen, Gunner; Sgt. Robert P. Adams, Gunner; Sgt. C. B. Sherburne, Jr., Gunner; Sgt. Anthony E. Frosini, Gunner and Sgt. Sam Bay, Gunner.

Lt. Campbell's aircraft was hit by flak at the target and on the return to base he ran out of gasoline just at the spur of the Italian boot, between Viesta and Peschici. Badly damaged and flying with two engines out, Campbell ordered the crew to bail out at 800 feet, nearing the coast. Lt. Bernstein, F/O Ryan and Sgt. Cohen landed in the water. Lt. Bernstein was Killed In Action, when his chute failed to open. His body was recovered by F/O Ryan and sent to Bari, Italy for burial. The balance of the crew landed safely within 500 feet of the shore. Sgt. Thompson was injured in landing and was sent to the 61st Station Hospital at Foggia, Italy. F/O Ryan was treated for shock and exposure before returning to the field.

22 November 1944: 1st Lt. John F. Priddy Jr., Pilot, 780th Squadron, flew a B-24G, #42-78259, Call Letter Red "N" named "Bugs" to bomb the South Oil Refinery at Blechhammer, Germany with crewmembers, Lt. Michael J. Pollot, Co-Pilot; Lt. Modesto Pellecchia, Navigator; Sgt. David N. Holdsworth, Nose Turret Gunner; Sgt. John G. Fekays, Flight Engineer-Gunner; S/Sgt. Francis J. Josselyn, Radio Operator-Gunner; S/Sgt. George E. Crawford, Gunner; Sgt. James G. Rush, Gunner and Sgt. Carrol G. Dempsey Tail Turret Gunner. There was a solid undercast and their aircraft was last sighted at 12:40 hours over Germany. This was a nine-man crew.

Eyewitness, Sgt. Robert N. Stickles, 780th Squadron, "On combat mission of 22 November 1944, enroute to bomb Munich, Germany, the formation turned off to bomb the secondary target due to extremely bad weather conditions. At this time Lt. Priddy's plane was still with the formation. Before we reached the first alternate target, this plane began to drop back and was lost from sight in the undercast. The reason for this was apparently due to engine trouble, because we had not passed through any accurate flak."

Lt. Priddy, "We led to an altitude of 23,000 feet and it was too much for the old engines. We left the formation approximately, 100 miles east of Switzerland on a heading of 276 degrees. The entire crew bailed out and all chutes opened as confirmed by secret GFW in the Gestapo Office at Villach, Germany."

Lts. Priddy, Pellecchia, and Pollot and Sgts. Holdsworth, Fekays and Crawford, went out through the bomb bay. Sgts. Rush, Dempsey and Josselyn, all went out through the rear escape hatch. Lt. Pellecchia bailed out in the vicinity of Ratzcbach or Villach Germany. He was not injured prior to bailing out, but was injured slightly after landing in the mountains.

Lt. Priddy said, "My last conversation with him was a position report and heading to the nearest safe landing area. This officer was taken prisoner by the Germans and was in Stalag Luft 1, in Barth Germany. The engineer, Sgt. Fekays, was not injured prior to bail out and he had done all that he deemed possible to get the engines back into operation before bailing out.

When last seen he was on the flight deck of the aircraft. I received information on Fekays and other missing crewmembers from my nose gunner who evaded capture and returned to the old bomb group and that the British Intelligence reported to Partisan forces that Fekays alone, of the entire crew was not taken prisoner by the Germans. This leads me to believe that Fekays along with other members of my crew now missing were taken into custody by a German Army Unit.

I was told by the secretary in the Gestapo Office in Villach Germany that two members of my crew were dead but that all had been seen in their parachutes after we had exited the plane. Gunners, Rush and Dempsey were not injured prior to bail out. I had no conversation with them prior to that time, but they were last seen in the tail section by some of their fellow crewmembers. The co-pilot, Lt. Pollot spoke to Rush, Fekays and Dempsey on the interphone. He told Fekays to jettison the guns. My radio operator told me that when he was captured the Germans showed him the Mae West that Dempsey was wearing at the time and it had two bullet holes in it and it was covered with blood. The Germans said, "See what happens to your comrades". He must have been shot upon landing from his jump."

The nose gunner, Holdsworth, landed in snow about five miles south of Villach, and climbed up a mountain south of the town. After looking over the terrain, he decided to start out the following morning. He spent the night on the mountain wrapped in his chute. On the morning of 23 November 1944, he made his way down the mountain and approached a small house near the railway. After watching the house for some time and only seeing an old woman and a child, he went to the house to ask for assistance. The woman was very friendly and gave him food and dried his clothes. He told this woman that he was an American and that he wanted to catch the train where it passed the house.

After waiting until 19:00 hours the train came by and he jumped on between the cars. After riding for about a mile a German conductor opened the door and found him. A brief struggle occurred in which he overcame the conductor and jumped off the train. He then made his way back to the house from which he started, found a place in the barn, and spent the night of 23/24 November 1944. On the morning of 24 November the Italian woman hid him among the straw and went out to find some Partisans. The Partisans arrived that night and he walked with them for thirty-three days, without having any serious difficulties.

While on the march with the Partisans through the hills, Holdsworth was in a barn one night and a Partisan, who had just arrived, and who claimed to have served in the British Navy and could speak a little English, told him that three of his "Komrads" had been shot and one taken prisoner by the Germans as they tried to cross railway lines. The report was later repeated to him by a British Major and Captain who had reached the first British Mission at Slovens, Partisan Headquarters, just before he did and who had been informed of the shooting by the Partisans. Passing along the Partisan chain of communication, Holdsworth eventually arrived at a British Mission near Partisan Slovenic Headquarters at Preggrad.

Holdsworth stated that the Partisans were well organized in the mountains of northern Yugoslavia but further south in the Trieste area they are scattered and disorganized. After staying at the British Mission for three days, he left on 27 December 1944, in a BAC "C-47" plane, together with 16 other American airmen. He landed at Foggia and came down to Bari by truck. Lts. Priddy, Pollot and Pellechia, and Sgts. Crawford and Josselyn, were captured and made Prisoners of War. Sgt. Holdsworth evaded capture and returned to duty. Sgts. Fekays, Dempsey and Rush were Killed In Action.

2 December 1944: 1st Lt. Frederic B. Withington Jr., Pilot, 780th Squadron, flew a B-24H, Call Letter Red "M" to bomb the South Oil Refinery at Blechhammer, Germany with crewmembers, Lt. Charles D. Softy, Co-Pilot; Lt. Fulton W. Haight, Navigator; S/Sgt. Kenneth O. McMann, Flight Engineer-Gunner; S/Sgt. James W. Long, Radio Operator-Gunner; S/Sgt. Harry M. Weaver, Gunner; S/Sgt. Kenneth L. Hardisty, Gunner; S/Sgt. Gerald K. Jackelen, Gunner and Sgt. Julius Blumenfeld, Gunner. There was a heavy haze and their aircraft was last sighted over Germany at 13:30 hours. This was a nine-man crew.

Eyewitness, Sgt. Jacob J. Schneider, "Lieutenant Withington's plane (Red "M") was hit by flak over the target on operational combat mission of 2 December 1944. One engine was smoking extensively. This plane came off the target with the formation. As soon as we were out of the flak area, Lt. Withington feathered the smoking engine, and although he lost some altitude, he kept on following the formation. No chutes left the plane, and it seemed to be well under

118

control. It kept following us for a long time but was gradually dropping further behind. Just before this plane was lost to our range of vision, it appeared to turn to the left which indicated that the pilot had decided to leave the formation entirely and probably try to make a safe landing in the nearest friendly territory."

The mission was to bomb the Oil Refineries at Blechhammer. Lt. Withington's crew managed to reach the target and drop their bombs. Then they were hit by flak and lost number 4 engine and number 1 engine was giving them trouble. They also had a fuel leak on number 1 engine and the auto-pilot was out so they left the formation approximately 50 miles from the target and the pilot decided to head for Russia. They found a small landing strip and the crewmembers assumed the ditching positions as they prepared to crash land. Sgt. Long the radio operator said they were too low and the Russians were shooting at them. Lt. Softy the co-pilot said, "Brace yourselves," "we are going to land." Lt. Softy was injured seriously when both of his legs were mashed and the nerves were torn as they crash landed. They managed to get the co-pilot out of the plane with the aid of Russian soldiers and Polish farmers. The Russians then took them to a fighter field north of the town of Rzeszow, Poland. They stayed there for about seven days and then were flown to Poltava. Then went to Doheran and eventually were evacuated to Bari, Italy on 20 December 1944.

2 December 1944: 1st Lt. John W. Franklin, Pilot, 780th Squadron, flew a B-24H, #41-28761, Call Letter Blue "P" named "Perry And The Pirates" to bomb the South Synthetic Oil Refinery at Blechhammer, Germany with crewmembers, Lt. Calvin C. Espy, Co-Pilot; Lt. James W. Hilger, Navigator-Bombardier; Sgt. Horace H. Dobie, Nose Turret Gunner; Sgt. William E. Hill, Flight Engineer-Waist Gunner; Sgt. George E. Dunlap, Tail Turret Gunner; Sgt. John T. Ryan, Radio Operator-Waist Gunner; Sgt. Franklin K. Powers, Flight Engineer-Top Turret Gunner and Sgt. Thomas Cremeen, Ball Turret Gunner. Their aircraft was last sighted at 12:43 hours. This was a nine-man crew.

Eyewitness, Lt. Neal C. Harbin, "Over Blechhammer, Germany on combat mission of 2 December 1944, I was watching "Blue P" for "bombs away" so I could tell the bombardier. Just as I said "bombs away" I noticed fire coming out of the bomb bays. One man left the plane almost at the same time as the bombs, - at least not more than five seconds later. He came out of the rear hatch, and his chute opened. Then two others jumped, and I saw one of their chutes open. It appeared as though one came from the nose, and the other from the waist. The ship then nosed down to the left losing altitude, and was lost from my range of vision."

Sgt. Hill, "After about 10 minutes of very accurate heavy flak over the target, we were hit in our fuel panel which caused our plane to be a mass of flames immediately. The altitude was about 25,000 feet so we were forced to bail out and the co-pilot ordered us to leave as soon as we had a chance. I believe Sgt. Dunlap was killed prior to that time by a burst of flak we had received in the tail of the plane. I last saw him in his tail turret. Lt. Franklin was sitting in his pilot seat watching the flak, while Lt. Espy the co-pilot was flying the plane when we were hit the fatal blow. Franklin started out but I don't think he made it due to the hot fire between him and the exit."

The co-pilot said, "After I gave the bail out order, I started out myself but was still connected to the seat so I sat back down to free myself. I guess Johnny (John Franklin) thought I was hit for he started out but seemed to be stuck between the seats. I gave him a push and I think he was free but as I had taken off my oxygen mask I passed out and that's the last thing I remember.

I remember reaching for my ripcord and feeling a jerk, then I regained full consciousness with my chute open at about 9,000 feet. I don't know how I got out of the plane. I didn't see any other chutes around me and knew nothing of the crew until I was back in France after I was liberated."

Lt. Hilger the navigator was in the nose compartment of the ship with Sgt. Dobie the nose gunner. When Dobie got ready to jump Hilger was standing beside him ready to jump also. That is the last Dobie saw of any of the crew until they were captured. Lt. Espy and Sgts. Cremeen, Dobie, Hill, Powers and Ryan were captured and made Prisoners of War. Lts. Franklin, and Hilger and Sgt. Dunlap were Killed In Action.

6 December 1944: 1st Lt. Harold F. Owens, Pilot, 783rd Squadron, and crewmembers, Lt. Irvin K. Raatz, Co-Pilot; 1st Lt. Lloyd R. Findlay, Navigator; 1st Lt. John D. DePlue III, Bombardier; T/Sgt. Earl T. Behr, Flight Engineer-Gunner; S/Sgt. Thomas J. Curtis, Jr., Radio Operator-Gunner; S/Sgt. Hudson J. Davis, Gunner; S/Sgt. Edward E. McDonald, Gunner; S/Sgt. Charles E. Roberts, Gunner and Sgt. Robert B. Gordon, Gunner, were scheduled to bomb the Rangier Marshalling Yards at Bratislava, Slovakia. Lieutenant Owen's and his entire crew were Killed In Action as their B-24 blew up on take-off as they started on this mission to Bratislava.

11 December 1944: 1st Lt. Vern L. Larson, Pilot, 780th Squadron, flew a B-24J, #42-51421, Call Letter Yellow "O" named "Mission Belle" to bomb the South Ordnance Depot at Vienna, Austria with crewmembers, Lt. August S. Calabrese, Co-Pilot; Lt. Herbert R. Cohen, Navigator; Lt. Robert M. Wilson, Bombardier; S/Sgt. Edwin K. Pratt, Ball Turret Gunner; T/Sgt. Thomas E.

McKnight, Flight Engineer-Gunner; S/Sgt. Leslie R. Davis, Radio Operator-Gunner; S/Sgt. George J. Le Comte, Gunner; S/Sgt. Edward C. Wilson, Gunner; S/Sgt. Edward A. Orpikowski, Gunner and Sgt. Erwin H. Meyer, Voice Interrogator. The weather was clear and their aircraft was forced down over Austria. This was an eleven-man crew.

Eyewitness, Sgt. Kenneth E. Gebauer, 780th Squadron, "While over the target on combat mission of 11 December 1944, I saw Lieutenant Larson's plane (Yellow "O") shortly after it had been hit by flak. The plane nosed up and to the left and then went into a complete roll. Being directly over us, I was able to see the bombs still in the racks. The plane then went into a flat spin and dropped behind and below us. I did not see any chutes leave this plane because it was lost from my view."

Sgt. McKnight, "The crew bailed out over the city of Vienna. I saw Sgt. Le Comte before take off but I don't know if he bailed out. Sgt. Wilson was taken prisoner, I saw him in France on my way back to the States."

Sgt. Pratt, "I last saw Lt. Wilson on the flight deck after the plane was hit and he was getting his chute on. Wilson was standing and staring. I presume that he stood a minute too long and the plane went into a spin and he probably did not get out."

McKnight said, "Lt. Cohen, was seen leaving the flight deck to go to the nose of the plane. The shell burst directly under Lt. Larson and Lt. Calabrese, therefore it is probable that Cohen was hit since he was in the nose of the plane. The last conversation with Calabrese was about five minutes before the plane was hit. After the plane was hit I never saw him move. I was standing between Larson and Calabrese and my foot was wounded by flak, therefore it is highly probable that Calabrese too, was hit by flak."

Sgt. Pratt, "Lt. Larson, Sgts. McKnight, Meyer, Wilson, Orpikowski and me, bailed out the front bomb bay after the plane went out of control. Our aircraft struck the ground on the outskirts of Vienna. Sgt. Wilson, after serving as a prisoner of war at Stalag-Luft 1, was repatriated to the United States in June 1945.
I do not think Sgt. Le Comte bailed out. I believe he may have been killed or injured by flak. I have the impression of seeing him slumped over in his turret as I abandoned the plane which was in a dive then. He may have been dead or seriously injured but I believe Le Comte was killed outright by flak, otherwise he would have made some attempt to leave his crew position as the plane began its dive.

I do not think Lt. Wilson bailed out because he was injured by flak or frozen by the thought of jumping. I glanced at him as the plane dived down. I did not think he was injured because he was on his feet. He was last seen standing at his position, which was at that time, the right waist window. A German interrogator asked one of the surviving crewmembers if the enlisted men called Wilson by his first name. We thought it a very odd question particularly because no explanation was given for it, nor was any comment made.

Since all of the men from the waist of the plane, except myself, are still missing, and because I faintly recollect shattered waist windows caused by a near flak burst it would be logical to assume that the men were probably all injured to some degree, however, the last I saw of Lt. Wilson, he was standing and apparently was uninjured. That is the reason I did not tender him any assistance whatever. Since there was a spasmodic fire in Lt. Cohen's compartment he is believed to have been the first to bail out. I don't know if he was injured as he was already out when the rest of the crew began to leave so no one saw or spoke to him. He was last seen at his crew position, the navigator's compartment.

While imprisoned at Vienna one partly opened parachute was brought in by the Krouts. However, no comment was made as to whom it belonged. I believe there are only two possibilities concerning the fate of Lt. Cohen, either his parachute failed to open or he was killed by civilians when he landed. The civilians treated all of the returned crewmembers very roughly, so this is by no means an absurd supposition. As Lt. Cohen was not a regular member of our crew, I know nothing at all about him.

Lt. Calabrese is believed to have been fatally injured when struck in the throat area by large pieces of flak fragments. As the plane became disabled and began to dive in, Calabrese made no movement to bail out. He was last seen in his crew position, the co-pilots seat. Since Calabrese made no movement whatever after an enemy flak shell burst between the pilot and co-pilot it is my opinion that he was killed instantly. In any case, I believe it would be safe to say if he was not killed instantly, he was very seriously injured and unconscious. While imprisoned at Vienna a guard made a remark that, near the wreckage of a plane, of that days raid, the body of a large man with somewhat Mongolian features was found. In my estimation that might have been a very rough description of Lt. Calabrese."

Lt. Larson and Sgts. McKnight, Wilson, Orpikowski, Meyer and Pratt, were captured and made Prisoners of War. Lts. Calabrese, Wilson and Cohen and Sgts. Davis and Le Comte, were Killed In Action.

16 December 1944: Lt. Michael Blakita, Pilot, 781st Squadron, flew a B-24J, #42-51631, Call Letter Yellow "D" named "Flaming Mamie" to bomb the Synthetic Oil Refinery at Brux, Czechoslovakia with crewmembers, Lt. Marion A. Pitts, Co-Pilot; Lt. David B. Coleman, Navigator; Lt. William L. Cassel,

Bombardier; Sgt. Howard G. Weistling, Flight Engineer-Gunner; Sgt. Truman C. Leath, Radio Operator-Gunner; Sgt. Alvin Hellman, Armorer-Gunner; Sgt. Ralph W. Leach, Gunner; Sgt. Dean T. Otto, Gunner and Sgt. Donald D. Stern, Gunner. There was a heavy overcast and their aircraft was last sighted at 12:10 hours over Esternberg, Germany.

Eyewitness, Flight Officer, Massis M. Santigian, 781st Squadron, "On the mission on 16 December 1944, Yellow "D" flown by Lt. Blakita, jettisoned its bombs and pulled out of the formation at 12:10 hours. The pilot feathered the prop on either number 1 or number 2 engine. This was just before we reached Linz. There had been no flak or fighters up to this time. The ship was last seen flying away in the distance, under control. None of the crewmembers had abandoned the ship."

The aircraft left the formation over Passau and prior to bailing out the entire crew was standing by, waiting for the bail out order and all bailed out successfully. Lt. Coleman and Sgt. Otto left by the nose wheel hatch. Lts. Pitts, Blakita, and Cassel and Sgts. Leach and Weistling, left by the bomb bay. Sgts. Hellman, Stern, and Leath, left by the emergency hatch at the rear of the fuselage. All ten men landed on the outskirts of Linz and were all picked up at different places that same afternoon and became Prisoners of War.

The bombardier, Lt. Cassel, was assigned to fly with this crew because they went overseas as a nine-man crew without a bombardier. Lt. Cassel became ill about one and one half months after he was sent to Stalag Luft 1, in Barth, Germany. Cassel was taken to the prison hospital and was in a good English Doctor's care. Sgt. Stern ran an errand for him from his compound to the hospital the day before his death and talked to him a few minutes. Stern said, "Lt. Cassel seemed to be in high spirits and believed that he would be back with us within the next week. His throat was swollen quite large and we were told that it was a tonsil infection. The whole trouble turned out to be Leukemia and he lost consciousness and died that afternoon." Lt. Cassel was taken to the hospital ten days before his death and was under the care of the English Doctor, until his death. He died on Sunday, 10 March 1945 at approximately 12:45 P.M. He was buried in the city cemetery in Barth, Germany on 15 March 1945. Lt. Coleman was present at the burial along with Colonels Herbert Zemke and Frances S. Gabreski. This was Lt. Cassel's thirteenth mission. On his second mission he was shot down over Yugoslavia and walked back to base.

16 December 1944: Lt. William V. Fertig, Pilot, 782nd Squadron, flew a B-24H, #42-52564, Call Letter White "X" to bomb the Synthetic Oil Refinery at Brux, Czechoslovakia with crewmembers, Lt. Donald N. Christensen, Co-Pilot; Lt. William P. Kemper, Navigator; Lt. Arthur J. Kernahan, Bombardier; Cpl.

Franklin E. Young, Top Turret Gunner; Cpl. Mack J. Kirby, Flight Engineer-Gunner; Cpl. Arnold J. Roth, Radio Operator-Gunner; Cpl. Claud J. Behn, Gunner; Cpl. James E. Dennis, Gunner and Cpl. Alex O. Swanson, Gunner. Weather was clear and their aircraft was last sighted at 14:30 hours.

Eyewitness, Sgt. Endrick S. Winslow, 783rd Squadron, "On our way back from the target at Brux just after passing between the Linz-Salzburg area, the airplane White "X" seemed to be having trouble with number 3 engine. For about 20 minutes they kept up with the formation and all the time the pilot kept trying to feather the number three engine but was unable to do so, and it kept windmilling as he crossed the mountains. White "X" didn't appear to be losing any altitude and the altitude reading was about 16,000 to 17,000 feet. As the formation left the Alps White "X" dropped out of sight. I didn't see any smoke or chutes exiting from the plane."

The target was reached and bombed from about 21,000 feet. While rallying with the formation number 1 engine lost oil pressure and the prop was feathered. On the return journey with the formation passing them, the number 3 engine lost oil pressure over the Alps and this prop was also feathered. They left the formation about 45 minutes on course from the target. Equipment and guns were jettisoned to lighten the plane. After crossing the Alps number 2 engine lost oil pressure and that prop was feathered. Losing altitude at 500 feet per minute the pilot gave the order to bail out, somewhere in the area of Fiume. Eight of the crew left the plane safely. Lt. Fertig bailed out behind Lt. Christensen. Cpl. Kirby bailed out directly behind Fertig, through the bomb bay. The remaining crewmembers were not seen leaving the ship. Cpl. Young the top turret gunner was seen crawling out of the upper turret.

He landed through some trees, in mountainous country, and came to rest about 10 feet from the ground. After loosening his chute harness he dropped to the ground where there was deep snow, using the compass and map from his escape kit, he started walking southeast avoiding the coast. He spent the night in three feet of snow under a tree. As he was wearing "GI" shoes, fleece lined flying boots, heavy underwear and his O.D. uniform, he managed to keep reasonably warm. On the morning of 17 December he contacted a Yugoslav civilian who took him to his house where he was given some corn to eat - there being no other food in the house. Due to the proximity of a German garrison he and his guide left the house after half an hour and headed for a Partisan Headquarters.

Young discovered he was four days walk from Dreznica. German troops were encountered during their travels, but they never paid much attention to him and his companion who always got off the road. Lt. Kernahan suffered a broken ankle on landing and he put a splint on it and walked to some nearby farmhouses. On 18 December 1944 Young picked up Lt. Kemper and Kernahan in an unnamed village. With Kernahan going by horse, they traveled together to Dreznica arriving there about 20 December 1944 where they joined the other five members of their crew at the Partisan Headquarters.

At Dreznica Young and his American companions were well treated by the Partisan soldiers who were in charge of them. In spite of overcrowded and primitive conditions he felt he was well treated and that he was welcome. The Partisans produced a doctor who attended to Kernahan, but due to the lack of medical supplies the doctor was not able to do much good. On 21 December 1944 all the Americans left here on foot - a sleigh being provided for Kernahan - and walked via Mrkopalj to Delnice. At Skrad a British mission was reached on 24 December 1944. Here some more expert medical attention was given Kernahan. Young and his companions ate with the Partisans, as did the Captain from the Mission. Food was very poor and very short. After a drop was received by the Mission, the food improved to a certain extent, but was never very plentiful.

On 2 January 1945 they all left the mission with the exception of Kernahan and Young who had volunteered to stay and look after the injured man. While here Young and Kernahan were joined by Sgt. Kraemer, Cpls. Richardson, McLean, and Ferguson and Lt. Reynolds, and F/O Hague, who were all from other crews. Arrangements were made by the Mission to move Kernahan to Slovenia and on the morning of 10 January he was taken away on a sleigh under charge of the mission personnel. Young and his six companions left on the afternoon of 10 January to travel on foot to Vrbovsko. Partisan guides accompanied the party, which spent a night at Vrbovsko in a civilian house. Treatment at the hands of the Partisans begun to get a "little rough." They were casual in their treatment of the Americans and kept them standing about for long periods waiting for accommodation.

Lt. Christensen and Lt. Fertig were captured by the Germans and made Prisoners of War in Stalag Luft 1. Lt. Christensen received no information concerning the whereabouts of the crew while he was a POW, until his liberation when he ran into a pilot from his group who told him that Lt. Kemper returned safely by way of the Partisans. Lt. Kernahan the bombardier was taken by the Partisans to Italy, where he was returned to the U. S. from where he wrote Lt. Christensen's wife, giving her all the information concerning Christensen and Fertig that he had at the time. In February 1945 the remaining crewmembers were returned to Italy.

16 December 1944: Lt. Hugh P. Thompson, Pilot, 783rd Squadron, flew a B-24J, #42-51879, Call Letter Blue "A" to bomb the Synthetic Oil Refinery at Brux, Czechoslovakia with crewmembers, F/O Louis L. Rice, Co-Pilot; F/O Joseph J. Treglia, Navigator; F/O Abraham Haber, Bombardier; Sgt. Bernard E. Shott, Nose Turret Gunner; Sgt. Wayne D. Stanford, Top Turret Gunner; Sgt.

Harry J. Ganson, Ball Turret Gunner; Sgt. James E. Odom, Flight Engineer-Waist Gunner; Sgt. Louis J. Quaglietta, Radio Operator-Waist Gunner and Sgt. Steve J. Kotik, Tail Turret Gunner. Weather was clear and their aircraft was last sighted at 11:42 hours over northern Italy.

Eyewitness, Sgt. Joseph T. Dulack, Jr., 783rd Squadron, "Blue "A" was last seen by the tail gunner flying Blue "B" at 11:48 hours. This time was taken from the navigator's log. We last saw the ship losing altitude while still in the Alps. There was no smoke or chutes seen coming from the plane so apparently the pilot had mechanical difficulties. It was last seen heading into a cloud bank."

Flight Officer Haber, "The bomb bay doors failed to close after the bomb load had been dumped. The cause of the loss of the aircraft is unknown. Each man checked with the co-pilot at approximately 11:20 hours, about 10 minutes before the crash. We were 50 miles northeast of Salzburg at 14,000 feet when we left the formation. I ordered Sgt. Shott, to get ready to jump and he said, "You go first Haber." I waited a few seconds and said, "Ok this is no time to argue, follow me right out." When the bail out bell rang about a half minute later, I jumped and Shott bailed out a few seconds later. Our aircraft struck the ground in the Austrian mountains, 20 to 30 miles northeast of Salzburg or 25 kilometers east of Murag, Austria. The Germans said that no one else left the ship. The plane crashed and burned in a small Village near Glosbrecken, Austria. Lt. Thompson, and Flight Officers Rice and Treglia and Sgts. Quaglietta, Stanford, Odom, Ganson and Kotik, were all Killed In Action. Flight Officer Haber, and Sgt. Shott, were captured and made Prisoners of War.

17 December 1944: 1st Lt. Alfred W. Mullan Jr., Pilot, 781st Squadron, flew a B-24H, #42-52494, Call Letter Red "F" to bomb the South Synthetic Oil Refinery at Blechhammer, Germany with crewmembers, Lt. Hyman H. Newman, Co-Pilot; Lt. Lester Hershey, Navigator; Lt. Richard F. Heaney, Bombardier; S/Sgt. Earl J. Culpepper, Nose Turret Gunner; Sgt. Chester Mijal, Assistant-Engineer-Top Turret Gunner; S/Sgt. Deverett J. Allen, Armorer-Ball Turret Gunner; T/Sgt. John W. Hogan, Flight Engineer-Waist Gunner; T/Sgt. Melvin O. Gilliam, Radio Operator-Waist Gunner and Sgt. Crawford C. Barnhart Tail Turret Gunner. The weather was overcast and their aircraft was last contacted by radio at 13:25 hours.

Eyewitness, S/Sgt. Henry E. Black, 781st Squadron, "Red "F" flown by Lt. Mullan on the mission of 17 December 1944, had engine number 1 start smoking about 12:00 hours. At 12:45 hours the prop on number 1 engine came off and went spinning down. The plane started falling back and for about fifteen minutes was flying all alone. The pilot called on command and said he was going to join another group that was behind us, but he was unable to keep up with that group also. At 13:25 hours the pilot of Red "F" reported on command that he was going to try to make Russia. He called for fighter escort and got it. The plane had not been hit by flak or fighters. No one had abandoned the ship. Red "F" left the formation just north of Lake Balaton."

The mission was to bomb the South Oil Refinery at Blechhammer. The target was reached and the bombs were dropped. Number 1 engine ran away just after "bombs away" and it could not be feathered. The prop came off and the pilot headed back. We crossed Lake Balaton and we were running out of gas. Number 4 engine ran away so the pilot crash landed in a beet field about 15 kilometers north of Meko, Hungary. All of the crew got out a little shaken up, but there were no casualties. The pilot said that the aircraft was damaged so badly by the crash that it could not be made flyable again. The crew was picked up by the Hungarian civilians who took them to Meko where they stayed for eight days and were then taken to Brad. They stayed at Brad overnight and then went to Bucharest. They stayed in Bucharest for eighteen days and were evacuated to Bari, Italy arriving on 14 January 1945.

18 December 1944: 1st Lt. Donald E. Clodfelter, Pilot, 781st Squadron, flew a B-24H, #41-29414, Call Letter Yellow "E" named "Chief Jo Jon" to bomb the North Synthetic Oil Refinery at Blechhammer, Germany with crewmembers, Lt. Virgil R. Christian, Co-Pilot; Lt. Turner J. Atkins, Navigator; Lt. John A. Wilson, Bombardier; S/Sgt. Walter W. Leitgeb, Nose Turret Gunner; S/Sgt. Charles R. Hemphill, Top Turret Gunner; S/Sgt. Robert H. Munson, Ball Turret Gunner; S/Sgt. Robert W. Elliott, Flight Engineer-Waist Gunner; S/Sgt. Joseph C. Joublanc, Radio Operator-Waist Gunner and S/Sgt. Royal A. Wilson, Tail Turret Gunner. There was an undercast and their aircraft was last contacted by radio at 11:46 hours.

Eyewitness, Pvt. Michael J, Gidra, Jr., 781st Squadron, "On the mission on 18 December 1944, I heard the bombardier say, "There goes "E" he dropped his bombs." Then Yellow "E" turned off to the left and seemed to keep on going in that direction and not turning back. My pilot said that Lt. Clodfelter, the pilot of Yellow "E" called and he thought that Clodfelter intended to rejoin the formation after it came off the target. Yellow "E" had two superchargers out. The bombs were dropped by Yellow "E" about 11:46 hours."

The mission was to bomb the Oil Refinery at Blechhammer North. On the way to the target, the number 3 engine was not working properly, and then number 2 supercharger was in trouble. Just past the I. P. number 3 engine went out and was feathered. The bombs were jettisoned and the plane turned out of the formation. Then number 4 engine lost oil pressure and was eventually feathered. Then the aircraft turned on a 130 degrees heading for Lake Balaton. There was an undercast all the way and the plane got down under the undercast at about 4,500 feet, looking for an airfield, escorted by two P-51's. Number 1 engine started throwing flames, so the pilot gave the order to bail out. All crewmembers got out safely and the plane hit the ground about two miles east of Kalosca.

Lts. Clodfelter and Christian landed about a mile apart and were brought together at once by Peasants. Next day they went to another town, where Russian's took charge. Next day they went by truck to Szekszard and a day later to Pecs, Hungary. Four or five days later a convoy came through and took them to Subotica. Lt. Atkins was with the convoy. Atkins was shot at on the way down and two or three bullets hit his chute. After landing he was fired at some more and then approached by Russians. They kept him covered and took his gun, watch, and escape kit. An examination of his gun seemed to convince them of his nationality and later the gun, watch, and escape kit were returned to him. They took him by poor roads to Gzalasobalhns. There were many Cossacks around. He stayed there an hour or two and then by truck he went to another town, possibly Deg. There they were strafed and bombed by the Germans. Next day he went by jeep to Dunafeldvar, where there were some more Americans who were part of two other crews. The next day by jeep he went to Pecs where he met Lts. Clodfelter and Christian.

Right after landing, Lt. Wilson met Sgts. Elliott, Leitgeb and Hemphill at the town of Felsonan, Hungary and went about three miles south to another village where they met Sgts. Wilson, Joublanc and Munson. The seven men spent the night in a Peasant house in the country. The next day they went by wagon to another small town where there was a Russian Major General. They were forwarded to Czeaze to meet an American Captain whom the Russians thought that they might know, but they did not. They stayed there eleven days, thence by truck for three days to Szeged where they stayed for two nights. On 24 December Lts. Clodfelter, Christian and Atkins, went to Szeged and on to Timasoura, Rumania. Christmas day they left by train and four days later arrived at Bucharest. Lt. Wilson and the rest of the crew arrived at Bucharest four days later. Thence the entire crew was evacuated by C-47 to Bari, Italy on 18 January 1945.

18 December 1944: Lt. William F. Johns Jr., Pilot, 782nd Squadron, flew a B-24, to bomb the Blechhammer North Oil Refinery at Blechhammer, Germany with crewmembers, Lt. Leonard Unrath, Co-Pilot; Lt. Robert Gephart, Navigator; Lt. Marvin Schefrin, Bombardier; S/Sgt. Michael Hitchak, Armorer-Nose Turret Gunner; S/Sgt. Robert N. Windom, Top Turret Gunner-Assistant Engineer; Sgt. Samuel T. Nicastro, Ball Turret Gunner; T/Sgt. Paul H. Stieg, Flight Engineer-Waist Gunner; T/Sgt. Donald W. Brink, Radio Operator-Waist Gunner and Sgt.

Theodore A. Butler, Tail Turret Gunner. Their aircraft was last sighted at 11:46 hours.

Sgt. Windom, "As we approached the target area the ground was becoming obscured by clouds until there was a solid layer of clouds separating us from the ground. It was a beautiful picture painted by the Master Artist, beautiful blue sky above and the fleecy white clouds beneath and man made machines winging their way through this setting to spill death and destruction upon the enemy. Sgt. Theodore A. Butler broke the silence, "Tail to top turret." "Top turret to tail go ahead." 'Do you see the four planes in the distance at nine o'clock high?" "Yes I think they're P-51's." "They were to join us at 10:40 hours. I'll keep an eye on them however." "Roger." These four friendly fighters were followed by four more until they formed an umbrella of protection. What a beautiful sight.

As we neared the target we began to put on our flak suits, and we really treasured every piece of it today. Out in front I could see the planes flying through the black and red smoke. And it brought to mind the twenty-third Psalm. "Though I walk through the valley of the shadow of death." We were on the bomb-run and the planes opened up the bomb bay doors and dispersed in order to form a larger "bomb hits" area and to prevent severe turbulence in the air should a plane suddenly become enveloped in flames as a result of a direct hit in the bomb bay or gas tank.

There was complete silence on the interphone as we came in on our run, "Bombs Away" yelled the bombardier. "Let's get the heck out of here." But the number one engine was sputtering and quit, as the oil system had been hit and the engine froze from lack of oil and it had to be feathered. What's this, number three is on fire. The pilot asked the navigator for our position. We were supposed to be bombing near the Russian lines. "I'm not sure just where we are," said the navigator. Shortly after feathering number one engine, number two had to be feathered for the same reason as number one, lack of oil. We jettisoned equipment to maintain altitude, and then we abandoned our positions to prepare for bailing out. As the altitude dropped my heart rose. I stood looking through the open bomb bay with my parachute clutched tightly. There were the white clouds beneath and the blue sky above. I prayed to land, I know not where, it mattered not because God was there."

Sgt. Butler, "Sgt. Windom could see that the engines had failed and were on fire. Though the crew was prepared to bail out, Bill and Len managed to put out the fire, flipping fire control switches in the cockpit, which activated a fire extinguisher in the engine compartment. We were flying with one engine on each wing, the only way we could have remained in the air with two engines gone. Rapidly losing speed and altitude, we left the formation and headed for Russian territory. After convincing the pilot of a Russian fighter plane that we were Americans and we needed to land he directed us to an open field and as the third engine failed, we made a smooth landing as the wheels of our heavy plane sunk up to their hubs in the soft soil.

Bill told us to stay together when we got out of the plane. We were surrounded by Russian soldiers with rifles pointed at our heads. Bill called out "Amerikanskis! Amerikanskis!" We were taken to their base of operations near the town of Jakebaralles, Hungary. We were housed in a commandeered Hungarian farmhouse. We ate Borscht, a kind of beet and cabbage stew and drank Vodka, since all of the water was polluted. I watched the Russians butcher the farmer's hogs and everything was saved except the squeal. We were entertained by a group of young Cossack dancers. The soldiers both men and women, slept in a chicken house on boards in their clothes. One male soldier took advantage of a female soldier. The discipline was swift and final, the male soldier was taken out and shot.

We were living with the Russians twenty miles behind the German lines. We heard the guns and bombs in the distance. No one spoke English and we could not understand Russian. While in this area, we held a burial service for a fatally injured ball turret gunner, who with his crew, had bailed out but his chute did not open. The civilians cut off his pockets and any identification. I hope that his family had recovered his remains from the little churchyard in Velike Kikinda."

Sgt. Butler and the other nine members of his crew finally reached Belgrade and then they were flown in a U. S. C-47 to Bari, Italy and the 782nd Squadron.

18 December 1944: Lt. Curtis I. Eatman, Pilot, 782nd Squadron, flew a B-24, to bomb the Blechhammer North Oil Refinery at Blechhammer, Germany with crewmembers, Lt. Charles A. Haynes, Co-Pilot; F/O William E. Evans, Navigator; Lt. William T. McGee, Bombardier; Sgt. Joe R. Dearman, Nose Turret Gunner; Sgt. Edward W. Hahn, Top Turret Gunner; Sgt. Harry J. Wamser, Ball Turret Gunner; S/Sgt. Lemont H. Pakes, Flight Engineer-Waist Gunner; S/Sgt. James P. Powell, Radio Operator-Waist Gunner and T/Sgt. Andrew Jay, Tail Turret Gunner.

The aircraft dropped it's bombs over the target in formation, rallied left and was hit by flak in number 2 engine, knocking it out on the turn. The plane stayed with the formation until it reached the border of Yugoslavia, when number 4 engine lost all oil pressure and Lt. Eatman could not feather it. The plane was losing altitude and fell behind, following the formation until they were in the vicinity of Split, when number 1 RPM and manifold pressure began oscillating. Eatman sighted water through a break in the undercast as they were coming out of it. "Big Fence" gave him a heading to Vis, but he went through another break in the clouds, over land and gave orders to bail out. The entire crew cleared the ship safely. The ship crashed into the mountains.

Sgt. Pakes pulled the ripcord but his chute didn't open, as did the bombardier's. Both pulled their chutes open. Lt. McGee and Sgts. Dearman and Pakes landed close together on a mountain, joined immediately and stayed there until a young Partisan boy took them down to a small village, 5 miles from where the plane crashed. On the way F/O Evans and Sgt. Powell joined them. At the village they found Sgt. Jay who had landed nearby and fractured his leg. Late that afternoon Sgt. Hahn joined the party. He had landed on the same mountain alone and had walked to the village. Later on, a Partisan brought Sgt. Wamser in by mule and his leg was also fractured. At the local Partisan Headquarters the Partisans had splinted Wamser's leg but the crewmembers did not splint Sgt. Jay's because they were told that a Physician was coming. With the injured men on beds and the rest on the floor, they spent the night. The entire party left for Kupros, and met the Partisans Commanding Officer the next day. In the afternoon, Lts. Eatman and Haynes joined them here.

Eatman landed near a house on a mountainside and was invited into the cabin by the farmer. Haynes had to walk about a mile to reach the house from where he landed. Here they spent the night, and the next day with the Partisans, they started for Jojoc but two miles along other Partisans caught them and guided them to the small village where the rest of the crew had been the night before. Then the two walked on to Kupros to join the others. All ten spent the night here. The two injured rode by horses and the rest walked to Bugajno and they stayed at the Partisan Dispensary until the night of 21 December, when by train they traveled north to Jajce. The two injured men were taken to the hospital where a Partisan doctor set their legs.

On 24 December they all left by train for Sliniata and on 25 December they changed to a truck, which took them south to Clamoc. They continued to Livno on the early morning of 26 December where they met two other American Officers. They spent the night in the local Partisan barracks. The next day the party went to Sinj, where they ate and slept. On 27 December by train, they traveled to Split to the Partisan Liaison Office. They continued by boat to Vis, and on 28 December a B-24 took them to Bari, Italy.

19 December 1944: Lt. James W. Griffith, Pilot, 781st Squadron, flew a B-24J, #44-41106, Call Letter Blue "N" to bomb the Marshalling Yard at Maribor, Yugoslavia with crewmembers, Lt. Bruce Cosper, Co-Pilot; Lt. Ray L. Laughner, Navigator; Lt. James O. Burns, Bombardier; Sgt. Dempsey O. Brett, Nose Turret Gunner; Sgt. Richard O. Carlson, Top Turret Gunner; S/Sgt. Attilio A. Benvenuto, Ball Turret Gunner; Sgt. John E. Hart, Flight Engineer-Waist Gunner; S/Sgt. William Russell, Radio Operator-Waist Gunner and S/Sgt. Lee C. Stutzman, Tail Turret Gunner. The weather was cloudy.

Eyewitness, Lt. Gerald G. Schaefer, Air Corps, Assistant S-2, "Aircraft number 44-41106, Blue "N" was last seen at 13:25 hours, at which time it was observed to be heading east, away from the formation with the number 3 and number 4 engines smoking. This aircraft was observed to have salvoed it's bomb load at 12:40 hours, but continued on with the formation over the target and shortly after headed east. It's last known position was north of Maribor, Yugoslavia."

The aircraft left the formation just south of the target. About five or ten minutes before the crew bailed out, Sgt. Hart was sent from the flight deck to the waist to prepare the men there for bailing out. Lt. Laughner looked at Lt. Griffith for a final okay to leave the plane. Griffith was in the pilot seat when Laughner and Sgts. Carlson, and Brett, bailed out just ahead of Lt. Burns. Griffith said that he and Cosper intended to bail out right after Burns. Burns had talked on the intercom to Sgt. Russell and ordered him to bail out after Lt. Griffith. Burns had also talked on the intercom to Sgt. Benvenuto during the mission, but he didn't recall any other conversation with him. All men who bailed out went out through the bomb bays near Lake Balaton.

Lts. Griffith and Cosper, and Sgts. Hart and Stutzman were hung by the Hungarian civilians, (Killed In Action). Sgts. Benvenuto and Russell were found dead in the aircraft. (Killed In Action). Lts. Laughner and Burns and Sgts. Carlson and Brett met on the ground after their capture and were made Prisoners of War.

15 January 1945: Lt. Charles W. Matzger, Pilot, 783rd Squadron, and his crewmembers, Lt. Gilbert H. Kauffman, Co-Pilot; Lt. Paul E. Pfalzgraf, Navigator; Lt. Victor Hansen, Jr., Bombardier; Sgt. Alex J. Leslie, Flight Engineer-Gunner; Sgt. Richard L. Wise, Radio Operator-Gunner; Sgt. Elbert L. Scroggins, Gunner; Sgt. Verlin S. Williams, Gunner and Sgt. Raymond C. Wolferding, Gunner, were all killed on a practice mission. This was a nine-man crew.

20 January 1945: 1st Lt. Harold W. Shoener, Pilot, 783rd Squadron, flew a B-24 to bomb a target at Linz, Austria, with crewmembers, Capt. Arthur C. Tennille, Jr., Pilot; Lt. Raymond W. Eberhart, Co-Pilot; Lt. Russell J. Aurentz, Navigator; Lt. John N. Boeris, Bombardier; S/Sgt. Theodore S. Puckett, Flight Engineer-Gunner; S/Sgt. Francis T. Mulrooney, Radio Operator-Gunner; Sgt. John W. Bartlett, Gunner; S/Sgt. Richard K. Rutgers, Gunner and Sgt. Robert H. Arnold, Tail Turret Gunner.

All members of this crew, with the exception of Sgt. Arnold the tail gunner, were Killed In Action, when they attempted a crash landing on the Island of Vis off the coast of Yugoslavia. Sgt. Arnold wrote the following letter to Mrs. Tennille, some time later:

Dear Mrs. Tennille

Probably by this time you have heard from someone in the Squadron who told you the details of how your husband was killed. They might have told you that the tail gunner was the only one to get out alive. I was the tail gunner on that ship. I should have written you long ago, and I can't tell you how sorry I am that I haven't had the courage until now to do it. Even now I don't quite know what to write. I suppose you would like to know just what happened and why it happened. I can tell you just about what happened but I'm not sure about why.

The flak over Linz, Austria, which was our target, knocked out our No. 3 engine and punctured No. 1 tank. We lost a lot of gasoline before the engineer could get the gasoline transferred for No. 1 to the other tanks. Then he had to keep pumping just enough into No. 1 to keep it going and not so much that it would flow through the holes. As you can see this was rather a delicate operation. We didn't have enough gas to get over the Russian lines and just barely enough to make Italy, but we would have to fly over water, so the pilot, Lt. Shoener (?) decided the best deal would be to go to the Isle of Vis where there is an Emergency field. Vis is a little island just off the coast of Yugoslavia. Vis is a little farther but it would have been over land all the way and if we ran out of gas we could bail out with a pretty good chance of running into the partisans (?). (I was shot down last September and got out that way.)

He came in over the island and made one circle and came back at right angles to the runway. The control tower gave a green flare and told the pilot to make a left turn and come on in. We were about 200 feet off the ground at that time. Instead of going to the left the ship turned to the right into the dead engine. It started to slip and the nose came down. I had my chute on and the escape hatch was open. So I dived out and pulled the ripcord at the same time. My chute opened at almost the same instant the ship hit. I hit the ground a second later. The navigator dived out behind me but his chute didn't have time to open. Those on the flight deck didn't have a chance to get out. Capt. Tennille was riding on the flight deck but he was not the pilot or co-pilot. He was just riding along to get a mission in on order from Group HQ. I think that is really the most unfortunate part.

I know how you must feel about this and I do not know of anything I could say or do that would make it easier for you, but if there is anything

I can do please don't hesitate to write and tell me and I will do my best to help you in any way I can.

Robert H. Arnold

P.S. I hope you'll pardon me if this sounds too blunt for it is very hard for me to write exactly the way I would have said what I have just written. I hope you understand.

31 January 1945: Lt. John P. Frantz, Pilot, 782nd Squadron, flew a B-24J, #44-41159, to bomb the Moosbierbaum Oil Refinery, twenty two miles northwest of Vienna, Austria with crewmembers, Lt. Richard R. Coleman, Co-Pilot; Lt. Owen W. Maloney, Navigator; Lt. Chelsea H. Browne, Bombardier; Sgt. Robert E. Schroeder, Flight Engineer-Gunner; Sgt. Malcom A. MacDonald, Armorer-Gunner; Sgt. John L. Russell, Radio Operator-Gunner; Sgt. Miles C. Bozarth, Gunner; Sgt. John W. Dollman, Gunner and Sgt. Francis C. Wilson, Gunner. Their aircraft was last known to be in the Vienna area.

Eyewitness, Major R. C. Pease, Air Corps, S-2, "On 31 January 1945 while participating in an attack on the Moosbierbaum Oil Refinery near Vienna, Austria, Lt. John P. Frantz and crew were seen by other members of the formation to be behind and below the formation at the target. Interrogation of the crew has not been able to determine the nature of trouble or the whereabouts of the aircraft thereafter. This aircraft was not heard to call on the radio."

The crew bailed out and Lts. Frantz, Coleman, Maloney, and Browne and Sgts. Schroeder, MacDonald, Russell, Bozarth, Dollman and Wilson, were all captured and made Prisoners of War.

31 January 1945: Capt. Matthew B. Liles Jr., Pilot, 780th Squadron, flew a B-24L, #44-49084, Call Letter Yellow "U" to bomb the Moosbierbaum Oil Refinery, twenty two miles northwest of Vienna, Austria with crewmembers, Lt. Robert R. Caldwell Jr., Co-Pilot; Lt. John G. Carothers, Navigator; Lt. Gilbert R. Carter Jr., Navigator; Lt. Thomas P. Walton III, Bombardier; Lt. Clinton E. Dyess, Bombardier; Sgt. Donald B. Johnson, Nose Turret Gunner; T/Sgt. George Dippel, Flight Engineer-Gunner; S/Sgt. Homer C. York, Radio Operator-Gunner; S/Sgt. William R. Johnson, Ball Turret Gunner and S/Sgt. Dennis F. Gayner, Gunner. The weather was undercast at the target and their aircraft was last sighted over Zagreb, Yugoslavia at 14:00 hours. This was an eleven-man crew.

Eyewitness, S/Sgt. Leslie L. Miller, 780th Squadron, "On operational combat mission of 31 January 1945, from my position of tail gunner, I noted that Yellow

"U" fell back in the formation a few minutes before we reached the IP. At this time number 3 engine was being feathered. Although we were climbing, it was obvious that the plane was losing altitude. Instead of flying over the target, the pilot of Yellow "U" cut across to the left. After we had passed over the target, I again saw this plane, flying low about 7 o'clock. It continued to follow us, gradually falling behind. A few minutes before we hit Zagreb, Yugoslavia I lost sight of this plane entirely."

The mission was to bomb the Moosbierbaum Oil Refinery. The target was not reached as the bombs were jettisoned in the general target area after the aircraft lost an engine and now was losing oil pressure in another. The pilot, Lt. Liles, took up a heading to land at Pecs Airdrome where he ran off the end of the runway and crashed into a group of houses on the outskirts of the city.

Sgt. Donald B. Johnson, the nose gunner, was injured on landing and was removed at once to the Pecs hospital. His shoulder blade was chipped and all the muscles in his left arm were pulled. He remained in the Pecs hospital for thirty-five days and then was placed on a train for Bucharest, but when he felt he could no longer endure the hardships of traveling in a boxcar in his condition he asked to be allowed to get off at the next city, which was Subotica. At Subotica he was again placed in a hospital where he remained until 28 March when he was removed to Debrecen by American officers from that base. On 4 April he was evacuated by C-47 to Bari, Italy.

Sgt. Donald B. Johnson and Sgt. William R. Johnson both stated that the Russians have more respect for Americans with a gun but regardless, they will not tolerate any smart tactics and are very prompt to put you in your place if you get out of order. Don't discuss politics with Russians or Hungarians at any time. Hungarian soldiers should be avoided if possible, as some of them are hostile towards Americans because of our bombing of their cities. Lt. Dyess the bombardier, was injured on landing at Pecs and was confined to the hospital and claimed to have lost his memory in so far as remembering what happened to him before he regained consciousness in the hospital in Pecs. He was confined to the hospital on 31 January, the day of the mission, and remained in the hospital for forty-four days. He reported that he received excellent care. He was moved to Debrecen on 23 March 1945 where he was turned over to the American representatives. He was evacuated by C-47 to Naples on 27 March and taken to Bari, Italy on 28 March 1945. All members of this crew were evacuated.

5 February 1945: Lt. Robert C. Jones, Pilot, 781st Squadron, flew a B-24H, #42-52503, Call Letter Yellow "H" named "Belle Ringer" to bomb the Winterhafen Oil Storage Depot at Regensburg, Germany with crewmembers, Lt. William I. Dobbs, Co-Pilot; Lt. Arthur Silver, Navigator; Lt. Joseph E. Ormes, Bombardier; Sgt. Howard M. Fox, Flight Engineer-Gunner; Cpl. Charles H.

Duffield Jr., Radio Operator-Gunner; Cpl. Roscoe E. Fee, Armorer-Gunner; Cpl. Bernard J. Reardon, Gunner; Cpl. Carrol E. Elmore, Gunner and Cpl. Vernon M. Elsworth, Gunner. Their aircraft was last contacted by radio at 13:30 hours over the Adriatic Sea.

Eyewitness, 1st Lt. Argene Barnett, "While returning from the combat mission of 5 February 1945, I was listening to 4900 to the ships in the 465th Bomb Group. Yellow "H" was calling Able-1 and could not contact him so he called Easy -1 and told him to relay this message to Able-1. "He said he had an indication of 270 gallons of gas and he might not be able to make it back to the field." Later on he called Easy -1 and asked him to relay a message to Able-1. The message was "I don't think I can make it to the field and I am taking a heading of 165 degrees and going to Ancona." He also asked for the weather in northern Italy. The last call I received was about 50 miles south-southwest of Pola and that was when he said he was taking a 165 degrees heading."

Lt. Jones aircraft fell behind the formation as it left the coast of Italy, enroute over the Adriatic Sea to the base. The plane did not appear to be in any trouble on the return leg of the mission, and after leaving the coast of Yugoslavia. Jones had called Able - 1 and not getting any response, he called Easy -1, reporting that he had only 275 gallons of gas left and indicated that he was going to try to make the coast of Italy. Easy -1 advised him to call Big Fence for a heading. Big Fence replied and gave him a heading of 165 degrees to Ancona. Jones advised Big Fence that he did not have very much fuel and wanted to know the weather at Ancona. He was told that it was 100 feet. Jones then advised Big Fence that he was heading 165 degrees. No further transmissions were heard from Jones and no one reported seeing the aircraft again. It was assumed that they ditched not long after the last radio message and that the entire crew was, Killed In Action on this mission to Regensburg, Germany.

16 February 1945: Lt. William B. Lyon, Pilot, 783rd Squadron, flew a B-24J, #42-51871, Call Letter Blue "R" to bomb the Winterhafen Oil Storage Depot at Regensburg, Germany with crewmembers, Lt. William D. Wine, Co-Pilot; Lt. Leslie P. Turner, Navigator; S/Sgt. Owrie V. Brown, Flight Engineer-Gunner; S/Sgt. Charles A. Mangan, Radio Operator-Waist Gunner; S/Sgt. Raymond J. Collins, Armorer-Nose Turret Gunner; Sgt. David L. Busch, Armorer-Waist Gunner; Sgt. Herbert M. Gatling, Tail Turret Gunner and S/Sgt. Allen A. Honey, Armorer-Gunner. Weather was clear and their aircraft was seen to crash north of Straubing, Germany at 13:39 hours. This was a nine-man crew.

Eyewitness, S/Sgt. Alfonse J. Misuraca, "Fifteen minutes prior to target time, the nose-gunner reported number 1 engine was smoking on Blue "R." It continued smoking throughout the entire bomb run. Five minutes after bombs away, the martin gunner and left waist gunner saw the left wing explode and completely dismember itself from the rest of the plane. At this point, it was called to the attention of the tail gunner. The tail plane broke away from the fuselage. From the manner in which the plane was acting, it appeared that the pilot might have been fighting to regain control of it. The plane went into a spin, leveled off, nosed over and continued its crazy motions, until it crashed in a clear spot in a forest. Two chutes came out of the plane. One at approximately 15,000 feet and another at approximately 5,000 feet."

About thirty miles from Regensburg, the plane blew up with no warning. Lt. Wine was still in the co-pilot's seat, Lt. Turner, the navigator, was in the nose compartment. Sgt. Mangan, the radio operator, was in the waist, Sgt. Collins, was in the nose turret and Sgt. Gatling was in the tail turret about two minutes before the explosion and as the plane started spinning they did not have time to bail out. Lt. Lyon the pilot did not have his chute on and did not have time to bail out. He had given permission to Sgt. Brown, the flight engineer, to go into the bomb bay to help and the last time Brown saw Lyon he was standing at the entrance to the forward bomb bay with no chute holding out an oxygen hose to him. Sgts. Brown and Honey bailed out and were taken prisoner by the Germans. Sgt. Busch was in the waist by the window and he had taken his chute off to warm up just before the explosion. The German Airdrome Commandant told Sgt. Brown that Busch's body had been thrown clear of the plane and they had his identification tags. The following seven members of the crew were Killed In Action: Lts. Lyon, Wine, and Turner, and Sgts. Mangan, Collins, Busch and Gatling.

1 March 1945: 1st Lt. Frederic B. Withington Jr., Pilot, 780th Squadron, flew a B-24J, #44-41164, to bomb the Marshalling Yards at Maribor, Yugoslavia with crewmembers, Lt. Fred Jordan, Co-Pilot; F/O Edward M. Ryan, Navigator; F/O James C. McCloskey, Bombardier; S/Sgt. Kenneth L. Hardisty, Nose Turret Gunner; T/Sgt. John C. Schlomer, Flight Engineer-Gunner; Sgt. Martin L. Schlossberg, Radio Operator-Gunner; S/Sgt. Gerald K. Jackelen, Ball Turret Gunner; S/Sgt. Harry M. Weaver, Assistant Engineer-Gunner and S/Sgt. Harry Millington, Armorer-Gunner,

The weather over the target prevented bombing so the formation headed toward the alternate target. Near the north end of Lake Balaton, Lt. Withington's aircraft was hit several times by flak, which cut three hydraulic lines and the wires to the hydraulic system's electric pump. The formation continued on to the alternate target. Withington's bomb bay doors would not open entirely so over the target area the bombs were salvoed through part of the doors. Just after "bombs away" there was a direct flak hit on the left side just forward of the nose wheel, killing the bombardier, Flight Officer James C. McCloskey and mutilating his body from his chest upward.

There was a very close explosion or direct hit under the left wing just inside of the number 1 engine. There were also numerous large holes in the tail, in the vertical stabilizer. Throttle control cables to number 1 and number 2 engines were out. Both engines started leaking oil and fuel badly. Number 1 engine ran away and would not feather and finally froze and caused much drag. Number 2 engine kept running but gave little power. The Autopilot was about 80% of the instruments. The nose and flight deck interphone and nose oxygen systems were shot out. The aircraft turned on a 130 degree heading toward the center of Yugoslavia. When the condition of the aircraft became worse the pilot headed away from the towns, toward a hilly, wooded area, for bail out and all crewmembers bailed out safely leaving the bombardier's body in the aircraft.

The aircraft circled back, almost striking two men, then struck the ground and demolished near Brinjent. All crewmembers landed southeast of Zagreb in Croatia. F/O Ryan, the navigator broke his leg in three places, as his chute was swinging causing him to hit the ground hard. Sgt. Schlossberg, the radio operator had either a broken or badly sprained ankle from a hard landing. Sgt. Millington the tail gunner hung in a tree and had to let go and drop to get away from the approaching enemy and either broke or probably sprained his back. All crewmembers were collected together within five hours in the village of Kutinice. Ryan and Schlossberg were taken to a crude hospital. The rest of the crew spent the night in the town in Partisan hands. Lt. McCloskey was buried there the next day. On 2 March Millington was taken on a cart to the hospital, escorted by the rest of the crew. The rest of the crew then went on to Grannioa near Gravenitza and Cazma. They stayed there at an airstrip, waiting for it to dry out sufficiently to be used. On 8 March they were told that the enemy was attacking. In company with some British and some other Americans they walked to Sammoritza. The next evening they went to Novisole for about two hours and went on foot and by cart to Daravar. On this last stage they were accompanied by several hundred wounded Partisans from the hospitals near Novisole and the three injured members of their crew. From Daravar two days later, they were evacuated by C-47 aircraft to Belgrade and the next day they were evacuated by C-47 to Italy.

1 March 1945: 1st Lt. William J. Smith, Pilot, 781st Squadron, flew a B-24L, #44-48861, Call Letter Red "Y" to bomb the Oil Refinery at Moosbierbaum, Austria with crewmembers, Lt. Stanley J. Winkowski, Co-Pilot; Lt. Gaythor L. Cass, Navigator; Lt. Richard J. Bilger, Radar Navigator; 1st Lt. Arthur W. Bovett, Bombardier; T/Sgt. Charles J. Thein, Flight Engineer-Gunner; S/Sgt. Paul B. Ihde, Radio Operator-Gunner; S/Sgt. Robert B. Cohlmia, Gunner; S/Sgt. Arnold D. McElwain, Gunner; S/Sgt. Donald B. Postema, Gunner and

S/Sgt. James W. Hinton, Gunner. The weather was clear and their aircraft was last sighted near Lake Balaton at 14:26 hours. This was an eleven-man crew.

Eyewitness, Major Robert E. Scanlon, Air Corps, Hq. 465th Bomb Group, "On the combat mission on 1 March 1945, Lt. W. J. Smith, who was flying Red "Y" called the group leader and said that he was going to Russia. I presume he meant "Russian Territory." No one answered his call, so I acknowledged the call and reported it upon landing. I have no knowledge of his whereabouts at the time. My position was approximately thirty miles west of Lake Balaton."

On the mission to bomb the Moosbierbaum Oil Refineries, Lt. Smith's aircraft was damaged by flak while over the target but managed to salvo it's bombs with the other aircraft in the formation. Number 1 and number 3 engines were hit at the same time by flak and one caught on fire and the other one began throwing oil. The pilot asked Lt. Cass, for a heading for the Pecs Airdrome, which was easily located, and a successful landing was accomplished on a smooth surfaced, 3,000-foot runway. All guns, ammunition, flak suits and other loose equipment were jettisoned before reaching Pecs to insure the aircraft to maintain altitude. The crew was bent upon landing by two Russian Army Officers and identification was acknowledged without any difficulty. The Russian escape passes were recognized at once by those officers. A Russian guard was placed on the aircraft.

The crew had destroyed the radar equipment before landing and the Russian officials objected strenuously to this action, but it was too late, as the job had been effectively carried out. The crew was taken to the field Commandant's office after landing and here they were interrogated by an interrogator who took their name, rank and serial numbers and the serial number of the aircraft. The following day Lt. Smith was asked to sign a paper in quintuplicate, which the Russian Officer stated, was a receipt for the aircraft. The pilot was given one copy of this paper, which he retained.

On 3 March the crew was loaded in an open truck and started for Csovaly. Enroute the truck broke down and the driver came upon another truck, which also had just broken down, and between them they made one good truck out of the two. This operation included a complete engine change. At Csovaly the crew was housed in a small schoolhouse and given straw to sleep on. The food consisted of Barley soup and black bread three times a day. This was sometimes supplemented by tea at the evening meal but on the whole the food was very bad. The crew was able to buy eggs and other foodstuffs from the civilians in town and this aided considerably. On 10 March the crew left for Timisoara by freight car attached to a hospital train. They were given a few sausages and several loaves of bread each, to last them to Bucharest. They laid over in Timisoara to transfer to the Bucharest fast express in order to save time. This arrangement was made by a Major Baker, the ranking man in the group. At Timisoara they were housed with wealthy civilians and were treated quite well by them. From Timisoara they went by train to Bucharest where they were flown by C-47 to Bari, Italy on 22 March 1945.

2 March 1945: 1st Lt. Italo M. Gemmato, Pilot, 782nd Squadron, flew a B-24H, #42-52533, Call Letter White "O" named "No Love No Nothing" to bomb the North Marshalling Yards at Linz, Austria with crewmembers, Lt. Norman R. Stickney, Co-Pilot; Lt. Lawrence J. Smith Jr., Navigator; Sgt. William R. Snow, Flight Engineer-Gunner; Sgt. Leonard F. Day Jr., Armorer-Gunner; Sgt. Robert L. Linsley, Radio Operator-Gunner; Sgt. John C. Martin, Gunner; Sgt. Freeman L. Smith, Gunner and Sgt. Irving Eisenbaum, Gunner. There was a solid undercast and their aircraft was last sighted near Zagreb, Yugoslavia at 15:40 hours. This was a nine-man crew.

Eyewitness, Lt. Richard D. DeArment, 782nd Squadron, "On the rally at Linz, I saw White "O" in number five position. That was the last time that I saw him but my armorer gunner saw him fall back and at last sight, saw him approximately five miles back at seven o'clock, holding altitude at the position where Baker box bombs were dropped. There is a possibility that he was escorted by two P-38's however, the B-24 that was being escorted could not be identified."

Over a city near Amstettin, Lt. Gemmato's aircraft took a direct flak hit in the oil system of number 3 engine and it was partially feathered. He took a heading for Zara but fuel ran low and number 3 prop started windmilling and ran away. There was no undercast and all men bailed out safely and no injuries were sustained other than sprained ankles, and Lt. Stickney was knocked unconscious when he had a rough chute landing. The aircraft struck the ground and was completely demolished. All members of the crew landed within 10 miles northeast of Korsnice, Yugoslavia and they all met Partisans who fed them and kept them overnight at Korsnice. All crewmembers were together within twenty hours. They did not meet any Germans and had no trouble. The next night they went by Partisan truck to Lovenac. After one night there, they went by Partisan convoy to Grucac and stayed all night. The convoy ran out of gas and they continued in another convoy to Zara. From there they were evacuated to Italy by C-47 aircraft. Gemmato remained in the hospital at Bari for a few days due to the condition of his stomach, which resulted from food eaten during his evacuation. Lt. Stickney also remained in the hospital at Bari due to the concussion he suffered in bailing out. All other members of the crew were interrogated at 15th Air Force Headquarters, and returned immediately.

2 March 1945: 1st Lt. Robert E. French, Pilot, 781st Squadron, flew a B-24H, #42-52762, Call Letter Yellow "T" named "The Scorpia" to bomb the North Main Marshalling Yards at Linz, Austria with crewmembers, 1st Lt. Kenneth L. Parkhurst, Co-Pilot; F/O David Leslie Bowman, Navigator; Sgt. Denny W. Horton, Nose Turret Gunner; Sgt. Harold F. Quagan, Top Turret Gunner; Sgt. Francis M. Donohue Jr., Ball Turret Gunner; Sgt. William B. Briggs, Flight Engineer-Waist Gunner; Sgt. Frederick P. Wagner, Radio Operator-Waist Gunner and Sgt. Lehman V. Wood, Tail Turret Gunner. The weather was undercast at 10,000 feet and their aircraft was last sighted near Amstettin, Austria at 14:15 hours. This was a nine-man crew.

Eyewitness, S/Sgt. Douglas O. White, 781st Squadron, "On the combat mission on 2 March 1945, Yellow "T" flown by Lt. French, was flying right behind our ship. Between Linz and Amstetten, just before we reached Amstetten, Yellow "T" left the formation. Number one engine was smoking. There was an undercast at about 10,000 feet and I watched Yellow "T" until it went out of sight below the undercast. No one had bailed out and the plane seemed to be under control but it also seemed to be losing about six or seven hundred feet a minute. All men had plenty of time to bail out."

The aircraft was in heavy, accurate flak and took a hit in number 3 and number 4 engines and lost power intermittently in engines number 1 and 2. The aircraft lost altitude from 29,000 feet to 5,000 feet in forty-five minutes. Lt. French gave the order to bail out over the east side of Lake Balaton. The interphone was also knocked out, so Sgt. Wood the tail gunner, had little knowledge of the events leading up to the actual bailing out of the aircraft. Shortly after the plane came off the target, Sgt. Wagner the radio operator went to the tail turret and told Wood that their aircraft had been hit and they were heading for Russian territory. Later Sgt. Donohue the ball gunner came to Wood's position and told him to bail out immediately. Wood left his turret and went to the escape hatch, where he bailed out and he believes he was the first man to leave the plane.

He landed in a pond near a small village in Hungary. He sprained his ankle on landing and he also sustained groin injuries due to his parachute harness becoming tangled. His descent was made in a horizontal position and he landed almost face down. As soon as he got out of the pond, three Hungarian soldiers approached. He was struck by one of the soldiers and forced to take his clothes off at rifle point. While this was going on, Flight Officer Bowman the navigator, who had landed nearby came up with an English speaking Hungarian and they demanded that the soldiers return Wood's clothes. The soldiers refused until three Russian soldiers approached and took the clothes from the Hungarians and returned them to Sgt. Wood. The Hungarian soldiers were cuffed by the Russians and then hauled away in a cart with one of the Russians in charge. Wood was then taken to the nearby town where a civilian doctor treated his injuries.

That night he was taken to the Russian Commandant's house at Dumbovar, Hungary and from there he went to the hospital in that town. He remained there for two days and was then taken to Pecs, Hungary for two days and from there he was moved to Subotica, Yugoslavia. He remained there for about twenty days in the hospital. He was contacted by the Allied Mission in Debrecen, Hungary and they arranged for his transportation to Debrecen by jeep. He was evacuated from Debrecen to Bari, Italy on 4 April 1945. From the time Wood reached the small Hungarian village until his return to Italy, he was accompanied by Sgt. Donohue.

When Lt. Parkhurst the co-pilot bailed out, he drifted over a small village and landed in a farmer's field. In a matter of minutes he was surrounded by twenty-five or thirty very friendly Hungarians. In about five minutes two Russian soldiers rode up on horses yelling "Tovarich, Tovarich." They took Parkhurst to a small station house, stripped and searched him and when they saw his pack of Camel cigarettes, he was accepted as an American. He was then taken to the village of Taneshi and around midnight, Lt. French strolled in. They were assigned a Russian Sergeant to take them to an Allied Mission in Debrecen. They arrived in Debrecen at 11:00 P.M on 13 March 1945, returned to Naples and on 18 March they rejoined their Squadron. All members of French's crew returned safely.

Lt. Parkhurst, "Sgt. Wagner, the radio operator showed some guts, when he had to open his parachute while falling, with a knife that was sent to him by his brother just one week prior to this mission."

4 March 1945: 1st Lt. Curtis I. Eatman, Pilot, 782nd Squadron, flew a B-24H, #41-28906, Call Letter Red "Q" to bomb the Marshalling Yard at Szombathely, Hungary with crewmembers, Lt. Charles A. Hayman, Co-Pilot; Lt. William E. Evans, Navigator; Lt. Raymond Milakovic, Bombardier; T/Sgt. William E. Alvey, Nose Turret Gunner; S/Sgt. Edward W. Hahn, Top Turret Gunner; S/Sgt. James E. Stephens, Ball Turret Gunner; T/Sgt. Lemont H. Pakes, Flight Engineer-Waist Gunner; T/Sgt. James P. Powell, Radio Operator-Waist Gunner and S/Sgt. James S. Bugg Jr., Tail Turret Gunner.

When number one engine was lost, it was evident that the aircraft could not complete the mission. The target was not reached and the bombs were salvoed in open country near the I. P. at 11:35 hours. After the bombs were salvoed the aircraft took a heading to reach the briefed course for the home base. About fifteen minutes later, number 3 engine cut out and the pilot set course for the Pecs Airdrome. It was believed that the second engine was lost because of the stress put on the three remaining engines when the first engine was lost. Upon reaching

Pecs the aircraft did a 360 degree turn and let down through a hole in the overcast and landed without incident on a short but otherwise serviceable field.

Two red flares were fired by the Russians when the aircraft was on its final approach. The Russians identified the crew as American airmen without any hesitation or questioning and immediately set about to camouflage the aircraft with branches of trees. There were three other 15th AF B-24's on this Airdrome, one from the 465th Bomb Group, which was apparently intact. One from the 460th Bomb Group, which had been strafed and seriously damaged, and one from another group, but this aircraft could not be identified because it had been demolished by a German bomb. The aircraft flown by Eatman's crew needs two new engines to replace number one and number three, one air intake duct and gasoline. Eatman and his crew were eventually evacuated and returned to Bari, Italy.

14 March 1945: 1st Lt. Robert E. Martz, Pilot, 781st Squadron, flew a B-24L, #44-49085, Call Letter White "Y" to bomb the Marshalling Yards at Nove Zamky, Hungary with crewmembers, Lt. William A. Bradley, Co-Pilot; Lt. Lester Hershey, Navigator; Lt. Harold J. Long, Navigator; Lt. Herbert M. Volle, Radar Operator; Lt. Peter P. Renzo, Bombardier; S/Sgt. William M. DeForest Jr., Nose Turret Gunner; T/Sgt. Vincent A. Beeson, Flight Engineer-Gunner; T/Sgt. George M. Smith, Radio Operator-Gunner; S/Sgt. Edward Dworetzky, Waist Gunner; S/Sgt. Joseph A. Gallelli, Waist Gunner and S/Sgt. William J. Brannon Jr., Tail Turret Gunner. The weather was clear with good visibility when their aircraft was seen to crash, one mile south of the Marshalling Yards at 13:35 hours. This was a twelve-man crew.

Sgt. Beeson the flight engineer, is the only member of Lt. Martz's crew to have survived and this is his account of the mission: "It was a dark and cold morning when we were awakened for the mission. We went to briefing to hear about the flak, the target, the type of bombs, etc., then to the flight line to our assigned plane White "Y". Assembling at the plane were Lt. Robert Martz, his crew and an extra lead navigator and mickey operator (Radar) making it a crew of 12. We were to fly number two position on this mission to the Marshalling Yards at Nove Zamky, Hungary. We started engines, taxied out, took off and began a routine flight to the target area. On the bomb run the flak was not heavy but it was very accurate, bursting right into the formation.

Sgt. Brannon the tail gunner, reported the flak was following our airplane and then there were three bursts right behind the aircraft, with the last one 200 feet behind and the next burst was right into the plane underneath the pilot's seat. By this time the bombs had been dropped and we were just getting ready to rally off the target to the right. There was a small fire by the pilot's side and at a quick glance, I could see that Lt. Martz had been fatally wounded because of the amount of steam from his body and the blood and because of the part of his body that was not there any more. I hit the alarm button on the dash as Lt. Bradley the co-pilot, was trying hard to control the plane. The engines were out of control and running wildly.

Suddenly the plane veered sharply to the left, swung around and although I had no command to bail out, I grabbed my chest chute, snapped it on my harness, then fell off the flight deck and down into the bomb bay. I saw Lt. Renzo the bombardier, carrying his parachute in one hand and his boots in the other. He was not wearing an oxygen mask. Sitting on the catwalk, I rolled out, falling for quite a distance. Mistakenly, I had put my parachute on upside down and instead of the ring being on the right hand side, it was on the left hand side. Reaching over, I pulled the ring and the chute flared out in front of me and popped open. In those few seconds I felt sure the harness was going to unsnap as I had put it on backwards. As I was falling before the chute opened, I must have been on my back as I could see the aircraft above me going around in circles.

Shortly after my chute opened, I could hear small arms fire from the ground as people were shooting at me and I could hear people yelling and screaming and dogs barking. To the west of me, I could see the smoke and flames from the small town, which we had just bombed. I could not see where our plane had gone down. By this time I had landed in a small thicket of 25-foot trees. I landed in a tree and slid out of my harness and dropped to the ground. The chute was like a white beacon in the tree. I then ran into a little valley and hid behind a log. Then I heard some more yelling and I turned around to look. There were civilians looking down on me and pointing at me.

They marched me back to the tree and pulled the parachute cords off the tree and were going to wrap them around my neck and hang me. Fortunately, a German soldier came up to us, firing his rifle into the air. The civilians stepped back and released me. We ran out of the woods, across fields, and then to a barn, and I was locked in a stable that had no windows. I lay there for an hour, then a soldier came in who spoke English. He asked me about the crew but I said "No Capich." They were concerned who my fellow crewmembers were and how many were in the plane. As it was getting dark, they walked me to a town called Popa.

From there I was put in a civilian prison and spent 7 days there. Every night there were bombings, probably Russians. Leaving at night, we headed north, stopping during the day where we stayed in small barns. There were 7 of us now, including 2 Russians. The Russians could hardly walk as the Germans were beating them with sticks and fists. In some of the towns we went through, we were stoned and spit upon. The Germans let some of it happen, then would make the civilians stop it. From there we headed toward Bratislava. Then traveling some on rail car, but walking most of the time, we arrived in Vienna where a bombing mission was in progress. Our guards locked us in a small streetcar and they headed for the bomb shelters. We sat in the middle of a square and the bombing was in another part of the city. We could see the action but were not hit. After the raid, we spent the rest of the day in a small hut along the railroad. The Russians were now separated from the group.

We headed west and reached Linz and then Innsbruck then traveled north to Nürnberg. There my electric heated suit was taken from me, leaving me with long underwear and coveralls. They issued a square dog tag with their information on it, which I wore along with my regular dog tag. They took my wristwatch and pocketknife. Then we headed south to Moosberg. One morning on the march some P-47's came down shooting at us and when they realized we were prisoners they stopped shooting and came back over and did a victory roll. Soon the American troops showed up and the small contingent of Germans surrendered. Three days later we were in Camp Lucky Strike, France and were taken to a nearby port and boarded a ship for the USA.

Mister Willis M. DeForest the father of S/Sgt. Willis M. DeForest Jr., the top turret gunner, requested information concerning his son's fate and the following letter dated 10 September 1946 was written to him by a Mr. Zoltan Galambos, Pastor of the Reformed Church of Komarno, which is about 30 miles from Nove Zamky:

My text for today: O Lord, thou hast pleaded the causes of my soul; thou hast redeemed my life.

Reverend Sir, my dear friend and brother! In answer to your letter of June 11, I wrote at once. On July 20 and Aug. 17, I informed you that we had some results. Herein enclosed is my wife's account who, with my son Gedeon (who is a student of Theology), personally investigated the accident of DeForest. Jr. The account is my wife's. I thank God that he permitted us through this service to show our brotherly love.

I ask your kindly answer that I may be assured that my letter has reached you. Please inform M. Farkas about receipt of my letter at the following address: Budapest XII, Geal u. 10/a faz. 1. Hungary Europe.

With brotherly greetings in the Lord Jesus, Zoltan Galambos.

"At the time of the accident, there was a great deal of turmoil in this section of Europe. Air raids followed one upon the other and the front came nearer. The residents suffered greatly. For three months people lived in cellars and many were killed in the air raids. Many planes crashed in this region of whose fate we know nothing because of rapidity of events in this turmoil. At the time Mr. DeForest, there were terrible air raids about 30 kilometers from Komarno, as the crow flies, at Nove Zamky which brought about dreadful destruction in the city and it's populace. Even today the scene of the destroyed city fills one with dread.

We know we deserve our punishment from God for our sins, for our great unbelief. But is also good to know, that with all this, God wants to draw us closer to him. And how good it is that in recognizing, we can be brothers with those whose heart aches across the ocean. We know no one in Nove Zamky. There is but one affiliate church there without a Pastor, their church was destroyed in the bombing. Through official channels we got very little information, therefore through prayer I asked the Lord to guide our path and to bring to us men who were witnesses to the happenings. Miraculously, it was so. We came upon an upright working man who at that time worked with others at clearing away the fliers.

His name is John Agg and he lives at Nove Zamky. He readily told us everything. All planes that crashed were taken by the German soldiers and permitted no one to draw close to them immediately. Only when the dead were to be taken away did they order workers there, among whom was John Agg.

On this day in this region only one plane fell, that which Mrs. DeForest signified. Every passenger of this plane found his death, (except the one who parachuted to earth and took the news to Mrs. DeForest). To get a true understanding, it must be known that because of the conditions of war the dead could only be buried only a couple of days later. It is therefore likely that by the time the witness arrived by the dead they had been stripped of all things, articles of equipment, clothing, etc. John Agg says there were twelve bomber dead, but there was a name tag on one only. The machine burrowed deep into the ground and was mostly burned and of the crew the bodies of six were under the plane or in the wreckage. They were burned to a great extent, their clothing burned and there was no identification tag nor other metal thing on them.

Four were found without burns, three quite close to the plane but there were no tags on them by this time and they had also been killed, while one, the fourth, lay dead in a corn field. Only this one had a name tag on him which was taken by a German officer present, who put it into his pocket. This one remained uninjured with his clothes on because the tall corn hid him and they did not notice him nor strip him. When I read the names of the bomber's crew to John Agg who, at the reading of the name, Lester (Hershey) exclaimed: "Lester! That's it, I remember that certainly." This one name is definitely sad proof that the witnesses stood about the bodies of the victims of the "Liberator" we were seeking. He also remembered that there was among the dead, an exceptionally tall man whom they could hardly place upon the stretcher. The three lying close to the plane were similar tall blond (fair) ones. Ten dead were gathered together and taken in one auto to the cemetery in Nove Zamky. We went to the cemetery also and received the necessary information from the cemetery caretaker (gravedigger), whose name is Joseph Molnar, who personally buried them.

In this beautiful and orderly cemetery rest the ten dead American fliers in a common grave: IV tablet, 11 Row, 10 Grave, which is wider than the ordinary and not the rounded and unmarked kind in use here. Therefore, the gravedigger alone and my son and I, know who rest in the grave, we who stood beside the grave, sympathized from this great distance with their loved ones. I asked the gravedigger to raise the graves a little and to mark it with something. He said, if someone cared for the grave, or if he knew that some day their relatives might visit it, he would take better care of it. Should Mrs. DeForest desire to have a grave marker or some inscription be placed upon the grave, though we do not live in that city, we would be glad to take care of the matter, if we received authorization for it and if we live and are still here. Otherwise, about their graves are mostly the graves of the victims of the bombings. We also met two workmen here who were at the wrecked plane. Their witnessing agreed with that of John Agg.

One man augmented it with one particular, which ought to be submitted with much consideration and caution with relatives. He says that the wrecked plane may still be seen at the place it crashed and, according to his statement, slumped upon the steering apparatus of the plane, is a skeleton. This was probably the pilot (perhaps Robert Martz), the eleventh dead, inasmuch as only ten were buried. Up to this time, they were unable to remove him from the wreck. This, I submit with reservations, as I was not able to personally see it, because I would have had to walk many kilometers, but because of my weak heart, I could not volunteer for this.

That, which I received from the witnessing of John Agg and the stories of the other witnesses which agree with this, may be summed up and reconstructed as follows: The machine was damaged and Robert E. Martz was fatally wounded. Then one jumped out and returned to America. The machine crashed and burned. In these last moments, four others jumped, but because the machine was close to earth, their parachutes did not open. These must have been the three blonds (fair ones) and Lester Hershey. The others remained in the machine. We could not get official certificates at City Hall, because they were buried anonymously and the official, who might have said something, was on vacation. Should Mrs. DeForest, or others, come to visit the grave and should come to us, we should be glad to guide them. Mrs. DeForest says, she prayed that she might find out what happened to her son: God has given this to her. He will surely give her the strength to receive from his hand this great sorrow. So she will receive comfort not from man, but from God. Permit me to bid farewell with that word which is written in the letter to the Romans 8:32.

(You may write to us in English).

Lts. Martz, Bradley, Hershey, Long, Renzo, and Volle and Sgts. Smith, Brannon, DeForest, Dworetzky and Gallelli, were all Killed In Action. T/Sgt. Vincent A. Beeson Flight Engineer-Gunner was captured and made a Prisoner of War.

15 March 1945: 1st Lt. Richard Bodycombe, Pilot, 782nd Squadron, flew a B-24 to bomb the Marshalling Yards at Graz, Austria with crewmembers, F/O Joe Boone, Co-Pilot; F/O Jim Sgroi, Navigator; Sgt. Joe Boyle, Flight Engineer-Top Turret Gunner; Sgt. Pinky Conner, Radio Operator-Waist Gunner; Sgt. Bob Ersepke, Waist Gunner; Sgt. Ed Hollingsworth, Ball Turret Gunner; Sgt. John Weber, Tail Turret Gunner and Sgt. Jimmy Sanders, Nose Turret Gunner. This was a nine-man crew. Their aircraft was damaged by enemy Anti-Aircraft fire and they were forced to crash land on the Island of Vis. This is Lt. Bodycombe's account of that crash landing:

As the heavy bomber war (15th AF style) evolved in the Italian theater, Groups usually had four Squadrons assigned with anywhere from 10 to 14 aircraft assigned per squadron. Normally the tasking order would direct each Squadron to mount 7 airplanes in a combat box. The boxes were called quite naturally Able (lead Sq.), Baker (high Sq. to the right), Charlie (low Sq. to the left), and Dog Sq. (again to the right and the lowest of all). Within each Squadron the leader was rightfully #1, his Deputy on his right wing was #2, the left wing man was #3, the slot man #4, his right wingman was #5, left wingman was #6, and the poor guy in the low slot was "Tail End Charlie" or #7. Seniority within the Squadron was determined by the number of missions the crew had flown, so for the first month or two you were absolutely guaranteed to be stuck in #7 or #6 positions. As my crew and I survived December and January of 1945, a unique situation developed. It soon went from gossip to reality that my co-pilot (Joe Boone) was probably the best formation pilot in the outfit. Once the Squadron Operations became aware of Joe's potential, from then on when it was the 782nd's turn to lead the Group, Bodycombe's crew jumped a lot of seniority and wound up on the Old Man's left wing. So this was the situation on 15 March 1945.

The tasking order that day laid a heavy load on the 465th Group. The group was required to put up 36 aircraft, divided into two Task Forces of 18 aircraft each, the Red and the Blue. Major John Charlton was assigned to lead the Blue Force with Bodycombe's crew on his left wing. Take-offs started at 0825 hours, and all 36 aircraft got off safely. As I remember, everything was normal throughout the climb-out and transit over the Alps and into airspace over Austria. Evidently the weather was poorer than forecast, and the bombardiers were having trouble. Over the command radio we heard that the Task Forces should split, with the Red Force headed toward their alternate target of Bratislava, and the Blue Force to hit the Graz, Austria Marshalling Yards. After leaving the IP (Initial Point), we started to receive flak that the official report classified as "moderate, accurate, and heavy." Joe Boone was doing his usual good job of putting our right wing tip almost in the "old man's" cockpit, which left me to watch the flak bursts walking around in front of us. The bomb bay doors came open, and Joe asked for a little more power, so I brought the prop RPM up some (probably to around 2300). I remember one bright burst almost off our nose, and the airplane started to bounce a little.

Then a short time later out of the corner of my left eye, I saw a sight I will never forget! Out of the top of #1 engine cowling near the accessory section came a steady stream of critical parts of that wonderful P&R (Pratt & Whitney) W R-1830 engine. And then magically, #1 propeller very quietly and gracefully went into a full-feathered mode. I saw Joe's left hand start to jab the throttles to keep from falling out of position in the formation. I tapped his hand hard, and when he gave me a quick peek, I pointed to #1 standing at attention. Fortunately, the bombs went away a few seconds later, and we could ease out of the formation as we started to fall down and away.

Days later in our critique about what happened, we figured a shell went right through the wing and the rear of #1 engine without exploding. I think that was the best thing that happened to us all day. Blue Force turned south towards our home base, and started to descend. We were keeping them barely in sight, when #2 engine started to surge and the propeller kept trying to overspeed. Joe was still hanging on to the yoke, so I suggested on interphone that we slow up a little to try to keep #2 prop under control. To assist slowing, I went to the prop toggle switches (electrically controlled), and discovered to my horror that #3 and #4 were stuck at the high RPM I had set a few minutes earlier. By reducing the throttles a little more, we were able to keep #2 engine almost under control. By this time, the formation had left us behind. We were sinking about 300 feet a minute, but since we had started at 25,000 feet, altitude was not a problem at that time.

Then something happened that was a concern. We were slowly sinking into a cloudbank straight ahead, and almost instantaneously the front windshields became covered with ice. Now the US Army Air Corps had issued me a dandy little card back in the States during training that said I was "instrument rated." But that was in training under a blind-flying hood back in sunny Alabama and Arizona, plus quite a few hours in the pesky little Link trainer that often seemed like a torture chamber. So this became the first time either Joe or I had been in actual weather. We struggled to remember what the artificial horizon was trying to tell us, while both hanging onto the heading the navigator provided and still keep the wounded bird going down at a reasonable rate. But my troubles were far from over! With a giant "whoosh" my oxygen mask was forced off my face with a pressure blast, and within seconds all the oxygen at my crew station was gone. I motioned to Joe Boyle, the flight engineer who normally fired the top turret, who was then standing right behind me. He saw my problem, and because were still at 20,000 feet or so, he quickly brought me several of the small 3-minute yellow oxygen bottles to keep me going. Because of all this activity, I was hyperventilating big time! I was sucking up the 3-minute supply in a hurry until I got myself under control. Joe very efficiently gathered up all the small bottles on board, refilled them as necessary, and set up a little assembly line alongside my seat until we got down to a more breathable altitude.

In our descent, now slowed to about 100-150 feet per minute, we finally came out of the clouds and could see the mountainous region of Northern Yugoslavia. Joe Boyle and Joe Boone and I then began a nervous attempt to determine our fuel state. The fuel quantity gauges on a B-24 were four slender glass tubes located just around the corner of the bomb bay. Fuel sloshed up and down in these glass tubes, which supposedly were calibrated on the sides to indicate gallons of fuel remaining. In the rough air, it was very difficult to determine the real numbers of gallons remaining. Back in the States in training, we were advised to disregard these gauges. With the props stuck at high RPM and #1 engine shutdown, we had both a transfer of fuel and a shortage of fuel problem all rolled together. Collectively, the two Joe's and I were sure we couldn't get back across the Adriatic Sea to our base in Italy. Remembering our briefing that morning, I asked the navigator for a heading to the Yugoslavian island of Vis, which the command had listed as the preferred primary emergency recovery strip. This island, which was about 10 miles off shore, turned out to be a key command post for Marshall Tito's Partisan forces.

As we approached Vis, the radio chatter told us we weren't the only crew that had this in mind. The island was very rocky, and somehow the Partisans had carved about a 3,500-foot hard surfaced strip. The problem was the approach. You had the sea at one end and rocks at the other. There was plenty of activity when we got over the runway. The Brits were running the control tower, and as I found later, also the base hospital. They cleared us to land, and in a somewhat anioxic condition I started an awkward righthand overhead pattern. Joe Boone solemnly advised that there were crunched and burning B-24's on both sides of the runway. We felt sure the status of our hydraulic system was somewhat in doubt, but the landing gear clanked out right on schedule.

However, the wing flaps seemed to be acting peculiar and the brake pedals seemed sort of spongy when I tried them. Evidently my pattern was high and overshot to the left (mostly because #2 began cutting in and out). We were long and hot, and when we went out the far end of the runway I could still see 80mph on the airspeed. Rocks started coming through the nose, and we went up almost to a vertical position. As the nose began to compact together it bent slightly left, leaving me compressed into the yoke and the front dash. The fuselage split on the right side, and Joe Boone unsnapped his seat and literally stepped out on to the ground. The rest of the crew jumped out and started running away. Out of the corner of my eyes I saw little flames from #2 engine, but no fire developed only because we were out of fuel.

After my crew so unceremoniously left the area, my survival instincts kicked in. I knew I was mashed into the controls, but as the aircraft began to creak and settle back from it's almost vertical position I had a little more "wiggle" room each time it moved. Then to my great surprise, a huge bearded figure of a Yugoslavian Partisan appeared outside my side of the cockpit. He reached in through the broken window frame and started trying to pull me out. I yelled out in pain and tried to show him that I was pinned in from the waist down. He kept pulling and I kept yelling, and finally in desperation I made a sort of fist and tried to punch him. He recoiled back, and with a few choice Serbian words about my Welsh ancestry, he left. Now some period of time elapsed, and I knew I was going into shock. Once more the aircraft lurched into a near horizontal position, and I was able to push myself out. I took off running almost blindly into the rock-strewn airfield. Later, the British doctor told me that it was not possible that I could have run with my right leg in the condition that it was. But some of the corpsmen driving the ambulance that scooped me up confirmed my wild run until I collapsed. The rest of the mission was somewhat of a blur to me. I knew I was hurting badly that night in the British field hospital (a Quonset hut). Thankfully, a big Yugoslavian Partisan lady came by with a goatskin pouch filled with wonderful red wine. The man laying next to me had a broken back from his B-24 crash, so I tried to quit moaning. We were airlifted off the island several days later by a USAAF air-evac C-47 to the 15th Air Force hospital in Bari, Italy. They kept my crew together while I recuperated, and we flew 8 more missions before the end of the European war. Years later some of my crew told me what happened when they were able to return to the wreck later that same afternoon.

They saw US salvage experts, some civilian employees of Consolidated-Vultee corporation included, quickly unscrew all four engines, and throw a huge cable around the fuselage just behind the waist windows and separate it for use as spare parts. The remains of the aircraft were bulldozed off to the side into a giant pile of aluminum junk. In summary, and reading from the official report, I learned that "bomb strike photos show Blue Force made hits in the North end of the South Graz Marshalling Yards and the South end of the North Marshalling yards as well as striking buildings in the Engineering Works and the bridge construction works."

"33 aircraft landed at 1645 hours. 2 aircraft landed at 1900 hours after landing at friendly fields for refueling, and one aircraft landed at Vis and has not returned to base." And take it from me, that aircraft never will!

s/ Major General Richard Bodycombe (Ret).

22 March 1945: 1st Lt. William E. Herman, Pilot, 783rd Squadron, flew a B-24L, #44-49894, Call Letter Blue "U" to bomb the Helingenstadt Marshalling Yard at Vienna, Austria with crewmembers, Lt. David N. Reeher, Co-Pilot; Lt.

William W. Edwards, Navigator; Lt. Kern McIlhenny, Bombardier; Sgt. Billy J. Irwin, Nose Turret Gunner; Sgt. Thomas F. Dennick, Top Turret Gunner; Sgt. Ernest Fink, Ball Turret Gunner; S/Sgt. Earl E. Eiberger, Flight Engineer-Waist Gunner; Sgt. Doyle B. Mayo, Radio Operator-Waist Gunner and Sgt. Robert J. Canterbury, Tail Turret Gunner. Weather was clear and their aircraft was last sighted over Austria at 12:53 hours.

Eyewitness, Lt. Robert S. Anderson, "This is what I saw happen to Blue "U". About thirty seconds after bombs away a direct hit between number three and four engine, which exploded the gas tanks, and the whole wing, and side of the fuselage, was aflame. The ship went right, and down. The gunners saw two chutes, and we peeled to the right and lost sight for a moment. A few seconds later the whole tail assembly twisted off. This happened about 12:58 hours."

On the rally, after bombing the Vienna Marshalling Yards, the aircraft was hit by a direct burst of flak between engines number 3 and 4. A sheet of flame covered the entire wing and the aircraft went into a violent spin. The navigator, Lt. Edwards, bailed out after the bombardier. Edwards and Sgt. Dennick bailed out, with difficulty, due to centrifugal force. After his chute opened, Edwards saw the right wing come off the aircraft, which then crashed afire into Vienna and exploded. He landed on a roof and his left arm was injured in landing and he required assistance from civilians to get down. He was met by armed policeman, who took him to the street. Here they were met by a mob of about 200 people, armed with clubs, etc. They beat him thoroughly though the policeman made an attempt to protect him.

As he lapsed into unconsciousness, a group of soldiers with submachine guns rescued him. He regained consciousness in a car, just as they reached a city prison, used by the Gestapo. All of his personal belongings and flying clothing had been removed. In the prison a preliminary interrogation was made. A list was made of his belongings and he had to sign the list.

Sgt. Dennick bailed out of the front bomb bay. Both Edwards and Dennick were shot at on the way down, and Dennick's chute was hit 2 or 3 times. He landed on the roof of a hospital. The chute dragged him off of the roof, and then caught on the roof, leaving him dangling against the side of the building. He could hear a mob, and could see them below, pulling palings off a wooden fence and shaking them at him. He kicked in a window, and managed to get his straps off and get in. As he got in, he was met by the mob coming, and was well beaten. Five German-speaking soldiers came, one with a pistol, and four with submachine guns. They disarmed him, and took him through the street around and into a cellar. The street was filled with people, who were attempting to reach between the soldiers to reach Dennick. He removed his flying clothes, both for comfort and to change his appearance as much as possible, in case of another

152

encounter with the mob. An officer came and gave orders, and they went out to a truck. Dennick with four guards rode in the back of the truck.

In about ten minutes, they reached a police station, where a civilian joined them. Then they went to another place, where they all went in. Here a civilian and a stenographer checked his dogtags against a previous record they had taken. This civilian had jammed Dennick's 45 and had him clear it. He was then taken to the jail, where he met Lt. Edwards. There dog tags were taken, and put with their personal belongings. They were interrogated by a German officer, who spoke excellent English. He had formerly been professor of English at a University. He was very courteous, and apologized for their treatment by the civilians. They said that the soldiers had been very prompt and had been helpful in moving them from the mobs, when only a minute or two of delay would have meant death. The only time this officer seemed annoyed was when Dennick asked him how far Vienna was from Germany. The officer was momentarily indignant, and said, "This is Germany." They were told that this prison was used by the Gestapo, and was about 2 blocks from the Gestapo Headquarters. The prison was by the first bridge across the canal, the Gestapo Headquarters was by the third bridge. Civilian prisoners were taken to the Headquarters at times for questioning and brought back badly beaten. Some German deserters were also kept in the prison, pending probable execution.

The officer told them they would remain only over night, then they would be taken, 30 Kilometers to the Stalag. Edwards still needed medical attention. He and Dennick were put in a 20X20 foot room, with a toilet, six beds, and 16 other men. They were not allowed to lie down during the day. They were fed, with the room commandant distributing the food. There was bread for all, but only 16 pieces of meat; the guard saying there was no meat for the "gangsters." Later a man from the kitchen insisted that they both got some meat. The next morning there was a different guard, a much better one. They asked him, through an interpreter prisoner, when they would be moved. He said that typhus had broken out in the prison, and they would be quarantined until 15 April.

They protested, saying that as military prisoners, under the "Geneva Convention" they could not be held in the Gestapo prison, but must be put in a military prison. The guard said he knew that, but with the quarantine no one could go in or out of the prison. That afternoon the guard came back and said the quarantine was only until 6 April. It was very boring. Nothing was allowed in the room except the people - no pencils, games, etc. Newspapers, such as the High Beobachter, containing mostly Berlin communiqués came in daily, with much comment on the "American gangsters."

While there, they found the reason for the mobs. On 12 March (or possibly 8 March), American aircraft had bombed the center of town, destroying the theater and opera house, breaking down into the ancient catacombs, killing 750 people in the opera house and many more in the streets. Until then the Viennese had not been angry at the Americans, as they could understand the bombing of the marshalling yard and nearby houses, but they could not understand the bombing of the center of the town, where there were no military targets. It made the people very angry. The guard told them that, on their own raids, two aircraft were shot down, and that the two of them were the only ones who lived. The first day, Edwards and Dennick, found that there was supposed to be an American in the next cell, but the man spoke very poor English.

The original two guards alternated, 24 hours per shift. The good one, an Austrian, would often give them a little extra food in a separate room. The guard brought the other "American" to meet them. The "American" was dressed in old clothing, and said he was preparing to escape. However, his questioning made him sound like a spy. The room was being scrubbed with disinfectant three times a day, and all clothes were deloused and they were given a bath.

They got a little extra food and some cigarettes from a former government minister then in prison, and they gave him an improvised colt (pistol) for the cigarettes. Cigarettes in prison could normally be gotten only on the prisoner's black market, ten marks for any cigarette (newspaper wrapping or tailor-made), ten to twenty for a gold ring, etc. Water was brought in only once a day in two jugs. At other times during the day, the other prisoners would refill jugs from the back of the toilet, but Edwards and Dennick say they never got that thirsty. They got much information from a Czech, who spoke some English. He acted as an interpreter.

Prison life was very monotonous. About 3 April, they heard that the Russians had reached Baden. They also heard, from long-time French prisoners, who were acting as orderlies, that the Gestapo was burning all records and preparing to leave. The whole prison was excited. The Mayor of Vienna wanted to surrender Vienna as an open city, but the Governor of Vienna issued a proclamation that Vienna was to be defended. The SS took over the defense. News was smuggled to the prisoners, written on a piece of wax paper concealed in a jar, that there was a bad typhus epidemic in the city, that bread was short, and there was no supply of bread in sight for the next week. There had been no water, gas, or electricity in the city from 1 March until 27 March, and then there was only water, at infrequent intervals. By now the Gestapo had left, and the SS was in full charge.

Arrangements had been made for a place to go to hide, if the prison walls were breached by bombs or shelled. Lt. Edwards had the address in writing. Also written for him, in German, were questions as to the route. A Rumanian officer wrote for him, in French, the same sentence as was on his escape identity card, as there were many French workers in the city. Edwards also got 100 marks from a Yugoslav doctor. On 7 April the friendly guard said he might be able to get them out. He moved them into the cell with the other "American," of whom Edwards and Dennick were still suspicious. This man said he had lived in New York, was part of an American mission, and was traveling under a false name, but said he could tell them nothing else. They wrote the friendly guard a helper's chit, for his help. This guard said he was not a Nazi, but an Austrian, but that he had the choice of acting as a Nazi or not living.

About 16:00 hours, this guard brought an old guard, who told the three that he would be willing to help them escape, that the SS were checking people closely and that it was a 50-50 chance, that they would either escape or lose their heads. There was also the choice that they might stay in the prison and sweat out the Russian advance, but since the prisoners were mostly political prisoners, the SS might decide any day to wipe them out with guns or gas. The three Americans decided to try the escape. The Austrian guard got all of Lt. Edward's maps, personal effects, etc., back from the police. Most of Sgt. Dennick's things had been taken by soldiers, and could not be returned by the guard. The Germans had never been willing to return the food kits, but had sent them away for analysis. They thought some of the concentrated goods were poisonous, to be taken in case of capture. The two guards even brought their flying clothes and Mae West's, and some bread. The guards got some civilian clothes from some French, so they could wear these clothes over their uniforms. The old guard seemed to be in the position of authority.

They were each given an official "release from prison" showing them to be civilians and authorizing them to get ration cards from the Burgomeister. The guard said these might help. The third American was to answer any questions, ask the questioner which language he could speak, and then say Edwards and Dennick only spoke some other languages. This third man spoke Czech, German, and three or four other languages. They started walking through Vienna in civilian clothes with Edwards and Dennick, carrying their flying clothes in two big brown paper bundles. They had been unable to leave them behind, as other prisoners and prison personnel thought it was a transfer on which they would take their equipment. The streets were full of SS and German soldiers, with only a few civilians. They had to cross the canal to get to the proper address.

As the bridges were heavily guarded, they dumped the packages in a bomb crater in a park, and walked in an unconcerned manner across the bridge past the guards. Only packages or wagonloads of goods were being searched. They pretended to be carrying on a conversation, the third man talking in German and Edwards and Dennick answering "Ja, Ja." The three reached the house for which they were looking. Here they were met by a doctor who knew the third man. The owner greeted the third man with a hug, and under cover of this got information about Edwards and Dennick. He then gave them a big greeting and told bystanders that the three were his best friends, bombed out of Wiener Neustadt. They were taken into the cellar, which was partitioned off into sections for all the people to live in. However, the landlord complained about the extra people. Also, whatever nationality they claimed, someone there would be able to speak the language. So they got some extra clothes from the man, such as a coat and some better fitting clothes, and they went out again.

They had to go across the canal again, to a second contact. In case the landlord had been suspicious and spread an alarm, they went a long way, traveling about five kilometers to cover a one-kilometer distance. Lt. Edwards traveled with the Yugo doctor and Sgt. Dennick with the original Czech-American. Edwards reached the apartment all right. Dennick and the Czech-American were halted by three or four Volksturm and searched. The Volksturm were excited, too, and gave them only a casual search, the papers getting them through. These two then caught up with the first two. The woman doctor was not at her apartment, so the four went to the clinic where she worked. She came down with some food in a bag, and asked no questions. They all went directly to her apartment. This time, even though on the same route, they did not see the Volksturm (who, in this case, had been only fifteen or sixteen years old, but had bayoneted rifles).

The four men stayed in the apartment until 11 April, when the Russians got there. During this time, the woman furnished some food, which consisted of potatoes and more potatoes. The Germans searched some apartments in the house, and put a machine-gun nest in the corner apartment, next door. There was another machine-gun nest across the street, and snipers were all around. Edwards, Dennick and the other two, would sleep in whatever room seemed safest from the current shooting.

The Yugo doctor went out (after the Russians arrived, to get a Russian). He came back with a Russian officer, who was holding a gun in his back, in case it was a trap. There was a big celebration, with a bottle of Champagne, which the woman had. They could make all of the noise they wished, for the first time in five days. Previously they had to be very quiet, and tiptoe, as the neighbors around and underneath knew that only one person lived in that apartment. The Russian then took them to Corps Headquarters. Corps Headquarters could do nothing for them, so sent them back toward Division Headquarters. They walked to where it was, 7 kilometers away, and then found it had just moved into Vienna. They found it in the grounds of the hospital where the woman doctor worked, 7 blocks from where they stayed. At this headquarters the four were treated very well, and given a shave and haircut, and fed well. Edwards and Dennick, and the Czech-American, were started toward Army Headquarters on foot.

They left a chit for the woman doctor, with an official Russian stamp on it. The Russians gave them no papers, but accepted the escape identity cards as passports. The headquarters were in a village 15 kilometers away. Several times on the way, they were stopped by Russians, who were planning to put them to work at once, locally. The Russian language on the cards always brought an immediate release, kisses and apologies. In the village, no one seemed to know anything. A woman MP said the headquarters was another 8 kilometers away. She got them a truck ride part of the way, and then they walked a while. They found the headquarters eventually, and were sent, next day, to another place by truck. The Russians would never give them papers, but considered that they had enough already.

Two days later, they went to another village. The Americans were always treated better than anyone else, civilians, eating at soup kitchens while they got rations, cooked by civilians on Russian orders. They were then sent to Vesprin, where they met about 150 British ex-POWs. Here, at the British request, Lt. Edwards was put in charge of them, as they had no officer among them. In a few days the group left by train, with about 300 Belgians and 50 or 60 civilians. A Russian Lieutenant was in charge. At Bubotica they got some food from the Yugoslav Red Cross. The train was due to go to Timisoara, Bucharest, and Odessa. They saw no reason in going that route, so at Szeged they and a British S/M slipped off. The Czech-American would not come, as he had no papers of his own, and was now on Russian orders and covered by them.

The three had to leave everything behind, as the Russian Lieutenant would have arrested them if he thought they were planning to leave. They got back to Bubotica, then down to Belgrade, and eventually through the American mission to Italy, arriving 4 May 1945. Lt. Edwards and Sgt. Dennick met at the Vienna Police Station, they were imprisoned together, they escaped together and they returned to base together. They had no knowledge of the fate of any of their crewmembers but Edwards was told at the prison that he and Dennick were the only airmen who were alive from the planes that were shot down that day. This information came from the Austrian guards, French Resistance Forces and forced labor workers around Vienna and in the prison. This would indicate that all crewmembers were Killed In Action, with the exception of Lt. Edwards and Sgt. Dennick. However, the Commanding Officer of the 783rd Bomb Squadron determined that the conversation between Lt. Edwards and Austrian guards, French Resistance forces and forced labor workers was not final proof that these personnel were killed. In fact, Lt. Herman and Sgts. Eiberger, Canterbury, Irwin and Fink were Killed In Action. Lts. Edwards, Reeher and McIlhenny and Sgts. Dennick and Mayo were captured and made Prisoners of war.

22 March 1945: Capt. Edgel W. Richardson, Pilot, 782nd Squadron, flew a B-24L, #44-49566, Call Letter Yellow "X" to bomb the Helingenstadt Marshalling Yards at Vienna, Austria with crewmembers, 1st Lt. James A. Funk, Co-Pilot; Lt. Paul H Durckel, Navigator; Lt. Garth Atherley, Navigator; Lt. Walton H. Osborn, Bombardier; Lt. Ernest E. Alden Jr., Navigator-Radar Bombardier; T/Sgt. Robert N. Geibel, Flight Engineer-Gunner; T/Sgt. Wendell V. Galbraith, Radio Operator-Gunner; S/Sgt. Hans P. Jergensen, Armorer-Gunner; S/Sgt. Leonard E. Edgell, Gunner; T/Sgt. Alfred N. Maas, Assistant

Engineer-Top Turret Gunner and Lt. Col. McHenry Hamilton Jr., Observer. The weather was clear and their aircraft was last sighted over Vienna at 12:53 hours. This was a twelve-man crew.

Eyewitness, 1st Lt. Ralph W. Humphreys, 780th Squadron, "The airplane Yellow "X" was hit by a direct burst of flak in the number 3 engine. The bombs had been released just a few seconds earlier and the pilot had just started his rally off the target when the airplane was hit. The burst of flak set fire to the number 3 engine and the inner section of the right wing. The airplane did not go out of control, but went into a gentle diving turn to the right. The crewmen of my plane flying to the right wing of Yellow "X" reported seeing seven parachutes leave the airplane before losing sight of it near the ground. All of these chutes were seen to open."

Capt. Richardson bailed out of the window next to the co-pilot's seat, Lt. Funk bailed out of the window next to the pilot's seat. Lts. Durckel, Atherley and Osborn, bailed out of the nose wheel door. Sgts. Geibel, Jergensen and Edgell, all bailed out of the escape hatch in the waist section, Sgt. Galbraith, bailed out of the bomb bay. The fate of Lt. Col. McHenry Hamilton Jr., Lt. Ernest E. Alden Jr. and Sgt. Maas, is uncertain.

Lt. Osborn, who had suffered a shattered right leg and was banged up quite badly, was imprisoned with Sgt. Galbraith in a military hospital in Vienna, Austria. They were liberated by the Russians on 9 April 1945. The last time Galbraith saw Maas he was still in the top turret. Hearsay information is that Maas and Alden were both killed by the civilians. When an Austrian guard was asked about Alden the guard replied "Those things just happened" and he indicated that Lt. Alden had been killed. When the guard was asked about Sgt. Maas, he stated that Maas had received the same treatment. Lt. Alden and Sgt. Maas were both Killed In Action. Lt. Col. Hamilton, Captain Richardson and Lts. Osborn, Durckel, Funk, and Atherley, and Sgts. Geibel, Jergensen, Edgell, and Galbraith were captured and made Prisoners of War.

31 March 1945: 1st Lt. Harry C. Bartels Jr., Pilot, 783rd Squadron, flew a B-24L, #44-48990, Call Letter Blue "T" named "Margie The Magnificent" to bomb the Marshalling Yard at Villach, Austria with crewmembers, Lt. Amos D. Key, Co-Pilot; Lt. Martin D. Seiler, Navigator; Lt. Joseph E. McGrath, Bombardier; S/Sgt. William J. Mitchell, Flight Engineer-Gunner; T/Sgt. Joseph F. Swift, Radio Operator-Gunner; Sgt. Joseph T. Dulack Jr., Gunner; Sgt. Robert E. Shelton, Gunner; Sgt. Norman Kiellerson, Armorer-Gunner and Sgt. Howard H. Harvey, Gunner. The weather was clear and their aircraft was last sighted at 11:40 hours over northern Italy.

Eyewitness, Sgt. Stephen M. Pitoniak, "We were flying to the target when number one ship suddenly lost speed and dropped down about fifty feet. We followed them down and he peeled off to the right. The plane seemed to be under control at all times until he was out of my view. It looked to me as though he had a runaway prop. He was not hit by flak or fighters. I did not see any chutes."

Crossing the Alps, the prop on number 4 engine ran away, the altitude was then about 24,000 feet. Immediately the plane lost about 4,000 feet. It was impossible to feather the prop or hold altitude so the pilot decided to turn around and head for Zara or home base. The plane lost altitude steadily and after losing about 16,500 feet, the pilot gave the order to bail out. This was necessary as the plane was below mountain elevation and clouds covered the mountains. All of the crew bailed out successfully about 5 miles south of Cerknicka. The plane was seen to make a 180-degree turn and crash into the valley. It burned and was completely destroyed.

Lt. Bartels landed in a small river. After getting rid of his parachute, he swam across the river westward at the suggestion of a Partisan soldier who ran to the opposite bank of the river to aid him. After drying off, the Partisan took him south up into the hills to a Partisan camp about 2 miles away. There he was given food and a place to sleep. He also met up with Sgts. Kiellerson and Harvey and Lt. McGrath, who arrived at about the same time.

Kiellerson had landed on the opposite side of the river and immediately took to the hills where he met a girl who directed him to Bartels. Harvey and McGrath met very soon after landing, and after getting rid of some clothes and getting their bearings, they took off into the hills southeast. After walking for about two hours, they came upon a Partisan camp. It was a good-sized camp with six or seven tents and was believed to be the headquarters of the Commandant of the region. They were given something to eat and were later shown the way to the camp where Bartels and Kiellerson had been brought.

Lt. Seiler and Sgt. Shelton ran into each other about two hours after landing. They had landed near each other in the hills. They started walking south and came to what they believed was the Italian border. Not desiring to cross into Italy they then took a road running eastward. Going along this road, they heard shots and hid in the underbrush for a while. They then proceeded to a small town about a half-mile from the burning plane. They decided to go into the church but it proved to be empty. Lights were seen in a small farmhouse and they decided to go in there. They were warmly welcomed and given excellent food. Later they were brought into the woods to sleep under a tin shelter close to a Partisan soldier. The next day they were taken, mostly by horse and wagon, to the town of Drezld about ten miles southeast.

There they met Bartels, Kiellerson, Harvey and McGrath who had walked there during the day of 1 April 1945. Bartels, Kiellerson, Harvey, McGrath,

Seiler and Shelton, started walking at 06:00 hours with two guides who were soon exhausted. After wearing out several other teams they reached Prozid at about 16:00 hours. There they were given food at a local Partisan Headquarters and then were sent by cart to an un-named camp. This was the Partisan Headquarters for the area. A meal was eaten by all six who then proceeded to another small un-named town over the hill at which was a Partisan Garrison. There they spent two nights in a Partisan home and were given five meals. Lt. Key and Sgts. Mitchell and Dulack, arrived here on the 2nd. Mitchell and Dulack together and Key alone. The Partisans made contact by telephone with an American mission located nearby. It is believed by all crewmembers that the mission area was called Bellachini.

Sgt. Mitchell had landed alone on a hillside. He heard firing and headed south into the hills away from it. He walked alone through the woods for about five hours, hearing sporadic shooting, and then suddenly he heard the sound of somebody chopping wood. Crawling up carefully to about twenty yards of the noise, he saw a fire, a girl and four men in Partisan uniforms. He then decided to go to this gathering. He was soon brought up to a camp about 20 yards further on. He did not know exactly where the camp was situated. He spent the night at this camp and next morning started off with four Partisans and two women to another camp where there was supposedly an automobile. They walked due east all day until about 16:00 hours and they came to a Headquarters Camp. It had permanent buildings, 1 brick building and 3 wooden barracks. This camp was about 100 yards from the Yugoslav border on the Italian side. Here Mitchell met Dulack.

Lt. Key, after landing, was told by an old man that there was a German patrol about. He decided to head south and soon he heard a noise. Hiding, he saw two German patrols of eight pass by. He then continued walking all through the night and at 09:00 hours the following morning, he came upon the Partisan camp where he was later joined by Mitchell and Dulack. They were given food and a bed to sleep on (a very comfortable spot). The next day, 2 April, Key, Mitchell and Dulack started off on foot due east with four Partisans.

They reached Prezild at about 14:00 hours and were given an excellent meal. They then proceeded to Cabar about two miles southeast and then moved on to the un-named Partisan Garrison town where they joined other members of their crew.

On the morning of 3 April all of the crewmembers, with the exception of the radio operator, Sgt. Swift, started walking at 09:30 hours to Cabar due west where transportation was expected. Reaching there at 10:30 hours, they waited by the roadside for a jeep. They were taken to the mission about 55 miles west, arriving there about 20:30 hours. They spent two nights and the day of 4 April in the mission. They were well fed, with food from the British mission, cooked by a Partisan. On the morning of 5 April 1945 they walked out to the airfield and awaited the planes. At 13:50 hours they took off for Bari in a C-47 aircraft.

Sgt. Swift said, "I was the eighth man to bail out and my chest chute opened well and I landed in trees in mountainous country. I saw all chutes open but I landed alone. I headed for the plane, which I could see burning in a valley. I heard shots and shouting so I stayed in the woods and walked south through the mountains until I reached a road. I observed no traffic on the road so after dark I began walking south on it. The moon was bright and I heard men walking so I ducked off the road into some bushes breaking a stick as I went. Two men came up wearing steel helmets and leggings. They carried rifles with bayonets. However, the men were afraid to look in the bushes and passed on by.

I spent the night in the woods and continued walking through the mountains. I saw two barracks which I watched until I could see the soldiers one of which was wearing a dark green uniform and putties. The soldier had a colored patch on his shoulder but I could not distinguish the colors of the patch. I continued walking south in the woods until reaching a small village, which had a road leading to it, but none leading out. I slept in the woods nearby that night. On the morning of 2 April, I saw a civilian and made contact with him. He called a man who had lived in the U. S for 22 years. I gave the family of the first man I met, a chit on which I credited them with giving me one meal. The people were very friendly and said they would help to get me to the Partisans.

I was then taken to another house, given another meal and then met another man who had been in the U. S. I was told the name of the village was, Usha, which was located between enemy and Partisan territory and was occasionally visited by both, but mainly by Partisans for food. Two Partisan boys and one girl came to the village at night and I was told to leave with them. Before leaving I left chits with the family with whom I had lived and also with the man who acted as interpreter. After a 3-hour walk we came to a cabin in the woods where I found four other Partisans. I was well treated and given food and they told me I would be in Bari in six days. I had given my gun to one of the Partisans who had brought me to the cabin. I walked from here with the Partisans to a small Operational Headquarters in the hills just north of Clana and with Partisans to Cabar. Here I spent the night with a civilian woman to whom a chit was given. Partisans in Cabar notified the American Mission Headquarters at Slovina and arrangements were made for a jeep to pick me up. I traveled part of the way by truck and then met the jeep and was taken to the evacuation point. Here I was cared for by the British Mission but kept in a separate house away from the airfield. The Partisans would not allow me to stay with a nearby American Mission and I was constantly under guard - or as the Partisans call them "Couper." I was evacuated two days behind my fellow crewmembers."

25 April 1945: 1st Lt. William G. Shreve Jr., Pilot, 780th Squadron, flew a B-24L, #44-49905, Call Letter Red "D" to bomb the Main Station Marshalling Yard at Linz, Austria with crewmembers, 1st Lt. Robert D. Carter, Co-Pilot; 1st

Lt. Gerald M. Harriman, Navigator; Lt. Franklin C. Diederichs, Bombardier; T/Sgt. Calvin A. Page, Flight Engineer-Gunner; T/Sgt. Wallace R. Anderson, Radio Operator-Gunner; S/Sgt. Carlyle P. Nickler, Gunner; Sgt. Donald E. Wood, Gunner; Sgt. James W. Herndon, Gunner and Sgt. Fred S. Wightman, Gunner. Visibility was twenty miles and their aircraft was last contacted by radio at 13:37 hours.

Eyewitness, 1st Lt. Jack C. Fraser, 780th Squadron, "Approximately fifteen minutes after rallying from the target on the mission of 25 April 1945, the pilot of Red "D" called me and transmitted this message "I have one engine feathered and am getting no power from number 2 engine. I also have a wounded man aboard. I'm leaving the formation and going to Russia."

Lt. Diederichs, "Heavy, accurate, intense flak, was briefed and was received a few minutes before "bombs away." Number 1 engine had been acting up on the bomb run and was feathered just as our bombs were released. Not rallying as briefed, our formation swung over St. Valentin, also heavily defended. The ship was racked in the flak bursts. A large caliber flak shell tore through the right wing without exploding. Superchargers number 2 and 3 weakened, then finally went out completely. Lt. Shreve, radioed the Group Command of our intention of aborting the mission and he headed the ship for Russian territory. We quickly assessed our condition and found that the right landing gear was possibly damaged, number 4 gas tank was punctured and the gas was gone.

There was a large assortment of smaller holes and all wiring was shot out of the right wing, the instrument panel was chopped up, number 1 engine was out completely and superchargers number 2 and 3 were also out. With the subsequent loss of power we quickly dropped to 8,000 feet. Unable to cross the Dinaric Alps it was decided to remain airborne as long as possible and crash land in Russian controlled territory. Although our compasses and navigation instruments were shot to pieces, we managed to find the Russian front lines and safely passed over them. Shortly afterward the airfield of Wiener Neustadt was sighted and we debated a landing. As we neared the field six Russian Yak fighters rose into the air. We manned our guns, uncertain of their intentions and we were stunned to find them peeling off to attack. Lt. Carter, the co-pilot, was by this time calling frantically for American fighter protection. One or two P-38's were contacted and they advised our proceeding to a different field while they took care of our "allies," the Russian Air Force. A short time later we located an emergency landing strip near the small city of Pecs, Hungary. We lowered our landing gear and it looked all right so Bill set our crippled ship down beautifully and we rolled to a stop slightly off the end of the runway.

A Russian Captain ran up and shook hands all around and welcomed us. Soon a group of Russian soldiers came up in a 1920 vintage truck and included in the group was a Major who spoke English. He informed us that we were guests of the Russian Government, to destroy nothing in the ship, leave our flying equipment and climb aboard the truck. We were transported to Nader Grande Hotel in the city. We were given rooms, ate our first of many Russian meals of beef and potatoes and went to bed. The following day, Shreve contacted the Russian Commandant to turn in a list of our names to be wired to the American Envoy in Moscow. This, however, was never done. The rest of the day we spent chatting with three interned American doctors, drinking beer, eating ham and eggs and sampling wines. Finally the interpreter told us we were leaving and about five in the afternoon we boarded a train.

Food for three days was given to us, consisting of six loaves of black bread, ten links of smoked sausage, and one slab of raw sowbelly. At six in the evening our battered old train pulled out, our destination being a Russian Air Force Field believed to be in the vicinity of Szombathely where we were to be questioned. Our escort was an Ober-Lieutenant who resembled Stalin so closely that we nicknamed him "Joe." The train rumbled along at a good ten-miles-per-hour with people hanging on both inside and out. "Joe" began hitting a bottle of alcohol. Soon he was singing and joking and trying to seduce a Hungarian girl in the next coach. Russian troops on board drank wine with us and discouraged any attempts at sleep. The night went slowly; "Joe" was successful in his pro and there were a few fights between the "soldats" and the Hungarian citizenry. In the confusion we missed a "getting off" point and found ourselves fifty miles on the wrong road listening to front-line artillery on the Austrian border. We put our selves on the right road next morning and at two in the afternoon the train ran out of track due to bomb damage at a tiny village called Lepseny at the end of Lake Balaton.

Seemingly stalemated at this point (from here on the tracks were blown out) we made temporary Headquarters in a badly bomb damaged depot. Although it started raining shortly afterwards, we proceeded to scrounge, ending up with a dozen eggs of uncertain vintage, which we put on to boil. The Russian garrison of the village was in the throes of a binge and various "soldats" were throwing hand-grenades at each other. So we settled down for the night - .45's loaded. Next morning dawned clear, and "Joe" turned up with horse-carts which we loaded up and began the next leg of our journey on "Horse-cart Thru Hungary"!

Our destination for the day (28 April) was Vesprim on the north shore of Lake Balaton. At our rate of travel we were able to closely survey the devastation of war. This area was the one in which the attacks of the first part of April took place. Villages were shells with redoubts and trenches; fresh graves and strewn equipment; tanks and guns shelled and wrecked. Not hard to believe Russian claims of tanks captured. The day was nice, so we jogged along, viewing the countryside and eating our black-bread and gut on the go. We arrived at Vesprim about two o'clock where we really first came in contact with Russian front-line troops. The Commandant brushed us off with no promise of transportation. "Joe" was non-plussed-merely requisitioning a few Hungarian houses and moving us in. We shared some of our escape kit bouillion with the Hungarian hostess of our hovel, shook hands with the local Russian soldiers, traded guns, watched the Russian WAC direct traffic, and went to bed.

Early the next morning we sat down on the curb near the highway to await transportation. The Commandant continued brushing us off throughout the morning, and horse-carts could not be found. Finally at about three in the afternoon we succeeded in hitching a ride with an Artillery convoy going in our direction. The drivers were well loaded with wine and we drove "formation" at sixty mph down the battered road. Our truck was in a bad way and soon we stopped to repair a flat tire. The tools were taken out, a five-gallon can of wine, and a chessboard - and the repair job got underway. While the driver worked on the tire we shot at a nearby telephone pole with all the weapons we could find, drank wine, and then played a rousing game of chess in which the Russians thoroughly beat the Americans. A short distance ahead a "jeep" was also being repaired. It was dusk and soon became rather dark. At this point the Russian repairing the "jeep", in need of a light with which to work, simply set fire to a barn a short distance away. Light was plentiful. In a short while we proceeded on our way and pulled into a small village called Janosasha. Here we were welcomed with real hospitality. A feast was prepared - baloney, black-bread, and wine, and soon we were all quite stewed having put away a few dozen toasts to the United Nations. Each toast was a twelve-ounce glass downed at one gulp with a rousing cheer. Supporting each other we finally staggered off to our beds in various nearby houses.

We were awakened early and found that about six barbers had been found who soon had us shaved. A cow and a pig had been slaughtered and breakfast was served - an egg, beef, pork, and more wine. After eating "Joe" rounded up horse-carts and we continued on. Jogging along about two mph we passed thru many small war-torn villages, and late in the afternoon arrived at our destination - - Sarvar, a few kilometers from the reported position of the Red Air Force Base at Szombathely. It didn't take long to discover, however, that the Air Force had moved to Wiener-Neustadt in Austria. So, we sat down to await a hitch. Needless to say we were all rather exasperated with Russian efficiency and Communications by this time. However, not long afterwards, we snagged a ride on a truck and were on our way. And soon after we crossed the frontier into Austria. We noticed little immediate difference, tho, with the exception of Signposts in German. The countryside was still well plowed, rolling, green land of the Balkans. But now to the west the Alps could be seen rising rapidly from the foothills to snow-capped peaks, which we had so often flown over on our forays to Nazi-land. Now too, a greater number of well-armed Russians were noticeable moving to the west in an odd assortment of horse-carts, wheelbarrows, and on foot. Transportation that was motorized consisted mainly of American Lend-Lease vehicles.

As we passed through the first Austrian towns we noticed there was a great improvement in sanitation over Hungary and in modern devices. The Austrians, also, appeared much healthier and better dressed than their Hungarian neighbors. We quickly passed thru Sopron and arrived about six in the evening at Eisenstadt, a large town near our destination. At Russian Headquarters we unloaded for the night. Here in Eisenstadt, which was one of the major, headquarters of the Russian Army in Austria; we were objects of great interest to one and all both Russian and Austrian. We were ushered into the commandant's Office and put on exhibit. We finally made it clear that we were hungry and a sumptuous repast was spread before us - - - smoked "gut", black-bread, and "vino". After we had eaten and drank more than was necessary merely to wash the food down, billets were found for us and we staggered off thru the night quite inebriated to ramshackle hotels that had been requisitioned for us. As drunk as we were, Shreve and I were billeted with two Bulgarian soldiers just back from the front. They were well supplied with wine and although we couldn't converse, they would awaken us from our stupor at intervals and whistle cheerfully as they forced huge pitchers of wine on us. When we felt we couldn't hold another drop we unlimbered our 45's and soon made it clear we had had enough.

May 1st dawned clear. Red Army Day and the town was full of soldiers celebrating. We were routed out of our billets and given breakfast. Then we were put on the curb in front of the building to listen to Stalin's speech. Needless to say we were not at all impressed. Shortly afterwards "Joe" arrived in high spirits with a truck all for us. We climbed aboard and started our search for the Red Air Force. Within a short time it began raining. That and hangovers made it a miserable ride. We started west toward Wiener-Neustadt and soon were quite lost. None of us liked the out-look as the German front lines weren't too far off. However, we finally turned about and started looking elsewhere. After 5 hours on the truck we ended up 15 km. from our starting point at a small village called Trausdorf where the Air Force was located. We unloaded the truck and our old buddy "Joe" left us. Felt sort of lost without him. And again we split up and billeted with various Austrian families. The Navigator, Harriman, Co-pilot Carter and myself were put into the home of Frans Shimestitch.

From May 1 to 7 we stayed in Trausdorf. Gradually we became quite well acquainted with the family. "Papa", who had been in the Nazi Gendarmie until he couldn't take the gaff and quit, then went to work in an Oil Refinery in Vienna where he lived thru the bombing we gave the place. "Mama" who stayed in the village living in continual dread that "Papa" would be killed in the bombing, crouching on the floor when our bombers passed overhead, and hiding in the loft when the Russians roared thru. The three daughters - - - typical blonde peasant girls of the Balkans, not at all appetizing or desirable. And one son in the Nazi army in Norway. Life was very dull in the Village. We heard innumerable stories of Russians atrocities, which we took with a grain of salt. Heard tales of the battle against the Reds from crippled former "Supermen". And really saw the results of our bombing on the lives of even the peasant. The atrocities could have been true, tho, as we witnessed the rape of a young married woman working in the vineyards by a Russian soldier. That, of course, can be expected in any conquering army or country. What shocked us, however, was the "what a joke - - so what" attitude of the high officers when the crime was reported. We were told of about 100 women pregnant by Russians. However, on the other side were the terrible tales of SS atrocities against shot-down American and Russian flyers - - - the hangings, brutalities, horrors inflicted by these black uniformed monsters. However, the Russian method of "tooth-for-tooth" seems quite terrible. Eventually we were sent to Kiev and on 7 May 1945, we climbed into a Red Air Force C-47 and started for Odessa, on the Black Sea. The entire crew, returned to the States together."

25 April, 1945: 1st Lt. Italo M. Gemmato, Pilot, 782nd Squadron, flew a B-24L, #44-49914, Call Letter White "V" to bomb the Main Station Marshalling Yard at Linz, Austria with crewmembers, Lt. Norman R. Stickney, Co-Pilot; F/O Lawrence J. Smith Jr., Navigator; S/Sgt. John C. Martin, Nose Turret Gunner; Sgt. Freeman L. Smith, Top Turret Gunner; S/Sgt. John H. Chapman, Ball Turret Gunner; T/Sgt. William R. Snow, Flight Engineer-Waist Gunner; Sgt. Robert L. Linsley, Radio Operator-Waist Gunner and S/Sgt. Leonard F. Day, Tail Turret Gunner. Visibility was twenty miles and their aircraft was last sighted 30 miles northeast of Linz, Austria at 13:17 hours. This was a nine-man crew.

Eyewitness, S/Sgt. Irving Eisenbaum, 782nd Squadron, "It was on Wednesday, 25 April 1945, that I was flying as an enlisted Navigator on ship White "O" for "Oboe" piloted by Lt. Osterhoudt, when I saw Lt. Gemmato's aircraft struck by flak and the entire crew bailed out. Our target for that day was Linz Main Station in Austria, a target heavily defended by anti-aircraft. Our bombs were away at approximately 13:27 hours when my tail gunner shouted over the intercom "Navigator, White "V" is on fire." We were flying Able 6 and White "V" was flying Able 5 directly on my right wing. I stuck my face in the window and saw fire and smoke spewing forth from the bomb bays and number 3 engine. It had lost about 1500 feet of altitude when it was struck. It was approximately 7 minutes after that when I saw a figure hurtle out of the camera hatch. I presume and I am pretty sure it was Sgt. Robert L. Linsley, the radio operator. The reason I say this is because I was on that crew until a month ago and I know the position of each man. He fell at least 8,000 feet before he pulled the ripcord and I saw his parachute open. Our altitude at that time was 22,000 feet. It was 30 seconds after his parachute opened that I saw 2 more figures leap out, S/Sgt. Leonard F. Day, the tail gunner and S/Sgt. John H. Chapman, the ball gunner. They cleared the ship, somersaulted once and their parachutes opened. Right after that 2 figures leaped out of the nose wheel door, Flight Officer Lawrence Smith Jr., the navigator and S/Sgt. John C. Martin the nose gunner, whose parachutes opened immediately.

Following them came 2 more figures, this time from the bomb bay doors, T/Sgt. William R. Snow the engineer and Sgt. Freeman L. Smith, the top turret gunner. Their parachutes opened immediately. About 20 seconds later came 2nd Lt. Norman R. Stickney, the co-pilot and his parachute opened immediately. It was a good 2 minutes later that I saw the pilot 1st Lt. Italo M. Gemmato leave the ship and his chute also opened immediately. I was very much relieved because this meant the full crew of 9 men had safely parachuted out. The ship evidently was trimmed up; for at this time I could see no fire, just smoke billowing out. She made a turn to the left, flying level and I last saw it losing altitude headed directly towards the city of Linz. The coordinates I plotted for the last man to leave the ship put them exactly 30 miles northeast of Linz. There was a 25 knot northwest wind blowing at the time."

All crewmembers bailed out except the pilot and co-pilot. The co-pilot, Lt. Stickney was in shock, due to being wounded. As he bailed out, his pilot chute hung up on the bomb rack shackles and he hung there for about two minutes, then the chute came free and as he fell free, he wondered if it had been damaged enough to prevent its opening. Fortunately the pilot chute pulled the main parachute out and he floated to the ground. The pilot followed the co-pilot out immediately and the plane exploded within ten seconds after they jumped. All crewmembers were captured and made Prisoners of War.

Following is a letter to Lt. Stickney's father, Mr. Frank Stickney from Mr. Erwin Kump.

Since my wife cannot read English well enough in order to translate this letter, I am sending it to you in the German language.

(Lt. Stickney's parents had the letter from Mr. Kump, translated by a college professor in Iowa:)

Erwin Kump
Vienna LV.
Schaumburgergasse (- street) 18

Vienna
July 23, 1946

To - Mr. Frank Stickney
Smithland, Iowa.

Your son, Lieutenant Norman Stickney, took part with his airplane in a heavy bomb-attack on Linz on the Danube, Upper Austria, the 25th of April, 1945. The airplane was damaged in this mission, so that the crew of nine men, among them your son, who was severely wounded on the right foot by a flak fragment (from an antiaircraft gun), was forced to jump by means of parachutes east of Linz and in fact between Perg and Baumgartenberg.

I was at that time a captain of reserves and a company chief of a militia company in Linz in charge of guarding those prisoners of war which were put to work in the city of Linz and in the district of Perg. Because I had suffered on the 22nd of February, 1945, during an air-raid alarm a complicated fracture of the tibia (shin-bone) and the fibula (calf, of the leg, bone), I was on leave of absence April 25, 1945, in Pitzing near Baumgartenberg at the home of a peasant named Zickerhofer, and at the time had my thigh and lower leg in a plaster cast.

Your son landed on a field about 300 meters from my dwelling house. My wife and a Polish woman farm worker, who was working for the peasant with whom I was living, were the first to reach your son, who was sitting helpless on the ground, holding his arms up as a sign of surrender. Then your son applied a tourniquet to his thigh, and himself cut his shoe off. In the meantime several peasants and some soldiers who were quartered nearby, as well as two prisoners of war who were working for my peasant friend and for a neighbor, had arrived on the spot. Your son was carried to the house of the neighbor, was given some whiskey from the prisoner of war of my neighbor Hickersberger, after your son had given himself an injection to allay his pain.

Because a hostile mood was now evident among those present who were bitter on account of the bombing attack and because a few remarks made me fear for the life of your son, I gave the command to carry your son to the home of my peasant friend, where I had him put to bed on a sofa and given some milk. Since the foot wound was bleeding in spite of the first aid bandage and the twisted bandage on the thigh, my wife brought my mattress and with it elevated the leg.

The already mentioned Polish woman farm worker was sent by me to Baumgartenberg for the Polish physician of that place, who however, in spite of my request, refused to attend to the wounded man. I then sent to Saxen for another Polish physician, who promised he would come. In the meantime an unwounded, forced-down American was brought in. I had him taken to your son, and the two spoke together a short while, with my permission. I then gave the command to the corporal who had taken the unwounded American to the staff of the pioneer battalion in Klam, to ask the troop doctor of the battalion to come to me.

My wife, who knows some English, spoke with your son, who was afraid he would be put into prison. I had him told that he should not worry, that I had already sent for doctors, and would continue to take care of him. Since he was also afraid that his papers and money would be taken away from him in captivity, he gave them both to my wife and wrote your address on a card (or possibly: map) with the request that the money and papers be sent to you. This took place after I had had the room cleared of people who kept coming in.

Since the doctor from Saxen did not arrive and I was afraid that your son might bleed to death, I had a wagon hitched up, straw put into it, and your son laid on the straw bed. To head sergeant-major Mast of my company I gave the command to ride along to the doctor in Saxen and after the service of surgical aid to carry out the transportation of the wounded man into the hospital in Perg about 14 kilometers distant. With serious wounds, I entrusted to my head sergeant major the responsibility for the life of your son and that was good, as I shall set forth later.

The wagon, your son and my head sergeant major had just started when the physician from Saxen came driving up. The doctor at once examined superficially the wounded man on the wagon, which had been stopped, and expressed doubt as to whether he would be able to stand transportation by wagon to the hospital in Perg, since the artery was completely cut off and your son much weakened by the loss of blood, to say nothing of the fact that rather big portions of muscle were gone from the foot. Both wagons now went to Saxen.

About an hour later, the troop doctor that I had asked to come from the pioneer battalion, a head physician (First Lieut. Physician) came driving up in a passenger automobile. I informed him about what had happened, and told him that your son was in danger of his life, that I was of the opinion that we should no longer consider the wounded man as an enemy, but should do our very best to save his life. I begged him to drive to the civilian doctor in Saxen and if there was need to help him (the wounded man) and see to it that he got quick transportation to Perg.

Meanwhile the following had taken place in Saxen:

The mayor of Saxen, who was quite generally disliked and was named Walch, and who moreover was shot down by persons unknown on the day when American troops marched in, appealed, while your son was with the doctor in Saxen to the district manager of the NSDAP (These initials are unknown by the translator) in Perg and received from there, permission to kill your son. He challenged my head sergeant major to shoot down your son, an act which the former refused to commit, referring to the orders, which he had received from me. Next the mayor challenged a man from Vienna, whom I had formerly known officially, to put an end to your son. The man, however, just like chief sergeant major Mast, declined to do so.

The head physician drove on to Saxen, found your son still at the doctors where he had been bandaged well, but he could not make up his mind to amputate, because he had no technically trained assistants at hand. The two doctors examined the wound once more and took off a part of the foot, which could not be saved. *This done, the head doctor had your son taken at once in his auto to the hospital at Perg. In the hospital the whole foot had to be taken off. Head sergeant major Mast announced to me on April 26, 1945 that your son felt comparatively comfortable.

A few days later I went to the hospital, requested the superintendent, a staff physician-captain-doctor as well as the room doctor, to take charge of your son, and then I visited your son in company with my wife, who told him our address at that time. Through my head sergeant major your son received also a toothbrush and some English books. Your son, together with some Austrian and German soldiers, was housed in a little hospital room. The superintendent of the hospital told me later that he had placed another American soldier in the same room in order that your son might converse with him.

On the 7th of May 1945, American troops marched into the district of Perg and took your son away from the hospital. Where they took your son was not reported to the staff physician, and I was not able to find out either when I inquired about him in the American military government office in Linz at the beginning of June 1945.

I hope that your son is now with you, at home again and in comfortable circumstances, also that he gratefully remembers the good treatment he received in Austria as a wounded prisoner of war. I am truly sorry that he was so badly wounded that his foot could not be saved, though possibly he was able to preserve even his life, thanks only to the quick and intensive help of the doctors.

The leather pocketbook which your son turned over to my wife on April 25, 1945, contained the following: 6895 Italian occupation lire; 12 French occupation francs; 10 French francs, as well as Identification card; Officers Pay Data Card; Individual Issue Record; Overseas Gift Sales Receipt; Unit Exchange Ration Card; Pictures; Pilot Certificate, Operators License.

Since I could not without risk take upon myself the obligation of sending to you in a simple letter the money and documents of your son, I waited until today in the hope that the registered letter service with the United States of America would be started again. Since registered packages are however not yet possible, and on the other hand that the occupation money might later perhaps not be exchanged to your son in dollars, I beg you to inform me how and where I am to send to you or to your son the money and documents.

From my wife and me, the best of greetings to your son and, although we are not acquainted, to you.

(Signed) Erwin Kump

*(Lt. Stickney stated: "Instead of going to Perg, the driver took me back to Linz and showed me all the bomb damage and then to a German jet fighter

airfield where I saw one do a victory roll. Then he took me back to Perg and it was dark when we arrived at the hospital. A nurse told me later that by this time my leg had become gangrenous. She said they had discussed taking my leg off at the hip, but had no blood or antibiotics. I had a very high fever for days. On May 7th Americans came and took me back to a MASH Hospital that evening. Two German Ju88's strafed the hospital. Both were shot down, one pilot was killed and the other wounded and brought in to the hospital near me. He later died. From there I was taken to 1st General hospital in Paris and back to the States May 30, 1945. From there to Percy Jones Hospital in Battle Creek, Michigan. Left from there and was separated on March 10, 1946."

April 25, 1945 was the third time Lt. Norman R. Stickney had been shot down. Following are his comments on the two times previous to April 25, 1945:

"On December 20, 1944 our aircraft had been shot up and with two engines shot out and no brakes, we were forced to make a crash landing on the Isle of Vis in the Adriatic and ended up in a vineyard. Right after we crash-landed, George McGovern came and I congratulated him on a great landing, he said they had brakes. Then in March of 1945 we bailed out over Yugoslavia and were picked up by Partisans. I suffered a concussion and ended up in the hospital in Bari, Italy."

Gene F. Moxley

"THE 465TH. REMEMBERED"

IN THE YEAR OF NINETEEN FORTY THREE,
A NEW BOMB GROUP WAS SOON TO BE.
THIS GROUP WAS NUMBERED, FOUR SIX FIVE,
TO ACHIEVE PERFECTION EACH MEMBER DID STRIVE.

THEY FORMED FOUR SQUADRON'S,
OF BRAVE, YOUNG MEN.
SOME WOULD NEVER SEE,
THEIR LOVED ONE'S, AGAIN.

THE SQUADRON'S WERE NUMBERED, FROM
SEVEN EIGHTY, THROUGH SEVEN EIGHTY-THREE.
AN OUTSTANDING BOMB GROUP,
THEY WERE DESTINED TO BE.

THEY FLEW THE FAMOUS "B-24",
A HEAVY BOMBER, JUST RIGHT FOR THE CHORE.
LOADED WITH BOMBS, AND BRISTLING WITH GUN'S,
THIS WAS THE ONE, THAT PUT THE "HUN" ON THE RUN.

THEY WERE BASED AT PANTANELLA,
IN SOUTHERN ITALY.
WHERE THEY FLEW THEIR MANY MISSION'S,
TO KEEP ALL OF US FREE.

SO LET US SAY A PRAYER,
OF THANKS, TO ALL THESE MEN.
FOR WITHOUT THEIR GALLANT EFFORT,
WHO KNOW'S, WHAT MIGHT HAVE BEEN.

WE WILL NEVER FORGET YOU,
THOUGH MANY YEARS' HAVE PAST.
YOU LEFT WITH US AN IMPRESSION,
THAT WILL, FOREVER, LAST.

SO HERE'S TO THE MEN OF THE FOUR SIXTY FIFTH,
GOD BLESS YOU, ONE AND ALL.
YOUR JOB WAS TOUGH AND DEADLY,
BUT YOU COURAGEOUSLY, ANSWERED THE CALL.

DEDICATED TO ALL MEMBERS OF THE 465TH BOMB GROUP (H)

The following pages contain the Battle Casualty list for the 465th Bombardment Group.

KILLED IN ACTION

NAME - RANK - SQUADRON - DATE

Adams, S/Sgt. James R.	782nd	03 August 1944
Alden, Lt. Ernest E., Jr.	782nd	22 March 1945
Armstrong, Sgt. Chestley J.	782nd	01 September 1944
Arzt, Sgt. Bert D.	780th	11 October 1944
Aurentz, Lt. Russell J.	783rd	20 January 1945
Babcock, Lt. Seth C., Jr.	782nd	03 August 1944
Bakes, Sgt. Russell V.	780th	24 August 1944
Balke, Sgt. Richard M.	783rd	20 November 1944
Ballbach, Lt. Michael W.	780th	19 July 1944
Barker, Sgt. Rome L.	783rd	07 July 1944
Bartlett, Sgt. John W.	783rd	20 January 1945
Bassler, Lt. Kenneth R.	783rd	04 October 1944
Bates, 1st Lt. Cecil R.	783rd	07 August 1944
Beckman, Lt. Charles A.	782nd	11 October 1944
Behr, T/Sgt. Earl T.	783rd	06 December 1944
Bentrud, Lt. Raymond G.	780th	24 August 1944
Benvenuto, S/Sgt. Attilio A.	781st	19 December 1944
Bernstein, Lt. Arthur H.	780th	20 November 1944
Bernzott, Sgt. Arthur E.	782nd	01 September 1944
Boehme, Lt. Edwin B.	782nd	06 June 1944
Boeris, Lt. John N.	783rd	20 January 1945
Bowyer, S/Sgt. William B.	780th	24 August 1944
Bradford, Sgt. David D.	783rd	12 September 1944
Bradley, Lt. William A.	781st	14 March 1945
Brannon, S/Sgt. William J., Jr.	781st	14 March 1945
Brenner, Lt. Arthur O.	782nd	01 September 1944
Bressler, T/Sgt. Edward L.	782nd	11 March 1944
Broderick, S/Sgt. William H.	782nd	03 August 1944
Buck, Lt. Leroy O.	780th	24 August 1944
Bullock, S/Sgt. Victor E.	780th	03 August 1944
Burda, Sgt. Charles F.	783rd	20 November 1944
Burk, Lt. Robert J.	782nd	11 March 1944
Burroughs, Cpl. Redford J.	781st	01 February 1945

Busch, Sgt. David L.	783rd	16 February 1945
Calabrese, Lt. August S.	780th	11 December 1944
Campbell, Sgt. Argonne F.	782nd	13 September 1944
Campbell, Sgt. William R.	782nd	03 August 1944
Canterbury, Sgt. Robert J.	783rd	22 March 1945
Canyock, Lt. Calvin J.	781st	30 May 1944
Carlen, Lt. Robert C.	780th	24 August 1944
Cassady, Sgt. Jack E.	783rd	20 November 1944
Claytor, Lt. William L., Jr.	782nd	06 June 1944
Cohen, Lt. Herbert R.	780th	11 December 1944
Collins, S/Sgt. Raymond J.	783rd	16 February 1945
Conn, Sgt. Roy C.	780th	24 August 1944
Conrad, S/Sgt. Roland M.	782nd	11 March 1944
Cosper, Lt. Bruce	781st	19 December 1944
Couch, Lt. Harold F.	782nd	11 March 1944
Cox, Lt. Leonard S.	782nd	03 August 1944
Crane, Sgt. Francis A.	782nd	11 October 1944
Crary, Sgt. Willard D.	783rd	30 June 1944
Curtis, S/Sgt. Thomas J., Jr.	783rd	06 December 1944
Davis, S/Sgt. Austin C.	781st	30 June 1944
Davis, Sgt. Benjamin J.	783rd	12 September 1944
Davis, S/Sgt. Hudson J.	783rd	06 December 1944
Davis, S/Sgt. Leslie R.	780th	11 December 1944
Deegan, Lt. Orville J.	783rd	12 September 1944
DeForest, S/Sgt. William M., Jr.	781st	14 March 1945
Dempsey, Sgt. Carrol G.	780th	22 November 1944
Denning, Lt. Latham	782nd	03 August 1944
Denny, Sgt. Robert S.	783rd	04 October 1944
DePlue, 1st Lt. John D. III	783rd	06 December 1944
Dickason, Lt. Larry H.	781st	28 October 1944
Dobbs, Lt. William I.	781st	05 February 1945
Downey, Lt. William B.	783rd	30 June 1944
Duffield, Cpl. Charles H., Jr.	781st	05 February 1945
Dunlap, Sgt. George E.	780th	02 December 1944
Dworetzky, S/Sgt. Edward	781st	14 March 1945
Eberhart, Lt. Raymond W.	783rd	20 January 1945
Eckhardt, Sgt. Earl L.	782nd	11 October 1944
Egerton, S/Sgt. Henry P.	782nd	03 August 1944
Eiberger, S/Sgt. Earl E.	783rd	22 March 1945
Elmore, Cpl. Carrol E.	781st	05 February 1945
Elsworth, Cpl. Vernon M.	781st	05 February 1945
Emery, Lt. Lester E.	780th	24 August 1944

Faiver, Capt. Jack M.	782nd	03 August 1944
Fee, Cpl. Roscoe E.	781st	05 February 1945
Fekays, Sgt. John G.	780th	22 November 1944
Fiecoat, 1st Lt. Howard F.	782nd	03 August 1944
Finch, S/Sgt. William A.	782nd	11 March 1944
Findlay, 1st Lt. Lloyd R.	783rd	06 December 1944
Fink, Sgt. Ernest	783rd	22 March 1945
Flynn, Sgt. Paul Jr.	783rd	20 November 1944
Fox, Sgt. Howard M.	781st	05 February 1945
Frankhart, Lt. Paul J.	782nd	01 September 1944
Franklin, 1st Lt. John W.	780th	02 December 1944
Gallelli, S/Sgt. Joseph A.	781st	14 March 1945
Ganson, Sgt. Harry J.	783rd	16 December 1944
Garber, Lt. DeWitt	780th	03 August 1944
Gatling, Sgt. Herbert M.	783rd	16 February 1945
Geohagan, S/Sgt. Hoyt O.	780th	03 August 1944
Giblin, Sgt. James T.	780th	11 October 1944
Godfrey, 1st Lt. Harry K.	780th	26 July 1944
Goldberg, Sgt. Arthur W.	782nd	01 September 1944
Goldsworthy, Sgt. Richard H.	783rd	20 November 1944
Gordon, Sgt. Robert B.	783rd	06 December 1944
Grabowski, Lt. Ernest V.	782nd	11 October 1944
Graham, Sgt. Harold N.	783rd	04 October 1944
Grahovec, Sgt. Joseph R.	782nd	01 September 1944
Griffith, Sgt. Clyde A.	780th	06 December 1944
Griffith, Lt. James W.	781st	19 December 1944
Gruber, T/Sgt. Carl W.	781st	22 July 1944
Gute, Sgt. Irwin R.	780th	24 August 1944
Hamilton, S/Sgt. Lawrence J.	780th	03 August 1944
Hansen, Lt. Herbert G.	782nd	31 May 1944
Hansen, Lt. Victor Jr.	783rd	15 January 1945
Hart, Sgt. John E.	781st	19 December 1944
Haustes, S/Sgt. Leonard M.	783rd	24 August 1944
Hayman, Lt. George W.	783rd	04 October 1944
Henderson, Sgt. Jesse L.	783rd	07 July 1944
Herman, 1st Lt. William E.	783rd	22 March 1945
Herrington, T/Sgt. Ralph W.	782nd	03 August 1944
Hershey, 1st Lt. Lester	781st	14 March 1945
Hilger, Lt. James W.	780th	02 December 1944
Hill, T/Sgt. Albert S.	782nd	03 August 1944
Hooper, Lt. William J.	780th	26 July 1944
Hoover, S/Sgt. Robert H.	781st	30 June 1944

Huebner, T/Sgt. Durward E.	783rd	07 July 1944
Huebner, T/Sgt. Norman B.	782nd	31 May 1944
Huey, Lt. Walton L.	780th	11 October 1944
Hulesberg, 1st Lt. Arthur F., Jr.	780th	24 August 1944
Irwin, Sgt. Billy J.	783rd	22 March 1945
Jabben, Sgt. Wallace G.	782nd	11 October 1944
Jackson, Lt. Robert P.	780th	11 October 1944
Jacovinich, S/Sgt. Tulio P.	780th	24 August 1944
Jaeger, Sgt. George F.	783rd	04 October 1944
Johnson, T/Sgt. C. E.	780th	24 August 1944
Johnson, Lt. Robert C.	782nd	03 August 1944
Jolicoeur, 1st Lt. Jerome F.	781st	30 June 1944
Jones, Lt. Robert C.	781st	05 February 1945
Jonkman, Sgt. Norman	782nd	11 March 1944
June, S/Sgt. Robert W.	782nd	31 May 1944
Kauffman, Lt. Gilbert H.	783rd	15 January 1945
Kelley, S/Sgt. James D.	781st	07 February 1945
King, Sgt. Billy B.	780th	11 October 1944
King, Lt. Robert M.	782nd	31 May 1944
Kissel, 1st Lt. Ralph F.	780th	24 August 1944
Kolago, F/O Michael	783rd	20 November 1944
Kostick, S/Sgt. John	782nd	03 August 1944
Kotik, Sgt. Steve J.	783rd	16 December 1944
Kresnak, S/Sgt. Andrew S.	782nd	03 August 1944
Landi, S/Sgt. Joseph L.	782nd	31 May 1944
Laub, T/Sgt. Sherman	782nd	06 June 1944
Le Comte, S/Sgt. George J.	780th	11 December 1944
Ledney, S/Sgt. Paul	782nd	06 June 1944
Lee, Sgt. Richard F.	780th	24 August 1944
Lemieux, Sgt. Joseph A.	782nd	01 September 1944
Lemley, Sgt. John W.	782nd	03 August 1944
Lengvenis, 1st Lt. Harry F.	780th	24 August 1944
Leslie, Sgt. Alex J.	783rd	15 January 1945
Lewis, S/Sgt. Robert L.	783rd	24 August 1944
Lokker, Lt. Col. Clarence J.	783rd	20 November 1944
Long, S/Sgt. Eugene C., Jr.	782nd	31 May 1944
Long, Lt. Harold J.	781st	14 March 1945
Lovey, 1st Lt. Alexander	781st	13 October 1944
Lowman, Sgt. Robert H.	783rd	20 November 1944
Luce, S/Sgt. John J.	783rd	29 May 1944
Lyon, Lt. William B.	783rd	16 February 1945
Maas, T/Sgt. Alfred N.	782nd	22 March 1945

Mangan, S/Sgt. Charles A.	783rd	16 February 1945
Martz, 1st Lt. Robert E.	781st	14 March 1945
Matzger, Lt. Charles W.	783rd	15 January 1945
McAlister, Lt. Lester H.	782nd	11 March 1944
McCloskey, F/O James C.	780th	01 March 1945
McDonald, S/Sgt. Edward E.	783rd	06 December 1944
McGrath, S/Sgt. John R.	782nd	06 June 1944
McParland, Sgt. James P.	780th	24 August 1944
Melody, 1st Lt. Charles A.	782nd	11 March 1944
Mickler, Lt. Marvin F.	782nd	11 March 1944
Miller, 1st Lt. William A.	783rd	04 October 1944
Milum, Lt. Warren G.	782nd	31 May 1944
Miosky, S/Sgt. Edmund J.	783rd	20 November 1944
Montana, S/Sgt. Lupe	783rd	12 July 1944
Mooney, Sgt. Thomas J., Jr.	783rd	04 October 1944
Morse, Lt. Raymond F.	781st	13 October 1944
Mulrooney, S/Sgt. Francis T.	783rd	20 January 1945
Murphy, 1st Lt. Robert E.	782nd	11 March 1944
Musch, Sgt. Alvin I.	783rd	04 October 1944
Newborg, Lt. William T.	781st	05 July 1944
Nolen, T/Sgt. Edwin E.	782nd	03 August 1944
Odom, Sgt. James E.	783rd	16 December 1944
Oley, Lt. Wayne L.	782nd	01 September 1944
Ormes, Lt. Joseph E.	781st	05 February 1945
Owens, 1st Lt. Harold F.	783rd	06 December 1944
Payne, S/Sgt. George J.	783rd	29 May 1944
Pearson, S/Sgt. Albert A.	780th	03 August 1944
Pemberton, Lt. Ralph L.	782nd	06 June 1944
Perrone, S/Sgt. Frank	782nd	03 August 1944
Perry, Sgt. Carl R.	780th	10 September 1944
Pfalzgraf, Lt. Paul E.	783rd	15 January 1945
Pfeifer, Sgt. George T.	780th	24 August 1944
Pilegard, Lt. Ralph L.	783rd	07 July 1944
Poole, Lt. Theodore G.	782nd	03 August 1944
Pope, F/O Thomas	783rd	20 November 1944
Prince, Lt. George A.	781st	30 May 1944
Prince, Sgt. Jesse J.	780th	24 August 1944
Prince, S/Sgt. Willie L.	782nd	03 August 1944
Puckett, S/Sgt. Theodore S.	783rd	20 January 1945
Quaglietta, Sgt. Louis J.	783rd	16 December 1944
Raatz, Lt. Irvin K.	783rd	06 December 1944
Rabkin, Sgt. Jack	783rd	20 November 1944

Reardon, Cpl. Bernard J.	781st	05 February 1945
Renzo, Lt. Peter P.	781st	14 March 1945
Ricciotti, Lt. Anthony N.	782nd	11 March 1944
Rice, 1st Lt. Grosvenor W.	783rd	20 November 1944
Rice, F/O Louis L.	783rd	16 December 1944
Ritch, Sgt. Charlie C.	783rd	20 November 1944
Roberts, S/Sgt. Charles E.	783rd	06 December 1944
Robertson, Sgt. Bobbie T.	780th	11 October 1944
Ronan, S/Sgt. William J.	782nd	11 March 1944
Rousseau, Sgt. Napoleon	782nd	11 March 1944
Ruiz, S/Sgt. Joe P.	782nd	11 March 1944
Rush, Sgt. James G.	780th	22 November 1944
Russell, S/Sgt. William	781st	19 December 1944
Rutgers, S/Sgt. Richard K.	783rd	20 January 1945
Ryan, Lt. Daniel J.	783rd	29 May 1944
Saalfeld, Sgt. Harold W.	783rd	12 September 1944
Saxton, Lt. Frank G.	782nd	31 May 1944
Scherger, S/Sgt. Joseph E.	783rd	30 June 1944
Scroggins, Sgt. Elbert L.	783rd	15 January 1945
Sehnert, T/Sgt. Ralph P.	782nd	03 August 1944
Sellars, S/Sgt. Charles F.	780th	03 August 1944
Shanley, Sgt. Walter E.	780th	24 August 1944
Sherbon, S/Sgt. George	782nd	31 May 1944
Shoener, 1st Lt. Harold W.	783rd	20 January 1945
Silver, Lt. Arthur	781st	05 February 1945
Smith, T/Sgt. George M.	781st	14 March 1945
Smith, F/O John R.	783rd	12 September 1944
Stanford, Sgt. Wayne D.	783rd	16 December 1944
Stewart, Sgt. John E.	782nd	01 September 1944
Stringham, Capt. Irving R.	783rd	16 November 1944
Stutzman, S/Sgt. Lee C.	781st	19 December 1944
Swanzy, Capt. Robert	783rd	12 July 1944
Tarantino, Lt. Paul A.	783rd	0? October 1944
Taylor, Sgt. George E.	783rd	04 October 1944
Taylor, T/Sgt. Joe	783rd	07 August 1944
Tennant, Sgt. Edgar O.	782nd	11 March 1944
Tennille, Capt. Arthur C., Jr.	783rd	20 January 1945
Thomas, Lt. Richard E.	782nd	03 August 1944
Thompson, Lt. Hugh P.	783rd	16 December 1944
Thornton, Lt. James W.	782nd	03 August 1944
Tout, Lt. Richard E.	782nd	01 September 1944.
Treglia, F/O Joseph J.	783rd	16 December 1944

Tripp, T/Sgt. Carl L.	782nd	03 August 1944
Turner, Lt. Leslie P.	783rd	16 February 1945
Volle, Lt. Herbert M.	781st	14 March 1945
Walker, T/Sgt. Robert D.	782nd	31 May 1944
Walker, S/Sgt. William B.	780th	24 August 1944
Whelan, Lt. Joseph S.	783rd	20 November 1944
Whitman, Sgt. Lemuel L.	782nd	13 September 1944
Whyte, T/Sgt. Thomas R.	782nd	06 June 1944
Williams, Sgt. Verlin S.	783rd	15 January 1945
Wilson, Sgt. Bernard A.	783rd	07 July 1944
Wilson, Lt. Robert M.	780th	11 December 1944
Wilson, Lt. Weiser W.	783rd	07 August 1944
Wine, Lt. William D.	783rd	16 February 1945
Wise, Sgt. Richard L.	783rd	15 January 1945
Wolferding, Sgt. Raymond C.	783rd	15 January 1945
Wright, 1st Lt. Harvey D.	783rd	16 November 1944
Wynn, Lt. George A.	783rd	04 October 1944
Zamora, S/Sgt. Ernest R.	782nd	03 August 1944
Ziklo, Sgt. Victor S.	780th	11 October 1944

TOTAL KILLED IN ACTION - 262

Burroughs, Cpl. Redford J., 781st Squadron. Crew of this KIA is unknown.

Dickason, Lt. Larry H., 781st Squadron. Crew of this KIA is unknown.

Griffith, Sgt. Clyde A., 780th Squadron. Died of Anoxia. Crew of this KIA is unknown.

Gruber, T/Sgt. Carl W., Radio Operator on Lt. O'Brien's Crew, 781st. Squadron, was killed in an emergency landing at Brindisi, Italy.

Kelley, S/Sgt. James D., Gunner on Lt. Martz crew was hit in the neck by flak over Vienna and killed instantly.

Newborg, Lt. William T. killed while flying with the 464th Bomb Group.

Lt. Tarantino, who transferred on Detached Service to the 350th Fighter Group, was killed sometime after 14 October 1944, when he crashed while flying a P-47 on return from a mission.

Gene F. Moxley

PRISONERS OF WAR

NAME - RANK - SQUADRON - DATE

Adair, T/Sgt. Carl S.	783rd	19 July 1944
Adsit, S/Sgt. Hoyt F.	781st	06 June 1944
Albertson, T/Sgt. Jack Jr.	783rd	19 July 1944
Allen, Lt. John A.	783rd	03 August 1944
Allred, S/Sgt. Claire J.	780th	03 August 1944
Atherley, Lt. Garth	782nd	22 March 1945
Austin, Sgt. Charles L.	783rd	20 October 1944
Bailey, Lt. Fay C.	783rd	03 August 1944
Barnaby, Lt. John F.	783rd	07 July 1944
Baronoski, S/Sgt. Alexander	783rd	07 August 1944
Beeson, T/Sgt. Vincent A.	781st	14 March 1945
Benson, Lt. Benjamin P., Jr.	782nd	03 August 1944
Bernstein, S/Sgt. Jack	783rd	03 August 1944
Biddle, Lt. John S.	783rd	13 September 1944
Bier, Lt. Samuel	783rd	13 September 1944
Billings, T/Sgt. Lee R.	783rd	20 November 1944
Bitsco, Sgt. Edward A.	780th	10 September 1944
Bitterman, Lt. William N.	783rd	19 July 1944
Blackburn, Capt. James L.	780th	10 September 1944
Blakita, Lt. Michael	781st	16 December 1944
Bolinski, Lt. Daniel S.	783rd	19 July 1944
Bonds, 1st Lt. Thomas W.	783rd	19 July 1944
Borrelli, Sgt. James V.	780th	12 September 1944
Bourne, Sgt. James A.	783rd	20 November 1944
Bowen, Lt. William I.	780th	12 September 1944
Bozarth, Sgt. Miles C.	782nd	31 January 1945
Bracey, S/Sgt. Thomas L.	783rd	19 July 1944
Bracken, S/Sgt. Leonard E.	780th	03 August 1944
Bradford, S/Sgt. William M., Jr.	780th	26 July 1944
Brady, S/Sgt. Paul B.	781st	16 July 1944
Brett, Sgt. Dempsey O.	781st	19 December 1944
Brimhall, Lt. Delbert C.	783rd	16 November 1944
Britton, Lt. George H.	780th	03 August 1944
Brooker, S/Sgt. Walter A.	782nd	13 June 1944
Brown, T/Sgt. Karl K.	781st	13 October 1944
Brown, S/Sgt. Owrie V.	783rd	16 February 1945
Browne, Lt. Chelsea H.	782nd	31 January 1945

180

Browning, Lt. Woodrow W.	783rd	07 August 1944
Bruscinski, T/Sgt. Henry S.	783rd	03 August 1944
Buol, S/Sgt. Vernon H.	783rd	10 September 1944
Burda, Lt. Vernon L.	781st	16 July 1944
Burns, Lt. James O.	781st	19 December 1944
Burton, T/Sgt. William C.	780th	03 August 1944
Capps, S/Sgt. Perry J.	783rd	22 September 1944
Carlson, Sgt. Richard O.	781st	19 December 1944
Carr, T/Sgt. Robert H.	781st	30 June 1944
Carroll, S/Sgt. Joseph E.	781st	30 June 1944
Carter, Sgt. Ernest W.	780th	12 September 1944
Carter, Lt. Guy M., Jr.	783rd	19 July 1944
Casadevall, Lt. Joseph M.	783rd	30 June 1944
Cassel, Lt. William L.	781st	16 December 1944
Chapin, S/Sgt. Edward J. F.	781st	13 October 1944
Chapman, S/Sgt, John H.	782nd	25 April 1945
Chessmore, 1st Lt. Louis C.	780th	10 September 1944
Christensen, Lt. Donald N.	782nd	16 December 1944
Christianson, Lt. Russell	783rd	24 August 1944
Clark, Lt. Francis R.	781st	13 October 1944
Clark, Capt. Thomas T., Jr.	783rd	24 August 1944
Clarke, 1st Lt. Lloyd N.	780th	03 August 1944
Clausen, S/Sgt. Walter	781st	13 October 1944
Cleworth, Sgt. Brian H.	780th	12 September 1944
Clutts, T/Sgt. Leonard D.	783rd	19 July 1944
Coburn, Sgt. William S.	783rd	13 September 1944
Cole, F/O Erwin J.	783rd	20 November 1944
Coleman, Lt. David B.	781st	16 December 1944
Coleman, Lt. Richard R.	782nd	31 January 1945
Conlin, Lt. Charles J.	783rd	07 August 1944
Connell, Lt. James L.	783rd	03 August 1944
Cooke, S/Sgt. Thurlie D.	780th	03 August 1944
Cooper, S/Sgt. John S.	780th	03 August 1944
Coote, Lt. Joseph J.	783rd	03 August 1944
Corn, Sgt. Wilford J.	783rd	20 October 1944
Crane, 1st Lt. Lawrence R.	780th	03 August 1944
Crawford, S/Sgt. George E.	780th	22 November 1944
Crawford, S/Sgt. Melton L.	781st	06 June 1944
Cremeen, Sgt. Thomas	780th	02 December 1944
Croston, T/Sgt. Conard D.	782nd	03 August 1944
Cutler, S/Sgt. Earl R.	783rd	03 August 1944
Davis, Sgt. Ray E.	781st	10 September 1944

Day, S/Sgt. Leonard F.	782nd	25 April 1945
Day, S/Sgt. Rex O.	780th	10 September 1944
Deironimi, S/Sgt. Michael J.	781st	16 July 1944
De Lucia, S/Sgt. Anthony J.	783rd	08 July 1944
Dennick, Sgt. Thomas F.	783rd	22 March 1945
Depp, Lt. Thomas G.	780th	12 September 1944
Deslatte, T/Sgt. Louis J.	781st	13 October 1944
Dickey, Capt. John R.	781st	30 June 1944
Dobie, Sgt. Horace H.	780th	02 December 1944
Dodd, Lt. Myron R.	782nd	03 August 1944
Dollman, Sgt. John W.	782nd	31 January 1945
Douglas, Sgt. William L.	783rd	19 July 1944
Drane, S/Sgt. Leroy M.	782nd	06 June 1944
Duckworth, Capt. Milton H.	783rd	20 November 1944
Duke, S/Sgt. John R.	781st	06 June 1944
Dumas, Sgt. Donald A.	783rd	30 June 1944
Dunderdale, S/Sgt. Otis W.	782nd	06 June 1944
Dunnagan, Sgt. Ernest N.	783rd	19 July 1944
Dunton, S/Sgt. Lloyd F.	783rd	19 July 1944
Durante, Sgt. Carmine M.	780th	12 September 1944
Durckel, Lt. Paul H.	782nd	22 March 1945
Dussault, Lt. Louis U.	783rd	10 September 1944
Dyer, S/Sgt. Francis E.	782nd	03 August 1944
Dyrda, Sgt. Albert	783rd	16 November 1944
Edgell, S/Sgt. Leonard E.	782nd	22 March 1945
Edmark, S/Sgt. Royal E.	783rd	20 October 1944
Edmonds, S/Sgt. Richard A.	783rd	10 September 1944
Edwards, Lt. Gordon L.	783rd	20 October 1944
Edwards, Lt. William W.	783rd	22 March 1945
Eicher, Lt. Ralph D.	783rd	03 August 1944
Elliott, 1st Lt. Wilbert	783rd	03 August 1944
Englehorn, S/Sgt. Leeland T.	780th	03 August 1944
Enzor, S/Sgt. Austin F.	783rd	22 September 1944
Espy, Lt. Calvin C.	780th	02 December 1944
Evans, Lt. Dean P.	783rd	20 October 1944
Evetts, S/Sgt. William N.	782nd	28 July 1944
Ewer, F/O James G.	783rd	10 September 1944
Falkoff, F/O Harry	783rd	22 September 1944
Farrar, S/Sgt. Harold B.	781st	16 July 1944
Fenski, Sgt. Robert A.	783rd	20 October 1944
Ferguson, Sgt. James A.	783rd	16 November 1944
Ferroll, S/Sgt. Robert W.	783rd	22 September 1944

Fertig, Lt. William V.	782nd	16 December 1944
Finley, Lt. Morris E.	781st	06 June 1944
Fischbach, Lt. Allen D.	783rd	13 September 1944
Fisher, Sgt. Paul S.	781st	10 September 1944
Foden, Sgt. Kenneth G.	781st	06 June 1944
Fowlie, F/O Gorden H. F.	783rd	20 October 1944
Frantz, Lt. John P.	782nd	31 January 1945
Funk, Lt. Glenford E.	782nd	06 June 1944
Funk, 1st Lt. James A.	782nd	22 March 1945
Gaines, 1st Lt. George Jr.	781st	13 October 1944
Galbraith, T/Sgt. Wendell V.	782nd	22 March 1945
Geibel, T/Sgt. Robert N.	782nd	22 March 1945
Gemmato, 1st Lt. Italo M.	782nd	25 April 1945
Geurrero, S/Sgt. Jesus Q.	782nd	11 October 1944
Gialo, S/Sgt. Pasquale A.	783rd	16 November 1944
Gibhart, Sgt. Albert J.	783rd	16 November 1944
Glos, S/Sgt. Robert L.	782nd	11 October 1944
Goins, T/Sgt. Edgar S.	782nd	13 June 1944
Goldstein, Sgt. Leonard J.	781st	13 October 1944
Goplen, Lt. Francis A.	783rd	19 July 1944
Gordon, Lt. Lewis C.	781st	10 September 1944
Grant, Sgt. Harold W.	781st	13 October 1944
Greco, S/Sgt. Natale E.	783rd	16 November 1944
Greenwood, 1st Lt. Thomas W., Jr.	783rd	19 July 1944
Grieble, Lt. Gordon A.	783rd	22 September 1944
Griesing, S/Sgt. Charles E.	783rd	19 July 1944
Griffin, Sgt. Orval E.	783rd	13 September 1944
Griffin, T/Sgt. Robert J.	783rd	03 August 1944
Groh, Lt. Edward A.	783rd	29 May 1944
Haber, F/O Abraham	783rd	16 December 1944
Hagen, Lt. Walter E.	782nd	28 July 1944
Hamilton, Lt. Col. McHenry Jr.	782nd	22 March 1945
Hamilton, Sgt. William T.	780th	10 September 1944
Harlin, Sgt. John R., Jr.	783rd	13 October 1944
Hartman, 1st Lt. John K.	783rd	16 November 1944
Haskins, Sgt. Herbert J.	783rd	30 June 1944
Hatch, Lt. Wilson M.	783rd	20 October 1944
Haugh, T/Sgt. Edwin W.	782nd	28 July 1944
Hausold, 1st Lt. Warren G.	781st	30 June 1944
Hellman, Sgt. Alvin	781st	16 December 1944
Hermanson, Sgt. Lyle A.	781st	10 September 1944
Heron, Lt. James P.	783rd	07 July 1944

Hill, Sgt. William E.	780th	02 December 1944
Hillman, 1st Lt. Harold A.	782nd	13 June 1944
Hinshaw, Lt. Donald E.	780th	10 September 1944
Hockman, 1st Lt. Robert M.	783rd	20 November 1944
Hoffman, Lt. Marvin E.	782nd	06 June 1944
Holcombe, T/Sgt. Hulitt L.	781st	16 July 1944
Holland, T/Sgt. Dennis A.	783rd	03 August 1944
Honey, S/Sgt. Allen A.	783rd	16 February 1945
Hongola, Lt. Russell I.	782nd	11 October 1944
Hooper, T/Sgt. William S., Jr.	782nd	03 August 1944
Hoyle, S/Sgt. Zane D.	783rd	16 November 1944
Hudson, S/Sgt. C. D.	781st	13 October 1944
Hutson, T/Sgt. Raymond H.	782nd	13 June 1944
Hylla, Lt. Frank T.	781st	30 June 1944
Ippolito, Sgt. Sam J.	781st	10 September 1944
Jackson, S/Sgt. Cleo H.	783rd	03 August 1944
Jackson, T/Sgt. Thomas R., Jr.	781st	06 June 1944
Jancarik, S/Sgt. Jarmar	781st	06 June 1944
Jasicko, T/Sgt. Frank R.	781st	16 July 1944
Jergensen, S/Sgt. Hans P.	782nd	22 March 1945
Jester, Lt. Herbert W., Jr.	783rd	10 September 1944
Jezowski, S/Sgt. Anthony J.	780th	03 August 1944
Johnson, T/Sgt. Hubert P.	783rd	29 May 1944
Johnson, Lt. Jackson C.	780th	19 July 1944
Jones, 1st Lt. Robert J.	783rd	24 August 1944
Josselyn, S/Sgt. Francis J.	780th	22 November 1944
Jumper, 1st Lt. Jesse T.	783rd	08 July 1944
Jurenec, Lt. George E.	780th	11 October 1944
Kanik, Lt. Frank J.	783rd	07 July 1944
Kapp, S/Sgt. Gilbert D.	783rd	03 August 1944
Kardas, Lt. Henry	783rd	24 August 1944
Keil, T/Sgt. Howard J.	780th	26 July 1944
Kennedy, S/Sgt. Clovis A., Jr.	782nd	03 August 1944
Kennedy, Sgt. Pierre J. J.	781st	13 October 1944
Ketron, T/Sgt. Herbert W.	782nd	28 July 1944
Kipp, Lt. Eugene M.	783rd	16 November 1944
Kline, Lt. Richard C.	782nd	06 June 1944
Klug, Lt. Richard C.	780th	11 October 1944
Knowles, F/O Murray	781st	13 October 1944
Korf, S/Sgt. Joseph J.	783rd	16 November 1944
Krzyzynski, Lt. Eugene M.	781st	16 July 1944
Kubanis, Lt. Ivan J.	783rd	08 July 1944

Kulczyk, T/Sgt. Eugene	783rd	08 July 1944
Kurtz, Lt. Robert R.	780th	03 August 1944
Kutger, 1st Lt. Joseph P.	783rd	20 November 1944
Lafata, S/Sgt. Donald F.	783rd	22 September 1944
Larson, 1st Lt. Vern L.	780th	11 December 1944
Latimer, Lt. Edward J.	783rd	16 November 1944
Laughner, Lt. Ray L.	781st	19 December 1944
Leach, Sgt. Ralph W.	781st	16 December 1944
Leath, Sgt. Truman C.	781st	16 December 1944
Lee, S/Sgt. Francis O.	782nd	03 August 1944
Leggate, 1st Lt. George H.	781st	10 September 1944
Leins, Lt. John A.	782nd	06 June 1944
Linsley, Sgt. Robert L.	782nd	25 April 1945
Little, Lt. Delbert	782nd	13 June 1944
Little, Sgt. Francis P.	781st	06 June 1944
Livesay, Lt. Owen W.	783rd	29 May 1944
Logan, 1st Lt. Patrick J.	780th	03 August 1944
Loomis, T/Sgt. Elwyn L.	782nd	06 June 1944
Lowenthal, Lt. Bernard L.	782nd	03 August 1944
Lunn, T/Sgt. Lowell M.	781st	13 October 1944
MacDonald, Sgt. Malcom A.	782nd	31 January 1945
Main, T/Sgt. Carl H.	783rd	07 August 1944
Maloney, Lt. Owen W.	782nd	31 January 1945
Marsh, S/Sgt. William A.	783rd	20 October 1944
Martin, S/Sgt. Gerard	780th	26 July 1944
Martin, S/Sgt. John C.	782nd	25 April 1945
Martin, 1st Lt. Kenneth M.	781st	06 June 1944
Matter, Lt. Leonard W.	782nd	03 August 1944
Mayo, Sgt. Doyle B.	783rd	22 March 1945
McCloskey, S/Sgt. James W.	783rd	19 July 1944
McCurley, Sgt. Robert L.	780th	12 September 1944
McDonald, 1st Lt. Richard F.	782nd	03 August 1944
McElyea, T/Sgt. Ralph W.	783rd	22 September 1944
McGuirk, S/Sgt. John W.	783rd	30 June 1944
McIlhenny, Lt. Kern	783rd	22 March 1945
McKnight, T/Sgt. Thomas E.	780th	11 December 1944
McNamee, T/Sgt. John F.	783rd	16 November 1944
McNew, Sgt. Thomas R. C.	781st	13 October 1944
Mead, Sgt. Egbert E.	783rd	16 November 1944
Merkel, S/Sgt. Donald L.	781st	06 June 1944
Messinger, T/Sgt. Robert H.	783rd	16 November 1944
Metzger, Lt. Charles H.	782nd	11 October 1944

Meyer, Sgt. Erwin H.	780th	11 December 1944
Miller, Sgt. Douglas F.	783rd	10 September 1944
Mitchell, 1st Lt. William	783rd	16 November 1944
Mock, Lt. Alfred R.	780th	12 September 1944
Monge, Sgt. Kenneth O.	783rd	07 July 1944
Monroe, S/Sgt. John C.	782nd	13 June 1944
Moore, Sgt. Carl D.	783rd	08 July 1944
Mroczkowski, S/Sgt. Matthew J.	782nd	06 June 1944
Mullins, Lt. James D.	783rd	08 July 1944
Murphy, T/Sgt. Alvin M.	783rd	03 August 1944
Murray, Sgt. Charles R.	781st	13 October 1944
Nashalsky, S/Sgt. Harold	783rd	08 July 1944
Nelson, Lt. John A.	781st	10 September1944
Ngoon, Lt. Chin I.	783rd	22 September 1944
Niemann, Sgt. Roger E.	781st	10 September 1944
Niven, S/Sgt. Robert N.	782nd	13 June 1944
Nunn, Sgt. Thomas A., Jr.	783rd	20 October 1944
Olsen, Sgt. Orville R.	783rd	10 September 1944
Orpikowski, S/Sgt. Edward A.	780th	11 December 1944
Osborn, Lt. Walton H.	782nd	22 March 1945
Otto, Sgt. Dean T.	781st	16 December 1944
Pace, Capt. Stanley C.	783rd	03 August 1944
Paluch, Lt. Edward J.	780th	03 August 1944
Parkison, 1st Lt. Herbert	783rd	10 September 1944
Pellecchia, Lt. Modesto	780th	22 November 1944
Perkins, S/Sgt. Dwight G.	783rd	03 August 1944
Petitti, Lt. Norman J.	780th	26 July 1944
Petrole, Sgt. William G.	782nd	13 September 1944
Phillips, Sgt. Stanley A.	783rd	13 October 1944
Pitman, S/Sgt. Merton P.	783rd	29 May 1944
Pitts, Lt. Marion A.	781st	16 December 1944
Pohlman, Sgt. Victor E.	783rd	20 October 1944
Pollot, Lt. Michael J.	780th	22 November 1944
Powell, Lt. Wilmer	782nd	28 July 1944
Powers, Sgt. Franklin K.	780th	02 December 1944
Pratt, S/Sgt. Edwin K.	780th	11 December 1944
Priddy, 1st Lt. John F., Jr.	780th	22 November 1944
Printz, T/Sgt. Harold M.	780th	26 July 1944
Radebaugh, S/Sgt. Melvin J.	783rd	19 July 1944
Ralston, S/Sgt. Albert D., Jr.	781st	16 July 1944
Ratliff, Sgt. William R.	780th	11 October 1944
Rebottaro, Sgt. Louis A.	783rd	16 November 1944

Reeher, Lt. David N.	783rd	22 March 1945
Reents, S/Sgt. Arthur F.	782nd	03 August 1944
Reifsnyder, S/Sgt. Harry G.	783rd	19 July 1944
Reuss, Sgt. Harry	781st	10 September 1944
Reynolds, S/Sgt. Roy E.	780th	10 September 1944
Rhinevault, Sgt. George B.	783rd	20 October 1944
Richardson, Capt. Edgel W.	782nd	22 March 1945
Riley, S/Sgt. Robert E.	783rd	10 September 1944
Rinard, Lt. Ralph Jr.	783rd	19 July 1944
Roberts, Lt. Melvin O.	783rd	20 October 1944
Robinson, S/Sgt. Edward D.	783rd	08 July 1944
Robinson, T/Sgt. Fred J.	783rd	07 July 1944
Rogers, S/Sgt. Oscar C.	782nd	03 August 1944
Rumble, Sgt. Kenneth M.	780th	10 September 1944
Russell, Sgt. John L.	782nd	31 January 1945
Rutan, S/Sgt. William T.	783rd	16 November 1944
Ryan, Sgt. John T.	780th	02 December 1944
Sabin, Sgt. Howard A.	780th	12 September 1944
Salmon, Sgt. Robert W.	782nd	03 August 1944
Sams, S/Sgt. William D.	783rd	19 July 1944
Sanford, Lt. Joseph C.	783rd	03 August 1944
Sapenoff, Lt. Howard L.	781st	06 June 1944
Satterfield, F/O Lloyd B.	782nd	13 June 1944
Scalese, S/Sgt. Thomas	781st	06 June 1944
Schilleman, Lt. Valmore A.	781st	10 September 1944
Schroeder, Sgt. Robert E.	782nd	31 January 1945
Schultz, S/Sgt. Steve	783rd	03 August 1944
Sedlak, T/Sgt. Frank C.	783rd	08 July 1944
Shaughnessy, S/Sgt. James A.	782nd	06 June 1944
Sheridan, 1st Lt. William P.	783rd	24 August 1944
Shott, Sgt. Bernard E.	783rd	16 December 1944
Simmons, S/Sgt. Gerald J.	781st	06 June 1944
Simpson, S/Sgt. Harold A.	782nd	13 June 1944
Smith, Sgt. Freeman L.	782nd	25 April 1945
Smith, F/O Lawrence J., Jr.	782nd	25 April 1945
Snow, T/Sgt. William R.	782nd	25 April 1945
Spontak, Lt. Joseph	780th	03 August 1944
Squyres, S/Sgt. Weldon D.	782nd	03 August 1944
Stern, Sgt. Donald D.	781st	16 December 1944
Stetz, S/Sgt. Nicholas	782nd	06 June 1944
Stickney, Lt. Norman R.	782nd	25 April 1945
Stoneham, Sgt. Lawson D.	782nd	13 September 1944

Strahan, S/Sgt. Samuel J.	783rd	03 August 1944
Stroud, Sgt. William D.	783rd	24 August 1944
Struble, Lt. Rex L.	781st	06 June 1944
Sullivan, T/Sgt. James T.	783rd	24 August 1944
Sullivan, Sgt. Thomas P.	783rd	24 August 1944
Swanson, Sgt. Robert E.	783rd	27 August 1944
Taft, Lt. Ernest R.	783rd	20 November 1944
Tannenbaum, Lt. Marvin	783rd	13 October 1944
Tiehen, Sgt. Lawrence J.	781st	13 October 1944
Teller, 1st Lt. William I.	783rd	03 August 1944
Thill, S/Sgt. Richard A.	781st	30 June 1944
Thomas, Sgt. Arla L.	782nd	11 October 1944
Thompson, M/Sgt. James F.	783rd	22 September 1944
Thompson, Lt. William D.	782nd	13 June 1944
Thurston, Sgt. Lawrence B.	783rd	10 September 1944
Tipton, 1st Lt. Dale C.	781st	16 July 1944
Toomey, Lt. Donald E.	781st	13 October 1944
Trimingham, Sgt. Richard H.	783rd	24 August 1944
Tucker, Lt. Fred G.	782nd	28 July 1944
Valentine, S/Sgt. Robert L.	783rd	03 August 1944
Vorheier, Sgt. Wilburn	781st	06 June 1944
Vorhies, Lt. William L.	783rd	29 May 1944
Wake, Lt. Donald K.	780th	26 July 1944
Ward, S/Sgt. Homer L.	783rd	29 May 1944
Ward, Lt. Royce L.	783rd	08 July 1944
Wayman, Lt. Emil E.	783rd	16 November 1944
Waymire, S/Sgt. Kenton	782nd	28 July 1944
Weber, S/Sgt. Grover J.	783rd	07 August 1944
Weiss, Lt. Eugene A.	781st	16 July 1944
Weiss, Lt. Sidney	781st	06 June 1944
Weistling, Sgt. Howard G.	781st	16 December 1944
Werner, Sgt. Earl J.	783rd	20 October 1944
Wightman, Sgt. William J.	783rd	13 September 1944
Wilby, S/Sgt. John J.	783rd	07 August 1944
Willett, S/Sgt. Joseph J.	780th	26 July 1944
Williams, 1st Lt. George W.	783rd	22 September 1944
Williamson, Lt. Robert L.	781st	06 June 1944
Wilson, S/Sgt. Edward C.	780th	11 December 1944
Wilson, Sgt. Francis C.	782nd	31 January 1945
Wilson, T/Sgt. George A.	781st	30 June 1944
Winston, Lt. Richard C.	783rd	19 July 1944
Wood, S/Sgt. Ernest J.	780th	26 July 1944

Yatkauskas, S/Sgt. Albert J.	783rd	07 August 1944
Yokitis, S/Sgt. Charles G.	783rd	29 May 1944

TOTAL PRISONERS OF WAR - 375

S/Sgt. Robert E. Swanson, Gunner, 783rd Squadron, bailed out near the IP. Crew of this POW is unknown.

EVADED CAPTURE

NAME - RANK - SQUADRON - DATE

Adams, Sgt. Robert P.	780th	20 November 1944
Allen, S/Sgt. Deverett J.	781st	17 December 1944
Alvey, T/Sgt. William E.	782nd	04 March 1945
Anderson, T/Sgt. Wallace R.	780th	25 April 1945
Arnold, Sgt. Robert H.	783rd	13 September 1944
Arnold, Sgt. Robert H.	783rd	20 January 1945
Atkins, Lt. Turner J.	781st	18 December 1944
Atkinson, T/Sgt. Thurman	780th	20 November 1944
Ayres, Lt. James	782nd	13 September 1944
Bailey, Sgt. Perry	782nd	13 September 1944
Barnhart, Sgt. Crawford C.	781st	17 December 1944
Bartels, 1st Lt. Harry C., Jr.	783rd	31 March 1945
Bay, Sgt. Sam	780th	20 November 1944
Beaubien, Sgt. Richard L.	782nd	13 September 1944
Beeson, Lt. Warren l.	781st	10 September 1944
Behn, Cpl. Claud J.	782nd	16 December 1944
Bentrud, Lt. Raymond G.	780th	07 August 1944
Betz, Sgt. Harry A.	783rd	13 October 1944
Bilger, Lt. Richard J.	781st	01 March 1945
Block, S/Sgt. Richard D.	780th	20 November 1944
Blumenfeld, Sgt. Julius	780th	02 December 1944
Bodycombe, 1st Lt. Richard	782nd	15 March 1945
Boone, F/O Joseph	782nd	15 March 1945
Bovett, 1st Lt. Arthur W.	781st	01 March 1945
Bowman, F/O David L.	781st	02 March 1945
Bowyer, S/Sgt. William B.	780th	07 August 1944
Boyle, Sgt. Joseph	782nd	15 March 1945
Briggs, Sgt. William B.	781st	02 March 1945
Brink, T/Sgt. Donald W.	782nd	18 December 1944
Brown, S/Sgt. Owrie V.	783rd	12 September 1944
Bugg, Sgt. James S., Jr.	782nd	13 September 1944
Bugg, S/Sgt. James S., Jr.	782nd	04 March 1945
Burda, Lt. Vernon L.	781st	31 May 1944
Burkhardt, Lt. Herbert V.	783rd	13 September 1944
Butler, Sgt. Theodore A.	782nd	18 December 1944
Caldwell, Lt. Robert R., Jr.	780th	31 January 1945
Campbell, 1st Lt. Ord A.	780th	20 November 1944

Carothers, Lt. John G.	780th	31 January 1945
Carter, Lt. Gilbert R., Jr.	780th	31 January 1945
Carter, 1st Lt. Robert D.	780th	25 April 1945
Cass, Lt. Gaythor L.	781st	01 March 1945
Cassel, Lt. William L.	782nd	13 September 1944
Christian, Lt. Virgil R.	781st	18 December 1944
Clark, Col. Charles A., Jr.	783rd	13 September 1944
Clodfelter, 1st Lt. Donald E.	781st	18 December 1944
Coahran, Lt. Robert A.	782nd	13 September 1944
Cohen, Sgt. Irving	780th	20 November 1944
Cohen, T/Sgt. Victor	783rd	13 September 1944
Cohlmia, S/Sgt. Robert B.	781st	01 March 1945
Conner, Sgt. Pinky	782nd	15 March 1945
Crabtree, Lt. Robert W.	783rd	12 July 1944
Crenshaw, T/Sgt. Leroy J.	783rd	13 September 1944
Cripps, S/Sgt. Charles A.	783rd	12 July 1944
Crist, S/Sgt. Robert E.	780th	20 November 1944
Cross, Lt. George R.	783rd	16 November 1944
Crowley, T/Sgt. John J.	781st	30 May 1944
Culhane, Lt. Cornelius V.	781st	10 September 1944
Culpepper, S/Sgt. Earl J.	781st	17 December 1944
Curtis, F/O James R.	783rd	20 October 1944
Dahl, Lt. Carl V.	781st	10 September 1944
Day, Sgt. Leonard F., Jr.	782nd	02 March 1945
Dearman, Sgt. Joe R.	782nd	18 December 1944
Deironimi, Sgt. Michael J.	781st	31 May 1944
Deitsch, S/Sgt. Theodore	780th	20 November 1944
Dennis, Cpl. James E.	782nd	16 December 1944
Diederichs, Lt. Franklin C.	780th	25 April 1945
Dippel, T/Sgt. George	780th	31 January 1945
Donohue, Sgt. Francis M., Jr.	781st	02 March 1945
Downs, Sgt. James F.	781st	30 May 1944
Dubinsky, Sgt. Abraham	781st	30 May 1944
Duckworth, 1st Lt. Milton H.	783rd	13 September 1944
Dulack, Sgt. Joseph T., Jr.	783rd	31 March 1945
Dyess, Lt. Clinton E.	780th	31 January 1945
Eatman, Lt. Curtis I.	782nd	18 December 1944
Eatman, 1st Lt. Curtis I.	782nd	04 March 1945
Eisenbaum, Sgt. Irving	782nd	02 March 1945
Elliott, S/Sgt. Robert W.	781st	18 December 1944
Ersepke, Sgt. Robert	782nd	15 March 1945
Evans, F/O William E.	782nd	18 December 1944

Evans, Lt. William E.	782nd	04 March 1945
Fairbrother, Lt. Edward F.	782nd	13 September 1944
Farrar, Sgt. Harold B.	781st	31 May 1944
Feely, S/Sgt. Weyland B.	783rd	13 September 1944
Ferrel, Sgt. Harley T.	782nd	06 November 1944
Finch, S/Sgt. Ralph C.	781st	06 June 1944
Fisher, Sgt. Roy D.	783rd	16 November 1944
Forbes, Sgt. Joseph C.	783rd	16 November 1944
Forsberg, Lt. Delbert E.	783rd	20 October 1944
Frank, 1st Lt. Aloys	783rd	13 September 1944
French, 1st Lt. Robert E.	781st	02 March 1945
Frosini, Sgt. Anthony E.	780th	20 November 1944
Gayner, S/Sgt. Dennis F.	780th	31 January 1945
Gehrki, Lt. Edward	782nd	13 September 1944
Gemmato, 1st Lt. Italo M.	782nd	02 March 1945
George, Lt. Robert L.	781st	06 June 1944
Gephart, Lt. Robert	782nd	18 December 1944
Gilliam, T/Sgt. Melvin O.	781st	17 December 1944
Guiffre, F/O Marvin	783rd	13 October 1944
Hahn, Sgt. Edward W.	782nd	18 December 1944
Hahn, S/Sgt. Edward W.	782nd	04 March 1945
Haight, Lt. Fulton W.	780th	02 December 1944
Hamann, Sgt. Karl J.	782nd	06 November 1944
Hardisty, S/Sgt. Kenneth L.	780th	02 December 1944
Hardisty, S/Sgt. Kenneth L.	780th	01 March 1945
Harper, Lt. James B.	782nd	13 September 1944
Harriman, Lt. Bruce	782nd	06 November 1944
Harriman, 1st Lt. Gerald M.	780th	25 April 1945
Harris, S/Sgt. Gerald L.	783rd	20 October 1944
Harrison, Sgt. Joseph E.	783rd	13 September 1944
Harvey, Sgt. Howard H.	783rd	31 March 1945
Harwood, S/Sgt. Mask W.	780th	13 October 1944
Hausner, Lt. Sigmund E.	783rd	12 September 1944
Hawn, S/Sgt. John W., Jr.	782nd	06 November 1944
Hayman, Lt. Charles A.	782nd	04 March 1945
Haynes, Lt. Charles A.	782nd	18 December 1944
Heaney, Lt. Richard F.	781st	17 December 1944
Hemphill, S/Sgt. Charles R.	781st	18 December 1944
Herndon, Sgt. James W.	780th	25 April 1945
Hershey, Lt. Lester	781st	17 December 1944
Hill, Lt. John M.	782nd	13 September 1944
Hinton, S/Sgt. James W.	781st	01 March 1945

Hitchak, S/Sgt. Michael	782nd	18 December 1944
Hoard, S/Sgt. James	782nd	13 September 1944
Hogan, T/Sgt. John W.	781st	17 December 1944
Holcombe, Sgt. Hulitt L.	781st	31 May 1944
Holden, Lt. Harold D.	781st	30 May 1944
Holdsworth, Sgt. David N.	780th	22 November 1944
Hollingsworth, Sgt. Edward	782nd	15 March 1945
Honey, S/Sgt. Allen A.	783rd	12 September 1944
Hooge, T/Sgt. Paul H.	783rd	12 July 1944
Horton, Sgt. Denny W.	781st	02 March 1945
Hulesberg, Lt. Arthur F., Jr.	780th	07 August 1944
Ihde, S/Sgt. Paul B.	781st	01 March 1945
Jackelen, S/Sgt. Gerald K.	780th	02 December 1944
Jackelen, S/Sgt. Gerald K.	780th	01 March 1945
Jacovinich, S/Sgt. Tulio P.	780th	07 August 1944
Jasicko, Sgt. Frank R.	781st	31 May 1944
Jay, T/Sgt. Andrew	782nd	18 December 1944
Jensen, Lt. James	780th	13 October 1944
Johns, Lt. William F., Jr.	782nd	18 December 1944
Johnson, T/Sgt. C. E.	780th	07 August 1944
Johnson, Sgt. Donald B.	780th	31 January 1945
Johnson, S/Sgt. William R.	780th	31 January 1945
Jordan, Lt. Fred	780th	01 March 1945
Joublanc, S/Sgt. Joseph C.	781st	18 December 1944
Kaiser, Lt. Robert	780th	20 November 1944
Keenan, Sgt. Richard A.	782nd	13 September 1944
Kemper, Lt. William P.	782nd	16 December 1944
Kernahan, Lt. Arthur J.	782nd	16 December 1944
Key, Lt. Amos D.	783rd	31 March 1945
Kiellerson, Sgt. Norman	783rd	31 March 1945
Kirby, Cpl. Mack J.	782nd	16 December 1944
Kissel, 1st Lt. Ralph F.	780th	07 August 1944
Klein, Sgt. Richard F.	782nd	13 September 1944
Knaus, Capt. John V.	783rd	13 September 1944
Knous, F/O John G., Jr.	783rd	16 November 1944
Kovar, Sgt. Charles P.	782nd	06 November 1944
Kraemer, Sgt. Francis A.	783rd	16 November 1944
Krzyzynski, Lt. Eugene M.	781st	31 May 1944
Kubitz, Sgt. Karl A.	782nd	06 November 1944
Lane, Lt. Homer W.	783rd	13 October 1944
Layne, Sgt. John P.	781st	10 September 1944
Leitgeb, S/Sgt. Walter W.	781st	18 December 1944

Lengvenis, 1st Lt. Harry F.	780th	07 August 1944
Leppla, F/O William Jr.	782nd	06 June 1944
Liles, Capt. Matthew B., Jr.	780th	31 January 1945
Linsley, Sgt. Robert L.	782nd	02 March 1945
Long, S/Sgt. James W.	780th	02 December 1944
Long, Lt. Lyle H.	783rd	20 October 1944
Love, S/Sgt. Frank D.	780th	20 November 1944
Maas, T/Sgt. Alfred H.	782nd	28 July 1944
MacFarlane, 1st Lt. John F.	781st	06 June 1944
Maher, S/Sgt. Robert T.	780th	07 August 1944
Mangan, S/Sgt. Charles A.	783rd	20 October 1944
Martin, Sgt. Adrian A.	781st	10 September 1944
Martin, Sgt. John C.	782nd	02 March 1945
Martinez, Sgt. Franklin B.	781st	10 September 1944
Mayo, Sgt. Charles	780th	13 October 1944
McCullagh, F/O Robert	780th	13 October 1944
McElwain, S/Sgt. Arnold D.	781st	01 March 1945
McGee, Lt. William T.	782nd	18 December 1944
McGrath, Lt. Joseph E.	783rd	31 March 1945
McMann, S/Sgt. Kenneth O.	780th	02 December 1944
McQuaid, T/Sgt. Albert P., Jr.	781st	06 June 1944
McWhorter, 1st Lt. John T.	780th	13 October 1944
Meehan, Sgt. William A., Jr.	780th	13 October 1944
Meute, Lt. Howard W.	780th	13 October 1944
Mijal, Sgt. Chester	781st	17 December 1944
Milakovic, Lt. Raymond	782nd	04 March 1945
Miles, Sgt. Dale D.	783rd	16 November 1944
Millington, S/Sgt. Harry	780th	01 March 1945
Miosky, Sgt. Edmund J.	783rd	13 September 1944
Mitchell, S/Sgt. William J.	783rd	31 March 1945
Morgan, Sgt. Forrest	782nd	13 September 1944
Mullan, 1st Lt. Alfred W., Jr.	781st	17 December 1944
Munson, S/Sgt. Robert H.	781st	18 December 1944
Musgrove, S/Sgt. Clare M.	782nd	28 July 1944
Napody, S/Sgt. Thomas	780th	13 October 1944
Nelson, 1st Lt. William A.	783rd	12 July 1944
Newman, Lt. Hyman H.	781st	17 December 1944
Nicastro, Sgt. Samuel T.	782nd	18 December 1944
Nickler, S/Sgt. Carlyle P.	780th	25 April 1945
Nolen, F/O Harry C.	780th	24 August 1944
Norman, 1st Lt. Joe Jr.	780th	20 November 1944
Nowak, S/Sgt. Edwin H.	780th	13 October 1944

Page, T/Sgt. Calvin A.	780th	25 April 1945
Pakes, S/Sgt. Lemont H.	782nd	18 December 1944
Pakes, T/Sgt. Lemont H.	782nd	04 March 1945
Parkhurst, 1st Lt. Kenneth L.	781st	02 March 1945
Patrick, Sgt. Jimmy	781st	30 May 1944
Payson, Sgt. Hollis E.	783rd	16 November 1944
Percy, Sgt. Howard J.	781st	10 September 1944
Perkins, Sgt. Richard E.	781st	10 September 1944
Pettigrew, Sgt. Jack C.	781st	10 September 1944
Postema, S/Sgt. Donald B.	781st	01 March 1945
Powell, S/Sgt. James P.	782nd	18 December 1944
Powell, T/Sgt. James P.	782nd	04 March 1945
Prouty, Sgt. William C.	783rd	13 October 1944
Quagan, Sgt. Harold F.	781st	02 March 1945
Rachow, Lt. William A.	781st	10 September 1944
Ralston, Sgt. Albert D., Jr.	781st	31 May 1944
Randel, Lt. Robert J., Jr.	782nd	06 November 1944
Reagan, S/Sgt. Edward M.	783rd	13 September 1944
Roberson, 1st Lt. Lubie M.	783rd	30 June 1944
Rogers, Lt. William F.	783rd	30 June 1944
Rolek, T/Sgt. Walter A.	782nd	06 June 1944
Rostedt, Sgt. Edwin J.	780th	13 October 1944
Roth, Cpl. Arnold J.	782nd	16 December 1944
Ruffalo, Sgt. Donald M.	783rd	12 September 1944
Rutgers, S/Sgt. Richard K.	783rd	20 October 1944
Ryan, F/O Edward M.	780th	20 November 1944
Ryan, F/O Edward M.	780th	01 March 1945
Sammons, S/Sgt. Cecil L.	782nd	06 June 1944
Sanders, Sgt. James	782nd	15 March 1945
Schefrin, Lt. Marvin	782nd	18 December 1944
Schlomer, T/Sgt. John C.	780th	01 March 1945
Schlossberg, Sgt. Martin L.	780th	01 March 1945
Schwarz, F/O Irwin	782nd	06 November 1944
Seiler, Lt. Martin D.	783rd	31 March 1945
Septoff, Lt. Murray	781st	30 May 1944
Seteropoulis, Sgt. William G.	781st	31 May 1944
Sgroi, F/O James	782nd	15 March 1945
Sheets, Lt. Collie E.	783rd	16 November 1944
Shelton, Sgt. Robert E.	783rd	31 March 1945
Sherburne, Sgt. C. B., Jr.	780th	20 November 1944
Shreve, 1st Lt. William G., Jr.	780th	25 April 1945
Smith, Sgt. Freeman L.	782nd	02 March 1945

Smith, T/Sgt. Harry M.	781st	30 May 1944
Smith, Lt. Lawrence J., Jr.	782nd	02 March 1945
Smith, 1st Lt. Ralph J.	783rd	12 July 1944
Smith, Sgt. Vernon L.	783rd	16 November 1944
Smith, 1st Lt. William J.	781st	01 March 1945
Snow, Sgt. William R.	782nd	02 March 1945
Softy, Lt. Charles D.	780th	02 December 1944
Sokira, S/Sgt. Charles B.	780th	07 August 1944
Stage, Lt. Anthony J.	780th	20 November 1944
Stephens, S/Sgt. James E.	782nd	04 March 1945
Stickney, Lt. Norman R.	782nd	02 March 1945
Stieg, T/Sgt. Paul H.	782nd	18 December 1944
Stinson, Lt. Robert T.	782nd	06 November 1944
Swan, Sgt. Roy C.	782nd	06 November 1944
Swanson, Cpl. Alex O.	782nd	16 December 1944
Swift, T/Sgt. Joseph F.	783rd	31 March 1945
Tardiglione, Sgt. Joseph	782nd	13 September 1944
Thein, T/Sgt. Charles J.	781st	01 March 1945
Thomas, 1st Lt. Robert B.	783rd	12 July 1944
Thompson, Sgt. C. M.	780th	20 November 1944
Tipton, Lt. Dale C.	781st	31 May 1944
Unrath, Lt. Leonard	782nd	18 December 1944
Urda, S/Sgt. Mike	780th	20 November 1944
Vaughan, T/Sgt. Wilber R.	783rd	12 July 1944
Vinophal, Lt. Thomas E.	782nd	13 September 1944
Volkman, Lt. Eric W.	783rd	13 October 1944
Wagner, Sgt. Frederick P.	781st	02 March 1945
Walsh, S/Sgt. Thomas W.	783rd	12 July 1944
Walters, S/Sgt. Jack A.	783rd	13 September 1944
Walton III, Lt. Thomas P.	780th	31 January 1945
Wamser, Sgt. Harry J.	782nd	18 December 1944
Weaver, S/Sgt. Harry M.	780th	02 December 1944
Weaver, S/Sgt. Harry M.	780th	01 March 1945
Weber, Sgt. John	782nd	15 March 1945
Weixelman, Sgt. Louis H.	783rd	30 June 1944
Wightman, Sgt. Fred S.	780th	25 April 1945
Williams, Sgt. Jack C.	781st	30 May 1944
Wills, 1st Lt. Robert F.	780th	20 November 1944
Wilson, Lt. John A.	781st	18 December 1944
Wilson, S/Sgt. Royal A.	781st	18 December 1944
Wilson, S/Sgt. Walter P.	783rd	12 July 1944
Wilson, Sgt. William W.	783rd	13 October 1944

Windom, S/Sgt. Robert N.	782nd	18 December 1944
Wine, Lt. William D.	783rd	12 September 1944
Winkowski, Lt. Stanley J.	781st	01 March 1945
Withington, 1st Lt. Frederic B., Jr.	780th	02 December 1944
Withington, 1st Lt. Frederic B., Jr.	780th	01 March 1945
Wood, Sgt. Donald E.	780th	25 April 1945
Wood, Sgt. Lehman V.	781st	02 March 1945
Wray, Capt. James W.	781st	31 May 1944
Yarbrough, S/Sgt. Edward L.	780th	07 August 1944
York, S/Sgt. Homer C.	780th	31 January 1945
Young, Cpl. Franklin E.	782nd	16 December 1944
Zacharias, Sgt. Michael H.	783rd	13 October 1944
Zewadski, Capt. William K.	780th	07 August 1944

TOTAL EVADEES - 302

INTERNED IN SWITZERLAND

NAME - RANK - SQUADRON - DATE

Barrett, Lt. Donald A.	781st	16 August 1944
Bergin, Lt. Richard A.	781st	16 August 1944
Bistarkey, F/O John	783rd	22 September 1944
Burchards, T/Sgt. Harold F.	781st	16 August 1944
Coleman, Lt. John N.	783rd	22 September 1944
Cook, Sgt. Robert A.	780th	16 August 1944
Curry, Sgt. William H.	783rd	22 September 1944
Davis, 1st Lt. Archie C.	780th	19 July 1944
Desmond, S/Sgt. Robert H.	780th	19 July 1944
Dodd, Lt. Francis C.	780th	16 August 1944
Emmel, S/Sgt. Leonard H.	781st	16 August 1944
Friedman, Lt. Eugene M.	780th	16 August 1944
Fulkerson, S/Sgt. Melvin R.	781st	16 August 1944
Gidley, Sgt. John	780th	16 August 1944
Golden, S/Sgt. Willie M.	781st	16 August 1944
Goldenbloom, Lt. Nathan	780th	19 July 1944
Goldman, Sgt. Robert E.	783rd	22 September 1944
Guertin, S/Sgt. Robert P.	780th	19 July 1944
Horne, Sgt. Joseph R.	783rd	22 September 1944
Hymans, T/Sgt. Dowie J.	781st	16 August 1944
Johnston, Sgt. Robert F.	780th	16 August 1944
Kraft, Lt. Roger L.	783rd	22 September 1944
Lyons, Lt. James J.	781st	16 August 1944
Meyers, Sgt. Lawrence C.	780th	16 August 1944
Moore, Lt. George E.	780th	16 August 1944
Moss, T/Sgt. Alva H.	780th	19 July 1944
Noyer, Lt. John L. E.	781st	16 August 1944
O'Brien, Lt. Earl	783rd	22 September 1944
Palmer, S/Sgt. Willie D.	780th	19 July 1944
Roberts, Capt. Lewis M.	781st	16 August 1944
Rosen, Sgt. Leonard T.	783rd	22 September 1944
Sangas, Sgt. John	783rd	22 September 1944
Secor, Lt. Howard J.	780th	16 August 1944
Shepherd, Sgt. Munroe E.	780th	16 August 1944
Sweet, Lt. Elliott B.	781st	16 August 1944
Truitt, Sgt. Brooks K.	783rd	22 September 1944
Weber, T/Sgt. Theodore L.	780th	19 July 1944

Wiley, S/Sgt. Robert A.   780th   19 July 1944
Womacks, Sgt. S. C.   780th   16 August 1944

TOTAL INTERNEES - 39

ABOUT THE AUTHOR

My wife Mary had an uncle named Frank Hutchcraft who was a S/Sgt. in the 780th Squadron of the 465thBomb Group (H). He was an Armorer-Top Turret Gunner on a B-24 Heavy Bomber named "Old Dutch Cleanser." He flew fifty combat missions with the 780th Squadron. "Old Dutch Cleanser" was shot down on 6 June 1944, while being flown by a crew of the 782nd Squadron. I began researching the 465th Bomb Group, fifteen years ago, to gain knowledge of Frank's tour of duty. I became engrossed in this research over the years and decided to compile a Chronological History of this Group and I completed the first two volumes titled, *The 465th Remembered*, book I and II. Before continuing with the compilation of the Chronology of the 465th, I have been asked by Major John F. Charlton, Pilot and Operations Officer of the 782nd Squadron, to record the events of the ninety-five B-24 aircraft that were shot down from the 465th Bomb Group in the last year of World War Two. Each B-24 normally carried a crew of ten men and each crew has a story to tell about their being shot down. I think this is an important part of military history that people of all ages might read and learn about the sacrifices made by the nine hundred and fifty four crewmembers of those ninety-five shot down aircraft and how some of them managed to survive

Printed in the United States
1096800002B/85-102